MW00905687

Knowing Mathematics

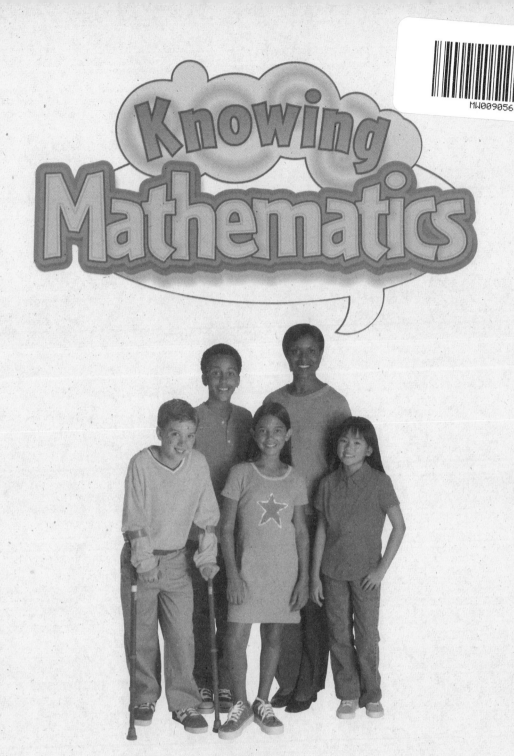

Authors
Dr. Liping Ma
Dr. Cathy Kessel

Green Level

HOUGHTON MIFFLIN BOSTON

Copyright © 2003 by Houghton Mifflin Company. All rights reserved.

No part of this work may be reproduced or transmitted in any form or by any means, electronic or mechanical, including photocopying or recording, or by any information storage or retrieval system without the prior written permission of Houghton Mifflin Company unless such copying is expressly permitted by federal copyright law. Address inquiries to School Permissions, 222 Berkeley Street, Boston, MA 02116.

Printed in the U.S.A.

ISBN-13: 978-0-618-24852-0 ISBN-10: 0-618-24852-8

6 7 8 9 10-HS-11 10 09 08 07

Table of Contents

Meet the Class

I'm Danny!

Hi! I'm Ms. Park!

I'm C.J.!

I'm Lily!

I'm Ana!

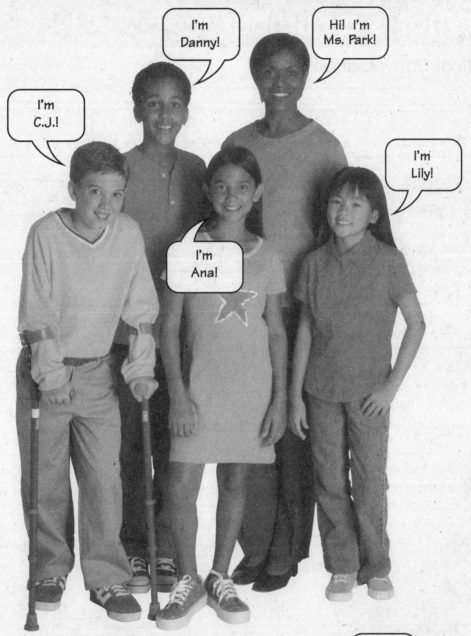

Ms. Park loves teaching math. Her students are Danny, Lily, C.J., and Ana, and they like to discuss math with Ms. Park. She always listens to them and helps them build their ideas about math!

Mr. K9 and his son Chip aren't part of the class, but they pay attention to what is happening. Read their comments to get some help in building your own ideas about math!

I'm Mr. K9!
I'm Chip!

Warm-up Exercises

$2 + 4 = $ 6 $3 + 3 = $ 6 $4 + 1 = $ 5 $2 + 2 = $ 4

$4 - 2 = $ 2 $5 - 2 = $ 3 $3 - 1 = $ 2 $4 - 2 = $ 2

1-1 What is a number?

Mathematical Conversation

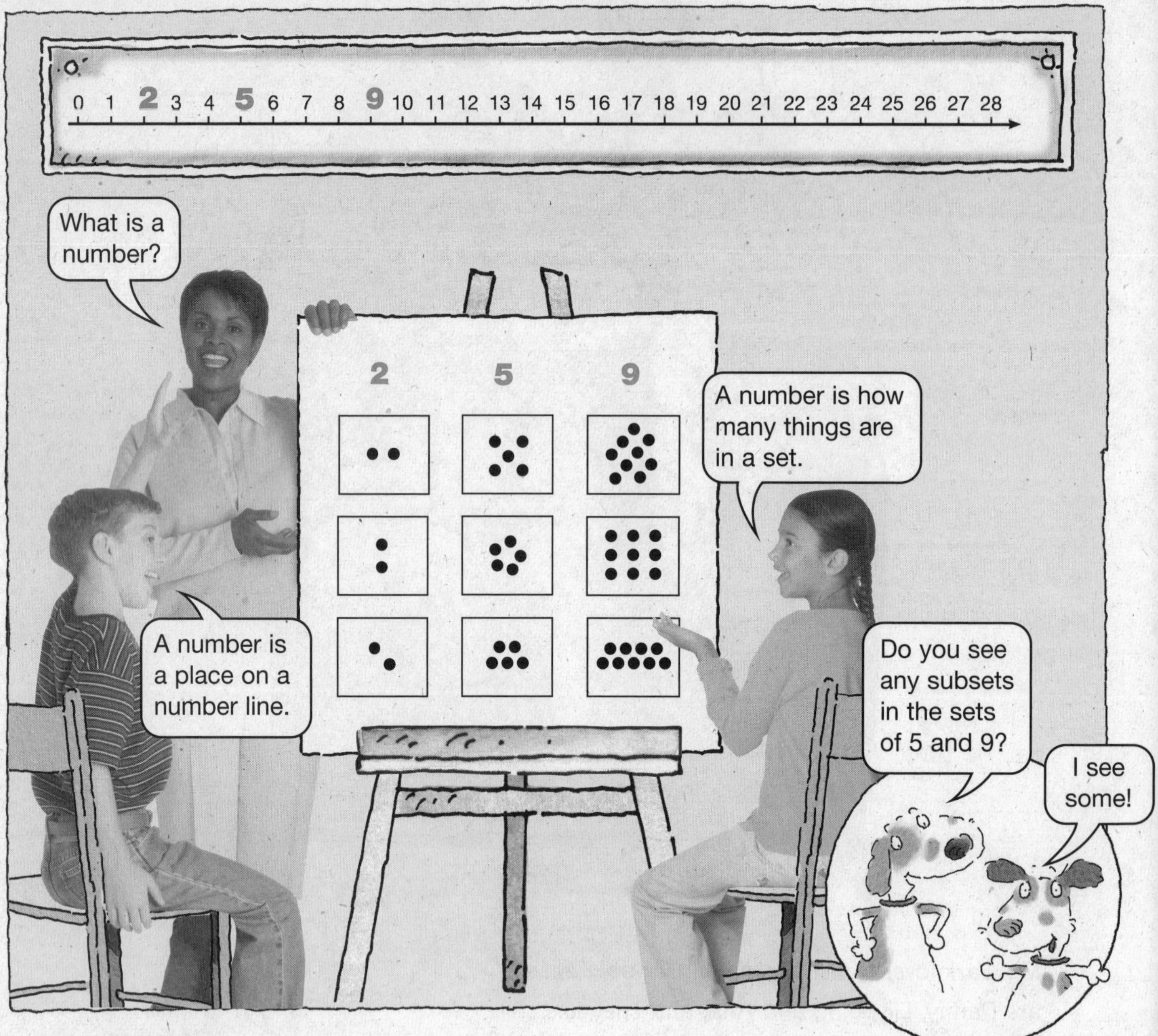

0 1 2 3 4 5 6 7 8 9 10 11 12 13 14 15 16 17 18 19 20 21 22 23 24 25 26 27 28

What is a number?

2 5 9

A number is how many things are in a set.

A number is a place on a number line.

Do you see any subsets in the sets of 5 and 9?

I see some!

Guided Practice

Circle the subsets that make up each group of dots. Write the number of dots in each set.

A. 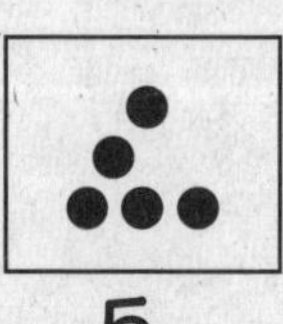
5

B. 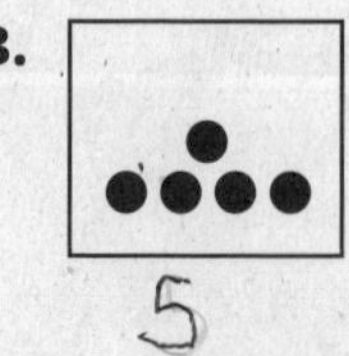
5

C. 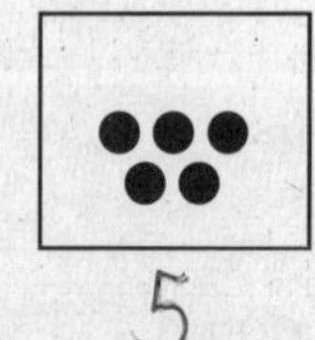
5

D. 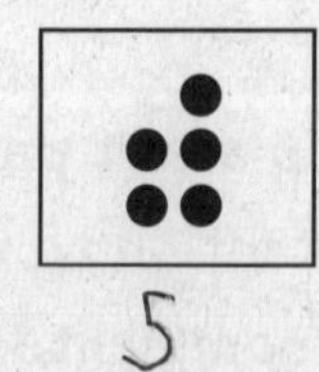
5

E. 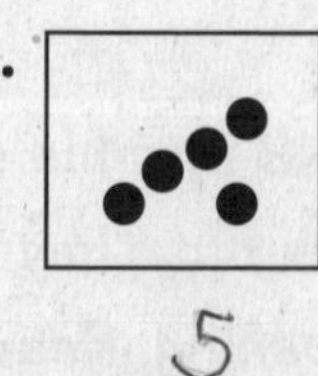
5

Lesson 1–1 Exercises

Write the number of dots in each set. Try to do it without counting the dots one by one. Circle subsets if it helps.

1.	2.	3.	4.	5.	6.	7.	8.
2	3	3	4	4	2	4	3
9.	**10.**	**11.**	**12.**	**13.**	**14.**	**15.**	**16.**
5	5	4	2	4	6	5	5
17.	**18.**	**19.**	**20.**	**21.**	**22.**	**23.**	**24.**
6	6	6	6	7	7	7	6
25.	**26.**	**27.**	**28.**	**29.**	**30.**	**31.**	**32.**
7	7	8	8	8	8	9	9
33.	**34.**	**35.**	**36.**	**37.**	**38.**	**39.**	**40.**
8	9	9	9	8	6	8	7

Word Problems

Write a mathematical expression to represent each problem. Then calculate and answer the questions.

41. Oscar has 3 green balloons and 3 red balloons. How many balloons does he have in all?

6 ballons

42. Mary has 2 pink balls and 5 purple balls. How many balls does she have altogether?

7 balls

43. Juan has 8 pens. He gives Tom 3 of them. How many pens does Juan have now?

5 pens

44. Ping has 9 stamps. Mary has 7 stamps. How many more stamps does Ping have than Mary?

2 stamps more

Reflection and Discussion

Look for two subsets in this set of dots and circle them. Which dots did you circle? How many dots are in each subset?

Warm-up Exercises

4 + 4 = 8	2 + 4 = ~~8~~ 6	7 + 2 = 9	6 + 4 = 10
6 − 2 = 4	5 − 1 = 4	7 − 2 = 5	10 − 6 = 4

1-2 Why is number 10 so special?

Mathematical Conversation

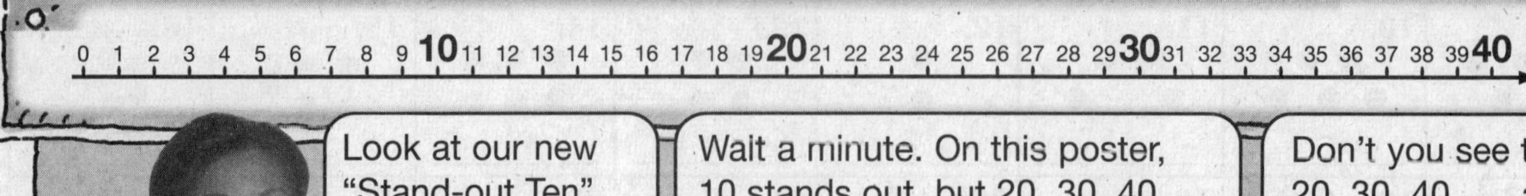
0 1 2 3 4 5 6 7 8 9 10 11 12 13 14 15 16 17 18 19 20 21 22 23 24 25 26 27 28 29 30 31 32 33 34 35 36 37 38 39 40

Look at our new "Stand-out Ten" number-line poster.
Wait a minute. On this poster, 10 stands out, but 20, 30, 40 . . . stand out, too. What do numbers like 20, 30, 40 . . . have to do with 10?
Don't you see that 20, 30, 40 . . . are all multiples of 10. 20 has two names. My friend says that "twenty" is its nickname, and "two tens" is its real name. And 30, 40, 50, 60 . . . all have two names, just as 20 does!

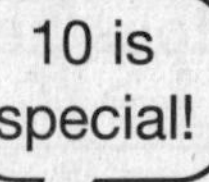
What's special about 10? Why don't the multiples of 3, 4, or 5 stand out?
You know what? I think 10 is a special organizer of numbers. See, 10 ones make a 10, 10 tens make a 100, 10 hundreds make a 1,000.
Good for you, Ana! This pattern works for decimals, too. 10 tenths make a 1.
10 is special!

Guided Practice

Write an expression to represent how each set of dots composes a 10.

A. 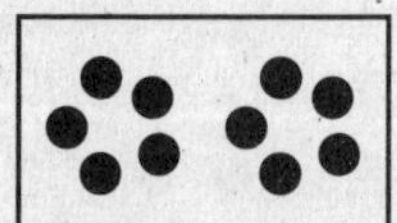

5 + 5 = 10

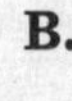

B. 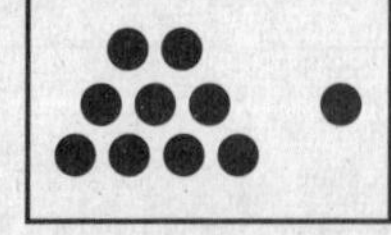

9 + 1 = 10

C. 

7 + 3 = 10

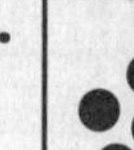

D. 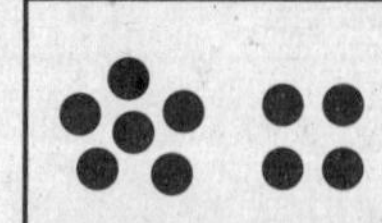

5+4=9

E. 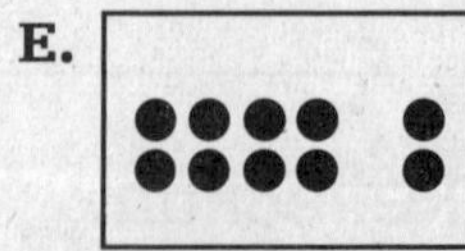

8+2=10

Lesson 1–2 Exercises

Fill in the answers. Calculate without using your fingers.

1. $9 + \underline{1} = 10$　**2.** $8 + \underline{2} = 10$　**3.** $7 + \underline{3} = 10$　**4.** $6 + \underline{4} = 10$

5. $1 + \underline{9} = 10$　**6.** $2 + \underline{8} = 10$　**7.** $3 + \underline{7} = 10$　**8.** $4 + \underline{6} = 10$

9. $10 - \underline{5} = 5$　**10.** $10 - \underline{1} = 9$　**11.** $10 - \underline{4} = 6$　**12.** $10 - \underline{3} = 7$

13. $10 - \underline{8} = 2$　**14.** $10 - \underline{9} = 1$　**15.** $10 - \underline{7} = 3$　**16.** $10 - \underline{2} = 8$

17. $5 + 5 = \underline{10}$　**18.** $4 + 5 = \underline{9}$　**19.** $6 + 4 = \underline{10}$　**20.** $7 + 3 = \underline{10}$

21. $4 + 4 = \underline{8}$　**22.** $2 + 5 = \underline{7}$　**23.** $3 + 4 = \underline{7}$　**24.** $3 + 3 = \underline{6}$

25. $10 - 5 = \underline{5}$　**26.** $8 - 5 = \underline{3}$　**27.** $10 - 4 = \underline{6}$　**28.** $10 - 3 = \underline{7}$

29. $9 - 4 = \underline{5}$　**30.** $7 - 5 = \underline{2}$　**31.** $8 - 5 = \underline{3}$　**32.** $9 - 6 = \underline{3}$

33. $8 + 1 = \underline{9}$　**34.** $7 - 4 = \underline{3}$　**35.** $8 - 2 = \underline{6}$　**36.** $9 + 1 = \underline{10}$

37. $6 - 5 = \underline{1}$　**38.** $10 - 6 = \underline{4}$　**39.** $4 + 2 = \underline{6}$　**40.** $2 + 7 = \underline{9}$

Write a number to complete each sentence.

41. Three tens make _______.　**42.** Five tens make _______.

43. Nine tens make _______.　**44.** Ten tens make _______.

45. Three plus seven is _______.　**46.** Ten minus seven is _______.

47. Six plus four is _______.　**48.** Ten minus six is _______.

Reflection and Discussion

How many tens are there in 110?

Warm-up Exercises

$10 - 1 =$ ____	$10 - 3 =$ ____	$10 - 2 =$ ____	$10 - 4 =$ ____
$10 - 9 =$ ____	$10 - 7 =$ ____	$10 - 8 =$ ____	$10 - 5 =$ ____

1-3 Can you turn addition into subtraction?

Mathematical Conversation

Do you know that a mathematical equation, such as 3 + 2 = 5, may have more than one version?
I know! Another version of 3 + 2 = 5 is 2 + 3 = 5.
Yes! The addends can trade places!

Now, can you turn 3 + 2 = 5 into a version with subtraction?

I can! Addition: 3 + 2 = 5 Subtraction: 5 − 3 = 2

Actually, I have two: 5 − 3 = 2 and 5 − 2 = 3.

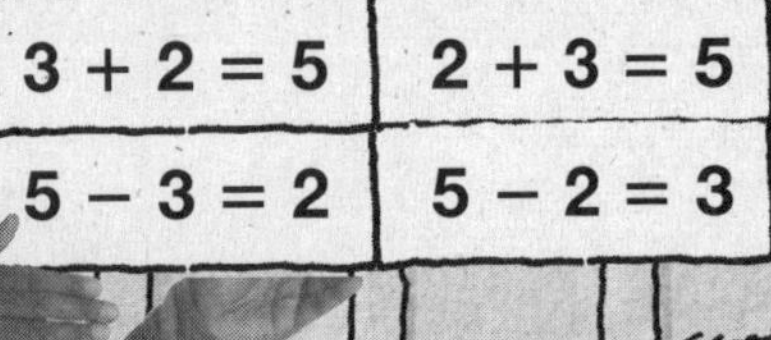

3 + 2 = 5
2 + 3 = 5
5 − 3 = 2
5 − 2 = 3

Hmm! Subtraction is the inverse of addition!

Ana got two! Cool!

Guided Practice

In each box, write three other versions of the equation.

A.	**B.**	**C.**	**D.**	**E.**	**F.**
$4 + 3 = 7$	$8 + 2 = 10$	$5 + 4 = 9$	$7 + 3 = 10$	$5 + 3 = 8$	$4 + 2 = 6$
$3 + 4 = 7$	________	________	________	________	________
$7 - 3 = 4$	________	________	________	________	________
$7 - 4 = 3$	________	________	________	________	________

Lesson 1–3 Exercises

In each box, write two addition and two subtraction equations that represent the number and organization of the dots.

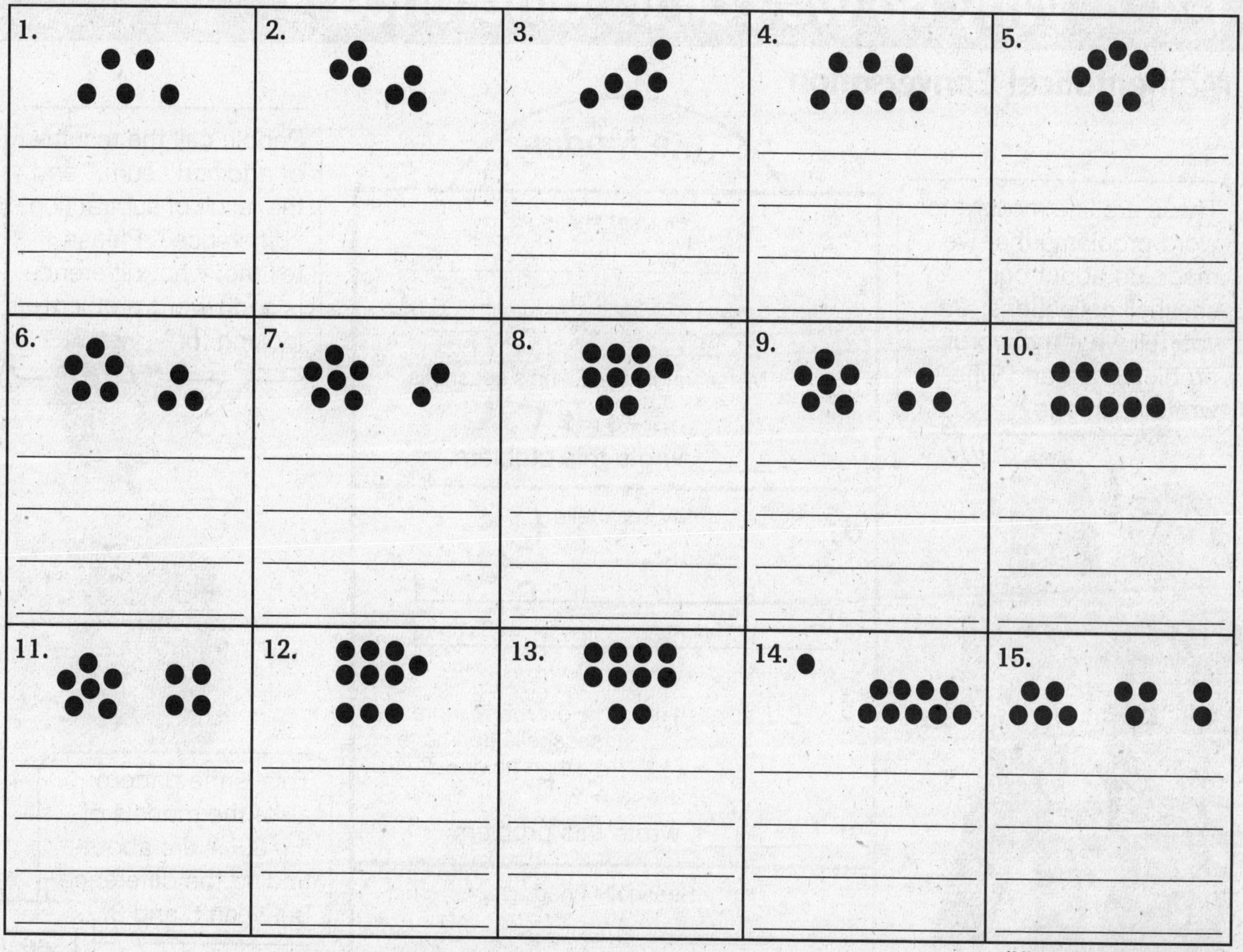

1.	2.	3.	4.	5.
6.	7.	8.	9.	10.
11.	12.	13.	14.	15.

(Hint: you can write a multistep equation for 15.)

Fill in the answers. Calculate without using your fingers.

16. Since $4 + 5 = 9$, then $9 - 5 =$ ______ and $9 - 4 =$ ______.

17. Since $2 + 6 = 8$, then $8 - 2 =$ ______ and $8 - 6 =$ ______.

18. Since $1 + 5 = 6$, then $6 - 5 =$ ______ and $6 - 1 =$ ______.

19. Since $10 - 7 = 3$, then $10 - 3 =$ ______ and $3 + 7 =$ ______.

20. Since $9 - 6 = 3$, then $9 - 3 =$ ______ and $3 + 6 =$ ______.

Reflection and Discussion

Can you find other versions for subtraction equations, such as $8 - 2 = 6$?

Warm-up Exercises

9 − 4 = ____	3 − 3 = ____	7 − 6 = ____	8 − 5 = ____
10 − 5 = ____	8 − 4 = ____	6 − 3 = ____	4 − 2 = ____

1-4 Why do we call it "difference"?

Mathematical Conversation

These are line models for word problems that we made up about our seashell collections. Can you tell what the word problems are and who wrote each one?

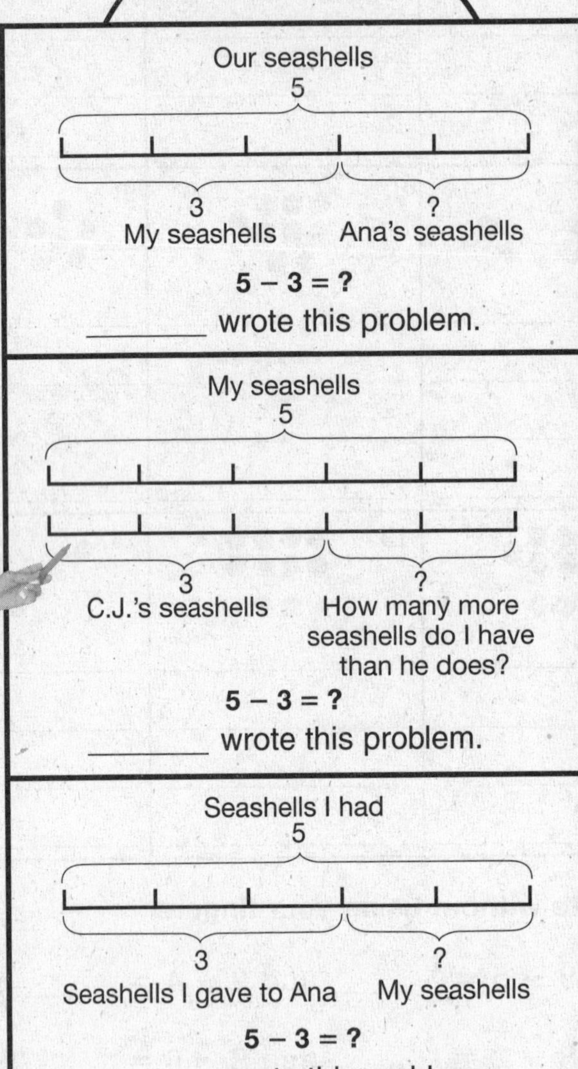

Line Models
Our seashells
5
3
My seashells
?
Ana's seashells
5 − 3 = ?
_______ wrote this problem.
My seashells
5
3
C.J.'s seashells
?
How many more seashells do I have than he does?
5 − 3 = ?
_______ wrote this problem.
Seashells I had
5
3
Seashells I gave to Ana
?
My seashells
5 − 3 = ?
_______ wrote this problem.

People call the result of addition "sum," and the result of subtraction "difference." Please tell me: what difference is each word problem looking for?

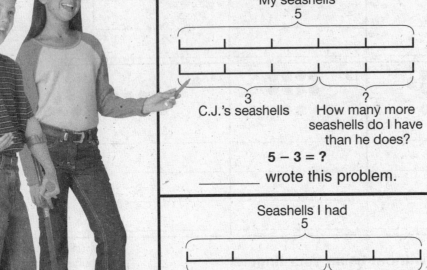

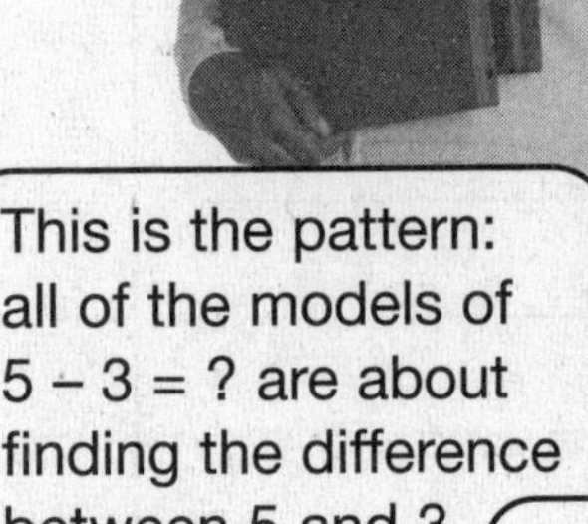

This is the pattern: all of the models of 5 − 3 = ? are about finding the difference between 5 and 3.

I see it!

Guided Practice

Create three different word problems that are represented by this equation.

Use the same topic for all three problems.

7 − 4 = 3

A. ________________

B. ________________

C. ________________

Lesson 1–4 Exercises

Create three different word problems that could be represented by each of these equations. Use the same topic for all three problems.

1. $10 - 6 = 4$

2. $8 - 3 = 5$

Draw a line model to represent each of the following expressions.

3. $5 - 3 =$ ____ 4. $6 - 4 =$ ____ 5. $4 - 1 =$ ____ 6. $3 - 2 =$ ____

7. $1 + 3 =$ ____ 8. $3 + 2 =$ ____ 9. $4 + 2 =$ ____ 10. $5 + 1 =$ ____

Write an equation for each problem.

11. What is the sum of 8 and 2? ____________

12. What is the sum of 3 and 4? ____________

13. What is the difference between 7 and 2? ____________

14. What is the difference between 6 and 10? ____________

15. How many more than 7 is 10? ____________

16. How many is 7 less than 10? ____________

Reflection and Discussion

We sometimes use line models to represent the difference between two numbers. Do we always use one line? Could we use two lines? How?

Warm-up Exercises

$6 + 4 =$ ____	$7 + 3 =$ ____	$9 - 2 =$ ____	$9 - 7 =$ ____
$8 - 2 =$ ____	$6 - 5 =$ ____	$5 - 3 =$ ____	$9 - 4 =$ ____

1-5 Review, Reflection, and Quiz 1

Mathematical Conversation

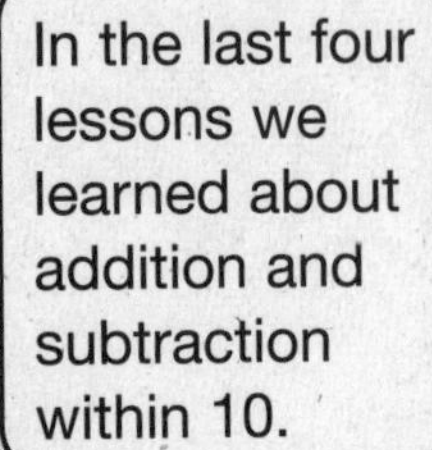
In the last four lessons we learned about addition and subtraction within 10.
But now I can do some addition and subtraction even beyond 10. Since 2 + 3 = 5, then I know that 20 + 30 = 50. Since 4 + 4 = 8, then I know that 40 + 40 = 80!
Cool! Since 20 is 2 tens, and 30 equals 3 tens, then 2 tens plus 3 tens equals 5 tens, 50! Since 40 is 4 tens, then 4 tens plus 4 tens equals 8 tens, 80!
Clever, huh?

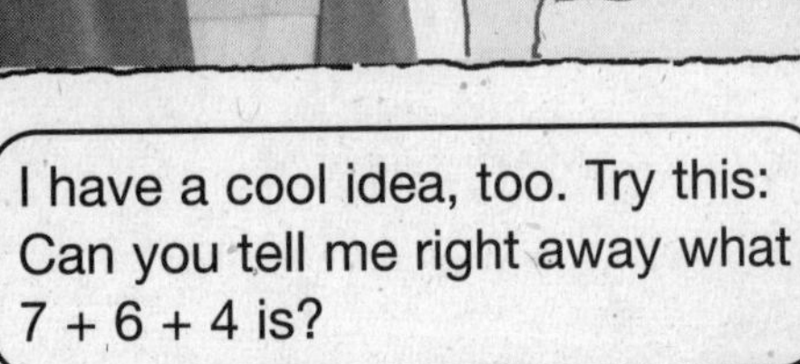
I have a cool idea, too. Try this: Can you tell me right away what 7 + 6 + 4 is?

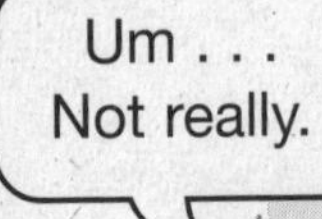
Um . . . Not really.
It's 17! Look, we know that 6 + 4 = 10, and that addends can trade places. So I composed 10 first, then added 7 to it. The answer is 17!
We can always learn new things by reflecting on what we've learned. Try the problems below.

Guided Practice

A. $40 + 30 =$ ____ **B.** $80 + 10 =$ ____ **C.** $60 + 40 =$ ____

D. $4 + 8 + 2 =$ ____ **E.** $7 + 7 + 3 =$ ____ **F.** $8 + 6 + 4 =$ ____

Quiz 1

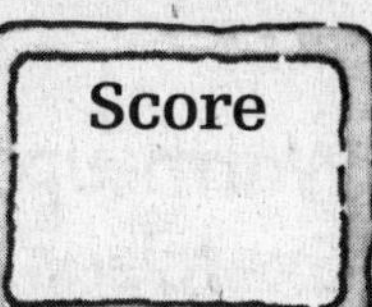

Score

Calculate without using your fingers and fill in the answers.

1. $2 + 2 =$ ____ 2. $3 + 2 =$ ____ 3. $4 + 4 =$ ____ 4. $4 + 3 =$ ____ 5. $5 + 5 =$ ____

6. $5 - 3 =$ ____ 7. $4 - 2 =$ ____ 8. $6 - 3 =$ ____ 9. $7 - 5 =$ ____ 10. $4 - 2 =$ ____

11. $5 + 2 =$ ____ 12. $6 + 3 =$ ____ 13. $7 + 1 =$ ____ 14. $5 + 4 =$ ____ 15. $7 + 3 =$ ____

16. $7 - 3 =$ ____ 17. $9 - 2 =$ ____ 18. $8 - 4 =$ ____ 19. $5 - 4 =$ ____ 20. $7 - 6 =$ ____

21. $5 +$ ____ $= 10$ 22. $6 +$ ____ $= 10$ 23. $7 +$ ____ $= 10$ 24. $4 +$ ____ $= 10$

25. $8 +$ ____ $= 10$ 26. $10 -$ ____ $= 6$ 27. $10 -$ ____ $= 5$ 28. $10 -$ ____ $= 1$

Calculate the answers. Then write three other versions of each equation.

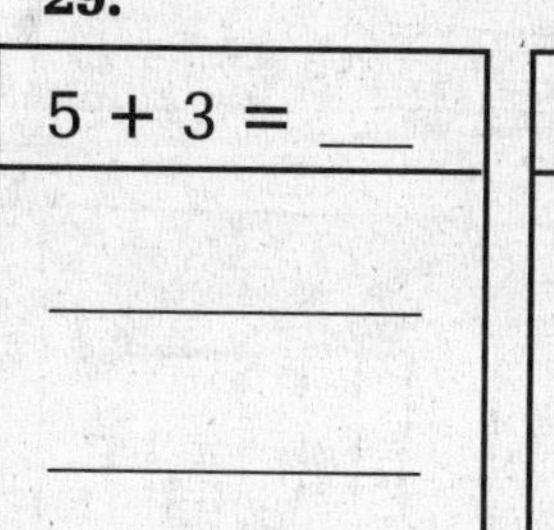

29.	30.	31.	32.	33.
$5 + 3 =$ ___	$4 + 2 =$ ___	$7 + 2 =$ ___	$9 - 3 =$ ___	$7 - 2 =$ ___
________	________	________	________	________
________	________	________	________	________
________	________	________	________	________

Word Problem

Draw a line model and write a mathematical expression to represent this word problem. Then calculate and answer the question.

34. Mary saw 5 birds in her yard when she got up. While she was having breakfast, 2 more birds arrived. How many birds are in the yard now? ________

Line Model:

Mathematical expression:

Challenge Yourself

35. $20 + 20 =$ ____ 36. $30 + 30 =$ ____ 37. $40 + 40 =$ ____ 38. $40 + 30 =$ ____

39. $50 + 30 =$ ____ 40. $5 + 8 + 2 =$ ____ 41. $9 + 9 + 1 =$ ____ 42. $6 + 7 + 3 =$ ____

Warm-up Exercises

10 + 1 = ____ 10 + 2 = ____ 10 + 3 = ____ 10 + 4 = ____ 10 + 5 = ____

10 + 6 = ____ 10 + 7 = ____ 10 + 8 = ____ 10 + 9 = ____ 10 + 10 = ____

1-6 What is the real name for "eleven"?

Mathematical Conversation

Ana mentioned before that 20, 30, 40 . . . have both real names and nicknames. Did you know that 11 also has two names?
I know! The nickname for 11 is "eleven." Its real name is "ten-and-one"!
Do you mean that all the numbers between 10 and 20 have two names? So the nickname for 12 is "twelve," and its real name is "ten-and-two"?

Yes! The nickname for 13 is "thirteen," and its real name is "ten-and-three"!
The real names for these numbers can help us make sense of them. Do you agree?
Here we see again that 10 is a special organizer of numbers!
Good for you!

Guided Practice

Write the "real names" for the numbers from 11 to 19.

A. Eleven ____________ **B.** Twelve ____________ **C.** Thirteen ____________

D. Fourteen ____________ **E.** Fifteen ____________ **F.** Sixteen ____________

G. Seventeen ____________ **H.** Eighteen ____________ **I.** Nineteen ____________

Lesson 1–6 Exercises

Calculate without using your fingers and fill in the answers.

1. 10 + 5 = ____	**2.** 10 + 2 = ____	**3.** 10 + 4 = ____	**4.** 10 + 8 = ____
5. 5 + 10 = ____	**6.** 2 + 10 = ____	**7.** 4 + 10 = ____	**8.** 8 + 10 = ____
9. 15 − 5 = ____	**10.** 12 − 2 = ____	**11.** 14 − 4 = ____	**12.** 18 − 8 = ____
13. 15 − 10 = ____	**14.** 12 − 10 = ____	**15.** 14 − 10 = ____	**16.** 18 − 10 = ____
17. 10 + 6 = ____	**18.** 10 + 3 = ____	**19.** 10 + 7 = ____	**20.** 10 + 9 = ____
21. 6 + 10 = ____	**22.** 3 + 10 = ____	**23.** 7 + 10 = ____	**24.** 9 + 10 = ____
25. 16 − 6 = ____	**26.** 13 − 3 = ____	**27.** 17 − 7 = ____	**28.** 19 − 9 = ____
29. 16 − 10 = ____	**30.** 13 − 10 = ____	**31.** 17 − 10 = ____	**32.** 19 − 10 = ____
33. 10 − 8 = ____	**34.** 8 − 2 = ____	**35.** 7 − 4 = ____	**36.** 9 − 3 = ____
37. 9 − 5 = ____	**38.** 7 − 2 = ____	**39.** 5 − 4 = ____	**40.** 9 − 6 = ____
41. $8 + \underline{5 + 5} =$ ____	**42.** $9 + \underline{8 + 2} =$ ____	**43.** $\underline{4 + 6} + 6 =$ ____	**44.** $\underline{7 + 3} + 4 =$ ____
45. $9 + \underline{9 + 1} =$ ____	**46.** $6 + \underline{7 + 3} =$ ____	**47.** 10 − 2 − 3 = ____	**48.** 10 − 8 − 1 = ____

Word Problems

Compare the two models. Write a mathematical expression to represent each problem. Then calculate and answer the questions.

49. I have 10 schoolbooks and 3 comic books. How many books is that?

____

Line model:

Bar model:

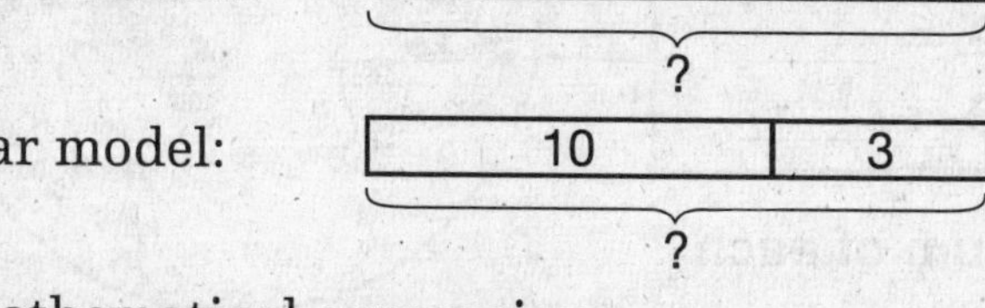

10
3
?
10
3
?

Mathematical expression:

50. I had 18 magazines. I gave away 8 of them. How many magazines do I have now? ____

Line model:

18
8
?

Bar model:

18
8
?

Mathematical expression:

Reflection and Discussion The nicknames of each teen number provide at least one hint of their real names with one exception. Do you know what these hints are? And what is the exception?

Warm-up Exercises

1 + 8 = ____	3 + 6 = ____	4 + 4 = ____	4 + 5 = ____
9 − 2 = ____	9 − 1 = ____	9 − 6 = ____	9 − 2 = ____

1-7 Do you know the trick for computing with 9?

Mathematical Conversation

Look, I've made an interesting list. Do you see the pattern? Can you fill in the blanks?

9 + 1 = 10
9 + 2 = 11
9 + 3 = 12
9 + 4 = 13
9 + 5 = 14
9 + 6 = ____
9 + 7 = ____
9 + 8 = ____
9 + 9 = ____

I made a list to go with Ana's list. Do you see the pattern? Can you complete my list?

Ana's List	My List
9 + 1 = 10	10 − 9 = 1
9 + 2 = 11	11 − 9 = 2
9 + 3 = 12	12 − 9 = 3
9 + 4 = 13	13 − 9 = 4
9 + 5 = 14	14 − 9 = 5
9 + 6 = 15	15 − 9 = ____
9 + 7 = 16	16 − 9 = ____
9 + 8 = 17	17 − 9 = ____
9 + 9 = 18	18 − 9 = ____

Here's another list that goes with Ana's list. Can you complete this one?

Ana's List	My List
9 + 1 = 10	1 + 9 = ____
9 + 2 = 11	2 + 9 = ____
9 + 3 = 12	3 + 9 = ____
9 + 4 = 13	4 + 9 = ____
9 + 5 = 14	5 + 9 = ____
9 + 6 = 15	6 + 9 = ____
9 + 7 = 16	7 + 9 = ____
9 + 8 = 17	8 + 9 = ____
9 + 9 = 18	9 + 9 = ____

So, what is the trick for computing with 9, and why does it work?
The number 1 seems to play a big role!
1

Guided Practice

Use the patterns that you found to figure out the sum of each pair of numbers. Memorize each sum.

	Sum	Numbers
A.	11	9, 2
B.		9, 3
C.		9, 4
D.		9, 5
E.		9, 6
F.		9, 7
G.		9, 8
H.		9, 9

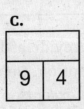

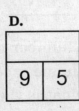

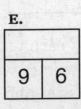

Lesson 1–7 Exercises

Calculate without using your fingers and fill in the answers.

1. 9 + 5 = ____ **2.** 9 + 2 = ____ **3.** 9 + 4 = ____ **4.** 9 + 8 = ____

5. 9 + 9 = ____ **6.** 9 + 3 = ____ **7.** 9 + 7 = ____ **8.** 9 + 6 = ____

9. 2 + 9 = ____ **10.** 5 + 9 = ____ **11.** 4 + 9 = ____ **12.** 3 + 9 = ____

13. 6 + 9 = ____ **14.** 0 + 9 = ____ **15.** 8 + 9 = ____ **16.** 7 + 9 = ____

17. 11 − 9 = ____ **18.** 18 − 9 = ____ **19.** 13 − 9 = ____ **20.** 14 − 9 = ____

21. 15 − 9 = ____ **22.** 16 − 9 = ____ **23.** 17 − 9 = ____ **24.** 12 − 9 = ____

25. 13 − 4 = ____ **26.** 14 − 6 = ____ **27.** 17 − 7 = ____ **28.** 17 − 8 = ____

29. 12 − 3 = ____ **30.** 11 − 2 = ____ **31.** 15 − 6 = ____ **32.** 18 − 9 = ____

33. 13 − 2 = ____ **34.** 18 − 7 = ____ **35.** 17 − 1 = ____ **36.** 16 − 3 = ____

37. 9 − 4 = ____ **38.** 15 − 5 = ____ **39.** 18 − 10 = ____ **40.** 17 − 6 = ____

41. 8 + 5 − 5 = ____ **42.** 9 + 2 + 8 = ____ **43.** 14 + 6 − 5 = ____ **44.** 17 + 2 − 1 = ____

45. 9 + 9 − 8 = ____ **46.** 6 + 5 + 5 = ____ **47.** 12 − 9 − 3 = ____ **48.** 14 − 9 − 2 = ____

Word Problems

Compare the models. Write a mathematical expression to represent each problem. Then calculate and answer the questions.

49. Ms. Park has 19 students in her class. There are 9 boys. How many girls are in her class? ________

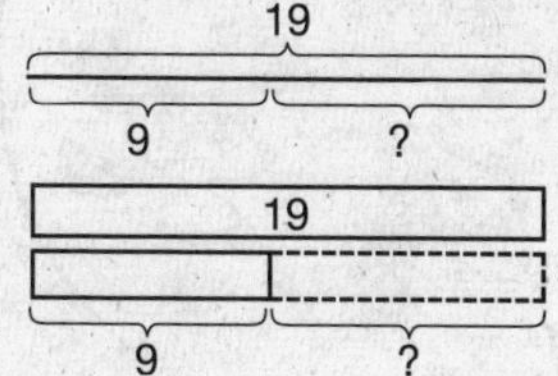

19
9
?
19
9
?

Mathematical expression:

50. Mary has 9 books. Sam has 7 books. How many books do they have altogether? ________

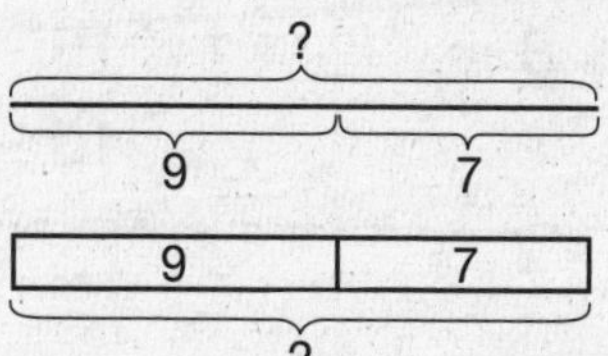

?
9
7
9
7
?

Mathematical expression:

Reflection and Discussion

Can you explain the trick for computing with 9?

Warm-up Exercises

9 + 4 = ____	6 + 2 = ____	7 + 1 = ____	9 + 8 = ____
9 − 1 = ____	8 − 3 = ____	9 − 2 = ____	8 − 5 = ____

1-8 Will computing with 8 be easier?

Mathematical Conversation

Are there any tricks for computing with 8? Can we revise the trick for 9 to make it work for 8?
8 + 3 = ?
You know what? I think the number 2 will be important.

I've got it! Here are the lists. Help me complete them. Don't forget to figure out the pattern.
Hey! The lists for 8 are shorter than the lists for 9.

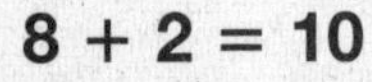

8 + 2 = 10	**2 + 8 =** ____	**10 − 8 =** ____
8 + 3 = 11	**3 + 8 =** ____	**11 − 8 =** ____
8 + 4 = 12	**4 + 8 =** ____	**12 − 8 =** ____
8 + 5 = 13	**5 + 8 =** ____	**13 − 8 =** ____
8 + 6 = 14	**6 + 8 =** ____	**14 − 8 =** ____
8 + 7 = 15	**7 + 8 =** ____	**15 − 8 =** ____
8 + 8 = 16		**16 − 8 =** ____

Unfortunately, "shorter" does not always mean "easier."
Really?

Guided Practice

Figure out the sum of each pair of numbers. Memorize each sum.

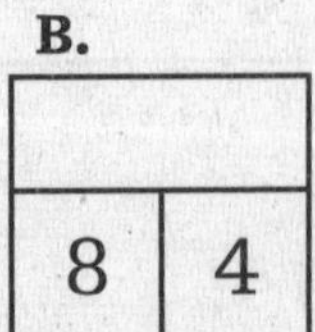

	A.	B.	C.	D.	E.	F.
Sum	11					
Pair	8, 3	8, 4	8, 5	8, 6	8, 7	8, 8

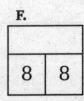

Lesson 1–8 Exercises

Calculate without using your fingers and fill in the answers.

1. 8 + 4 = ____ **2.** 8 + 3 = ____ **3.** 8 + 5 = ____ **4.** 8 + 8 = ____

5. 8 + 9 = ____ **6.** 8 + 2 = ____ **7.** 8 + 7 = ____ **8.** 8 + 6 = ____

9. 3 + 8 = ____ **10.** 6 + 8 = ____ **11.** 5 + 8 = ____ **12.** 2 + 8 = ____

13. 4 + 8 = ____ **14.** 0 + 8 = ____ **15.** 7 + 8 = ____ **16.** 8 + 8 = ____

17. 11 − 8 = ____ **18.** 18 − 8 = ____ **19.** 13 − 8 = ____ **20.** 14 − 8 = ____

21. 15 − 8 = ____ **22.** 16 − 8 = ____ **23.** 17 − 8 = ____ **24.** 12 − 8 = ____

25. 13 − 5 = ____ **26.** 14 − 6 = ____ **27.** 14 − 8 = ____ **28.** 17 − 9 = ____

29. 12 − 4 = ____ **30.** 11 − 3 = ____ **31.** 15 − 7 = ____ **32.** 18 − 10 = ____

33. 13 + 5 = ____ **34.** 12 + 7 = ____ **35.** 15 + 2 = ____ **36.** 14 + 4 = ____

37. 18 − 2 = ____ **38.** 15 − 1 = ____ **39.** 19 − 10 = ____ **40.** 17 − 1 = ____

41. 8 + 7 + 3 = ____ **42.** 9 + 4 + 6 = ____ **43.** 14 + 6 − 5 = ____ **44.** 17 + 2 − 1 = ____

45. 8 + 9 − 9 = ____ **46.** 2 + 5 + 8 = ____ **47.** 10 − 7 − 3 = ____ **48.** 16 − 2 − 2 = ____

Word Problems

Compare the models. Write a mathematical expression to represent each problem. Then calculate and answer the questions.

49. Tom ate 6 apricots on Monday and 8 on Tuesday. How many apricots did he eat during those two days?

____

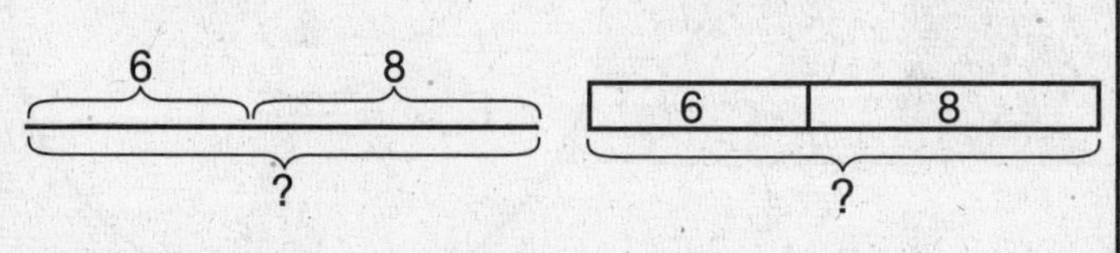

6
8
?
6
8
?

Mathematical expression:

50. There are 14 red cups and 6 white cups. How many more red cups than white cups are there?

____

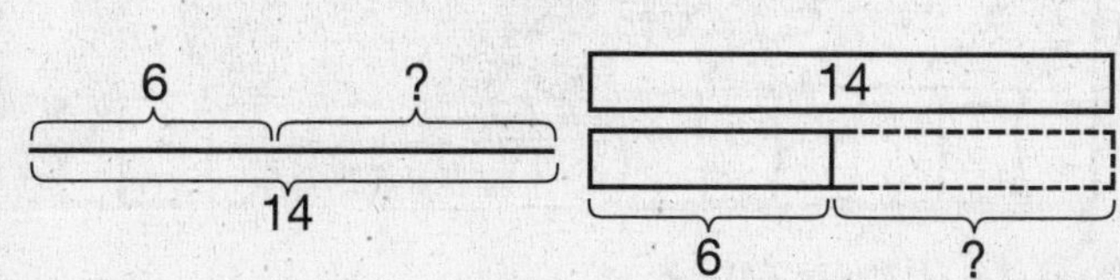

6
?
14
14
6
?

Mathematical expression:

Reflection and Discussion

Do you think that computing with 8 is easier than computing with 9? Why?

Warm-up Exercises

$8 + 8 =$ ____	$4 + 8 =$ ____	$10 - 2 =$ ____	$8 - 5 =$ ____
$9 - 2 =$ ____	$7 - 4 =$ ____	$7 + 3 =$ ____	$8 + 9 =$ ____

1-9 What are the equation lists for 7?

Mathematical Conversation

I guess today we will work on equation lists for 7.
I guess the lists for 7 will be even shorter than for 8.
For 7, you are going to complete all the lists by yourselves.

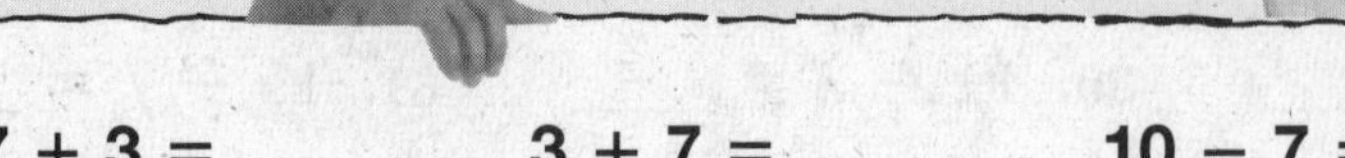

$7 + 3 =$ ____	$3 + 7 =$ ____	$10 - 7 =$ ____
$7 + 4 =$ ____	$4 + 7 =$ ____	$11 - 7 =$ ____
$7 + 5 =$ ____	$5 + 7 =$ ____	$12 - 7 =$ ____
$7 + 6 =$ ____	$6 + 7 =$ ____	$13 - 7 =$ ____
$7 + 7 =$ ____		$14 - 7 =$ ____

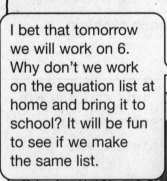

I bet that tomorrow we will work on 6. Why don't we work on the equation list at home and bring it to school? It will be fun to see if we make the same list.
Good idea. Let's do it.
Do you know why 7 + 8 and 7 + 9 are not in the list?

Guided Practice

Figure out the sum of each pair of numbers. Memorize each sum.

A.

7	4

B.

7	5

C.

7	6

D.

7	7

Lesson 1–9 Exercises

Calculate without using your fingers and fill in the answers.

1. $7 + 3 =$ ____	**2.** $7 + 4 =$ ____	**3.** $7 + 5 =$ ____	**4.** $7 + 6 =$ ____
5. $7 + 7 =$ ____	**6.** $7 + 1 =$ ____	**7.** $7 + 2 =$ ____	**8.** $7 + 0 =$ ____
9. $3 + 7 =$ ____	**10.** $6 + 7 =$ ____	**11.** $5 + 7 =$ ____	**12.** $2 + 7 =$ ____
13. $4 + 7 =$ ____	**14.** $0 + 7 =$ ____	**15.** $1 + 7 =$ ____	**16.** $8 + 7 =$ ____
17. $11 - 7 =$ ____	**18.** $13 - 7 =$ ____	**19.** $12 - 7 =$ ____	**20.** $14 - 7 =$ ____
21. $15 - 7 =$ ____	**22.** $16 - 7 =$ ____	**23.** $17 - 7 =$ ____	**24.** $10 - 7 =$ ____
25. $13 - 9 =$ ____	**26.** $14 - 9 =$ ____	**27.** $14 - 5 =$ ____	**28.** $17 - 9 =$ ____
29. $12 - 3 =$ ____	**30.** $11 - 4 =$ ____	**31.** $15 - 8 =$ ____	**32.** $18 - 8 =$ ____
33. $13 + 7 =$ ____	**34.** $10 + 5 =$ ____	**35.** $15 + 2 =$ ____	**36.** $12 + 4 =$ ____
37. $19 - 8 =$ ____	**38.** $15 - 6 =$ ____	**39.** $19 - 3 =$ ____	**40.** $17 - 6 =$ ____
41. $7 + 7 + 1 =$ ____	**42.** $9 + 7 + 2 =$ ____	**43.** $11 + 5 - 5 =$ ____	**44.** $14 + 2 - 2 =$ ____
45. $8 + 7 - 9 =$ ____	**46.** $3 + 5 + 8 =$ ____	**47.** $10 - 4 + 3 =$ ____	**48.** $14 - 2 - 2 =$ ____

Word Problems

Compare the models. Write a mathematical expression to represent each problem. Then calculate and answer the questions.

49. Oscar has 7 computer games. His older brother has 9. How many games do Oscar and his brother have in all? ____________

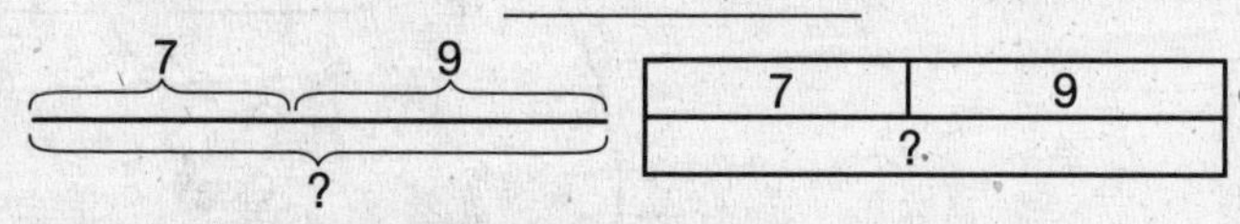

7
9
?
7
9
?

Mathematical expression:

50. Mary collected 11 scenic postcards and 4 animal postcards. How many more scenic cards than animal cards did Mary collect? ____________

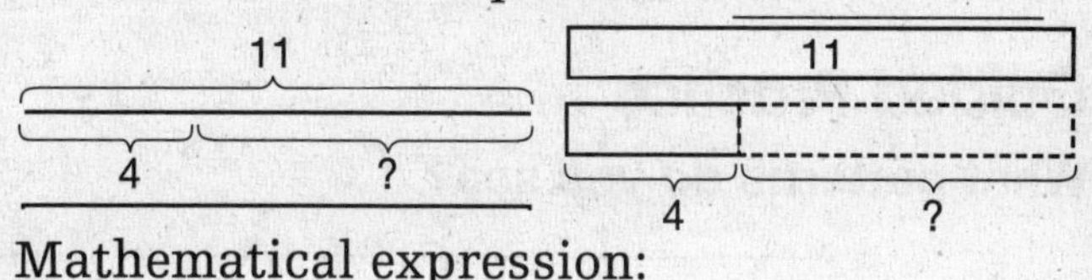

11
4
?
11
4
?

Mathematical expression:

Reflection and Discussion

Can you explain why $6 + 7 = 13$, using the idea of 10 as an organizer?

Warm-up Exercises

7 + 7 = ____	7 + 4 = ____	5 + 7 = ____	8 + 7 = ____
6 − 5 = ____	12 − 2 = ____	15 − 6 = ____	13 − 7 = ____

1-10 Review, Reflection, and Quiz 2

Mathematical Conversation

Here's my list for 6.
You forgot these versions.
Ana's List
6 + 4 = ____ 10 − 6 = ____
6 + 5 = ____ 11 − 6 = ____
6 + 6 = ____ 12 − 6 = ____
C.J.'s List
6 + 4 = ____ 4 + 6 = ____ 10 − 6 = ____
6 + 5 = ____ 5 + 6 = ____ 11 − 6 = ____
6 + 6 = ____ 12 − 6 = ____
Great!

There are twenty important pairs of numbers. Please memorize the sums of these pairs. You will find it very helpful to know them by heart.
1, 2, 3, 4 . . . 20! Wow, it *is* 20 pairs!
Actually, I *have* memorized the sum of these pairs.
9, 2 | 9, 3 | 9, 4 | 9, 5 | 9, 6 | 9, 7 | 9, 8 | 9, 9
8, 3 | 8, 4 | 8, 5 | 8, 6 | 8, 7 | 8, 8
7, 4 | 7, 5 | 7, 6 | 7, 7
6, 5 | 6, 6

But do you know them well?

Guided Practice

What patterns do you see?

9, 2	9, 3	9, 4	9, 5	9, 6	9, 7	9, 8	9, 9
	8, 3	8, 4	8, 5	8, 6	8, 7	8, 8	
		7, 4	7, 5	7, 6	7, 7		
			6, 5	6, 6			

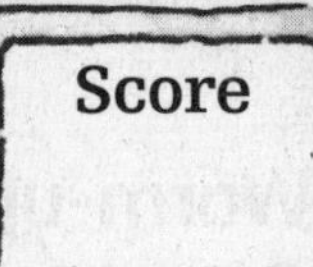
Score

Quiz 2

Calculate without using your fingers and fill in the answers.

1. 9 + 6 = ____ **2.** 4 + 9 = ____ **3.** 8 + 8 = ____ **4.** 7 + 4 = ____ **5.** 5 + 6 = ____

6. 2 + 9 = ____ **7.** 4 + 8 = ____ **8.** 7 + 5 = ____ **9.** 3 + 8 = ____ **10.** 7 + 5 = ____

11. 13 − 7 = ____ **12.** 12 − 6 = ____ **13.** 15 − 6 = ____ **14.** 17 − 9 = ____ **15.** 11 − 2 = ____

16. 11 − 3 = ____ **17.** 14 − 6 = ____ **18.** 16 − 8 = ____ **19.** 18 − 9 = ____ **20.** 12 − 4 = ____

21. 5 + ____ = 12 **22.** 6 + ____ = 12 **23.** 7 + ____ = 12 **24.** 4 + ____ = 12 **25.** 8 + ____ = 12

26. 15 − ____ = 6 **27.** 15 − ____ = 5 **28.** 15 − ____ = 8 **29.** 15 − ____ = 7 **30.** 15 − ____ = 9

Calculate the answers. Then write three other versions of each equation.

31.	32.	33.	34.	35.
8 + 7 = ____	7 + 6 = ____	9 + 8 = ____	13 − 6 = ____	12 − 4 = ____
____	____	____	____	____
____	____	____	____	____
____	____	____	____	____

Draw a model and write a mathematical expression to represent this word problem. Then calculate and answer the question.

36. Tom and his brother wrote 15 poems during their summer vacation. Tom wrote 8 of them. How many poems did Tom's brother write?

____

Model:

Mathematical expression:

Challenge Yourself

37. 60 + 60 = ____ **38.** 70 + 70 = ____ **39.** 80 + 40 = ____

40. 90 + 50 = ____ **41.** 50 + 40 = ____ **42.** 15 + 80 + 20 = ____

43. 29 + 90 + 10 = ____ **44.** 70 + 40 + 1 = ____ **45.** 20 + 50 + 50 = ____

Warm-up Exercises

8 − 7 = ____	5 + 4 = ____	4 + 3 = ____	7 − 6 = ____
9 − 4 = ____	2 + 6 = ____	1 + 7 = ____	5 − 3 = ____

1-11 Which is easier?

Mathematical Conversation

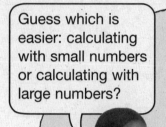

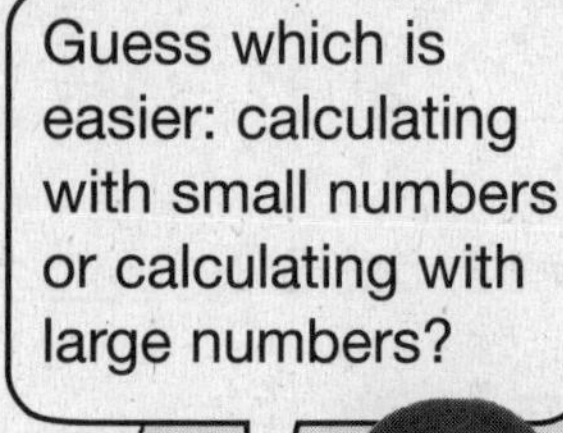
Guess which is easier: calculating with small numbers or calculating with large numbers?
Smaller numbers of course! The smaller the numbers, the easier the calculation.

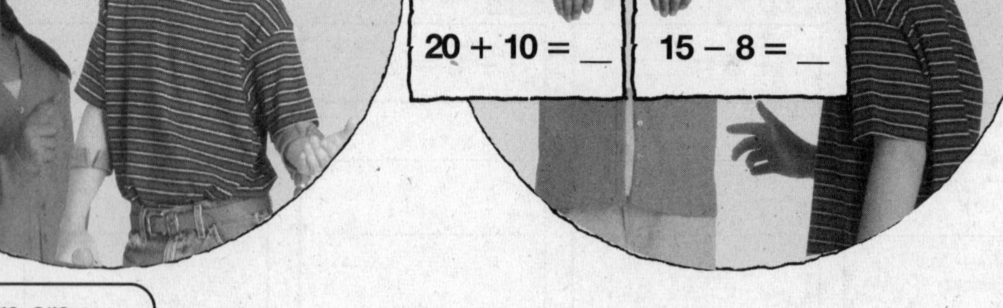
OK, look at this! Which is easier?
Hey, 2 tens and 1 ten make 3 tens—30! It's even easier than 15 – 8 = 7!
20 + 10 = _
15 – 8 = _

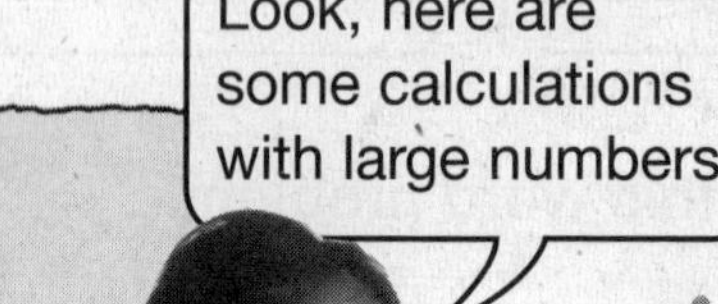
Look, here are some calculations with large numbers.

40 + 40 = ____
70 + 10 = ____
50 – 30 = ____
When you use the real names . . .
. . . these are simple!
Simple questions don't always have simple answers.

Guided Practice

Calculate and fill in the answers. Use the real names for the numbers to help you.

A. 30 + 20 = ____ **B.** 80 − 20 = ____ **C.** 35 + 21 = ____ **D.** 99 − 31 = ____

Lesson 1-11 Exercises

Calculate without using your fingers and fill in the answers.

1. $2 + 2 =$ ____ **2.** $5 + 3 =$ ____ **3.** $1 + 5 =$ ____ **4.** $4 + 3 =$ ____

5. $20 + 20 =$ ____ **6.** $50 + 30 =$ ____ **7.** $10 + 50 =$ ____ **8.** $40 + 30 =$ ____

9. $30 + 31 =$ ____ **10.** $40 + 14 =$ ____ **11.** $50 + 42 =$ ____ **12.** $10 + 83 =$ ____

13. $22 + 52 =$ ____ **14.** $73 + 23 =$ ____ **15.** $34 + 34 =$ ____ **16.** $65 + 11 =$ ____

17. $8 - 3 =$ ____ **18.** $4 - 1 =$ ____ **19.** $5 - 2 =$ ____ **20.** $9 - 3 =$ ____

21. $80 - 30 =$ ____ **22.** $40 - 10 =$ ____ **23.** $50 - 20 =$ ____ **24.** $90 - 30 =$ ____

25. $78 - 50 =$ ____ **26.** $67 - 30 =$ ____ **27.** $89 - 60 =$ ____ **28.** $95 - 20 =$ ____

29. $38 - 24 =$ ____ **30.** $43 - 21 =$ ____ **31.** $57 - 56 =$ ____ **32.** $70 - 70 =$ ____

33. $30 + 50 =$ ____ **34.** $20 + 70 =$ ____ **35.** $30 + 40 =$ ____ **36.** $60 + 30 =$ ____

37. $80 - 20 =$ ____ **38.** $50 - 10 =$ ____ **39.** $90 - 80 =$ ____ **40.** $70 - 40 =$ ____

41. $2 + 2 + 2 =$ ____ **42.** $20 + 20 + 20 =$ ____

43. $3 + 3 + 3 =$ ____ **44.** $30 + 30 + 30 =$ ____

45. $10 + 10 - 5 =$ ____ **46.** $20 + 2 - 1 =$ ____

47. $10 - 7 - 3 =$ ____ **48.** $40 - 2 - 8 =$ ____

Word Problems

Draw a model and write a mathematical expression to represent each problem. Then calculate and answer the questions.

49. A white hen laid 20 eggs. A black hen laid 30 eggs. How many eggs did the two hens lay in all? ____

Model:

Mathematical expression:

50. Ping's brother weighed 10 pounds two years ago. Now he weighs 30 pounds. How many pounds did he gain? ____

Model:

Mathematical expression:

Reflection and Discussion

Do you think computing $20 + 20$ is easier than computing $8 + 6$? Why?

Warm-up Exercises

40 + 4 = ____	32 + 5 = ____	52 + 7 = ____	23 + 4 = ____
66 − 20 = ____	58 − 10 = ____	70 − 40 = ____	85 − 30 = ____

1-12 Let's work on some hard computations!

Mathematical Conversation

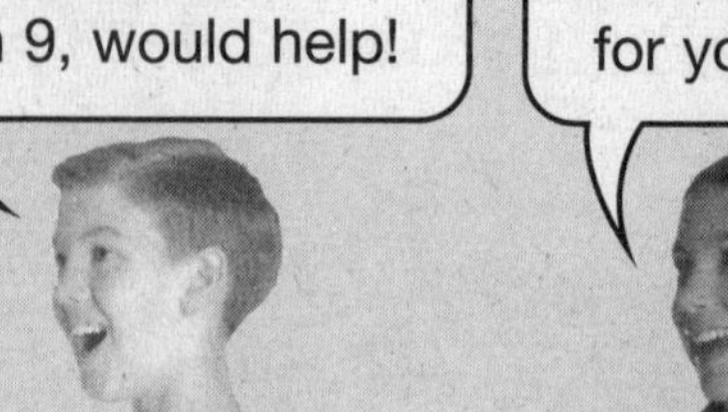

These computations are a bit harder than the ones we did in the last lesson.
You know what? What we learned before, the trick for computing with 9, would help!
Yes! Good for you!

29 + 3 = ____

49 + 7 = ____

32 − 9 = ____

57 − 9 = ____

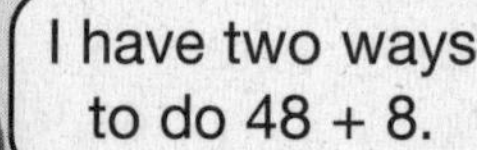
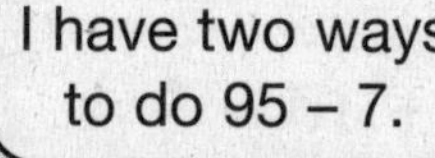

Here are more computations.
I have two ways to do 48 + 8.
I have two ways to do 95 − 7.

48 + 8 = ____

69 + 6 = ____

37 + 5 = ____

52 − 3 = ____

95 − 7 = ____

Way 1:
8 + 8 = 16 and
40 + 16 = 56

Way 2:
48 + 2 = 50 and
50 + 6 = 56

Way 1:
15 − 7 = 8 and
80 + 8 = 88

Way 2:
95 − 5 = 90 and
90 − 2 = 88

What is your strategy for doing these computations?

Guided Practice

Do these calculations and fill in the answers.

A. 38 + 4 = ____ **B.** 92 − 3 = ____ **C.** 75 + 6 = ____ **D.** 64 − 5 = ____

Lesson 1–12 Exercises

Calculate without using your fingers and fill in the answers.

1. 39 + 2 = ____ **2.** 58 + 3 = ____ **3.** 65 + 5 = ____ **4.** 27 + 4 = ____

5. 26 + 5 = ____ **6.** 47 + 4 = ____ **7.** 18 + 5 = ____ **8.** 38 + 3 = ____

9. 31 + 9 = ____ **10.** 32 + 9 = ____ **11.** 33 + 9 = ____ **12.** 34 + 9 = ____

13. 23 + 8 = ____ **14.** 55 + 6 = ____ **15.** 72 + 9 = ____ **16.** 66 + 4 = ____

17. 21 − 3 = ____ **18.** 24 − 5 = ____ **19.** 33 − 6 = ____ **20.** 92 − 3 = ____

21. 84 − 6 = ____ **22.** 77 − 9 = ____ **23.** 51 − 4 = ____ **24.** 34 − 8 = ____

25. 43 − 5 = ____ **26.** 56 − 7 = ____ **27.** 36 − 8 = ____ **28.** 85 − 6 = ____

29. 32 − 7 = ____ **30.** 43 − 6 = ____ **31.** 54 − 9 = ____ **32.** 90 − 8 = ____

33. 60 + 30 = ____ **34.** 40 + 20 = ____ **35.** 40 + 40 = ____ **36.** 70 + 30 = ____

37. 80 − 60 = ____ **38.** 50 − 40 = ____ **39.** 90 − 30 = ____ **40.** 60 − 50 = ____

41. 2 + 7 + 8 = ____ **42.** 29 + 3 + 3 = ____

43. 3 + 9 + 7 = ____ **44.** 15 + 6 + 9 = ____

45. 22 + 10 − 2 = ____ **46.** 20 + 7 − 6 = ____

47. 18 − 8 − 3 = ____ **48.** 32 − 3 − 9 = ____

Word Problems

Draw a model and write a mathematical expression to represent each problem. Then calculate and answer the questions.

49. C.J. hid 35 marbles. His sister found 7. How many marbles are still hidden? ________

Model:

Mathematical expression:

50. Ana's mom picked 22 tomatoes and 6 cucumbers. How many more tomatoes are there than cucumbers? ________

Model:

Mathematical expression:

Reflection and Discussion

What is your strategy for calculating 48 + 6?

Warm-up Exercises

39 + 2 = ____	58 + 4 = ____	37 − 8 = ____	15 + 6 = ____
22 − 6 = ____	28 + 8 = ____	72 − 5 = ____	48 − 9 = ____

1-13 One step further!

Mathematical Conversation

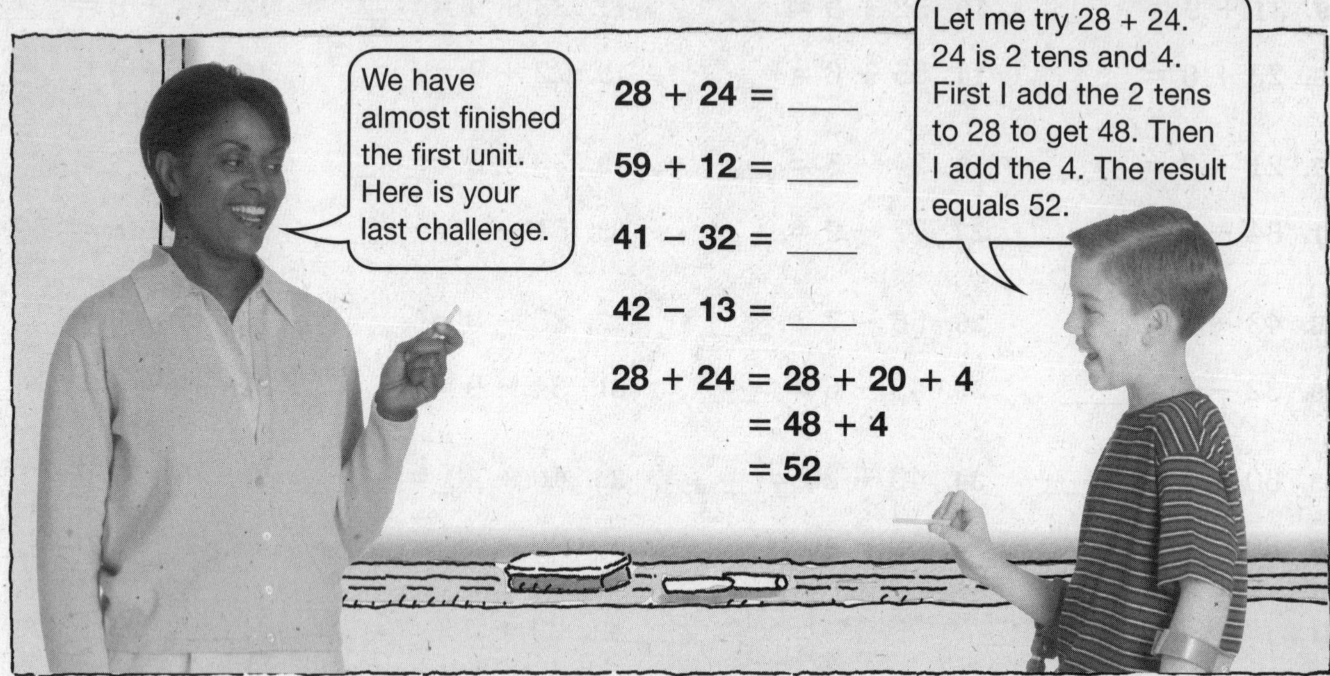
We have almost finished the first unit. Here is your last challenge.
28 + 24 = ____
59 + 12 = ____
41 − 32 = ____
42 − 13 = ____
28 + 24 = 28 + 20 + 4
= 48 + 4
= 52
Let me try 28 + 24. 24 is 2 tens and 4. First I add the 2 tens to 28 to get 48. Then I add the 4. The result equals 52.

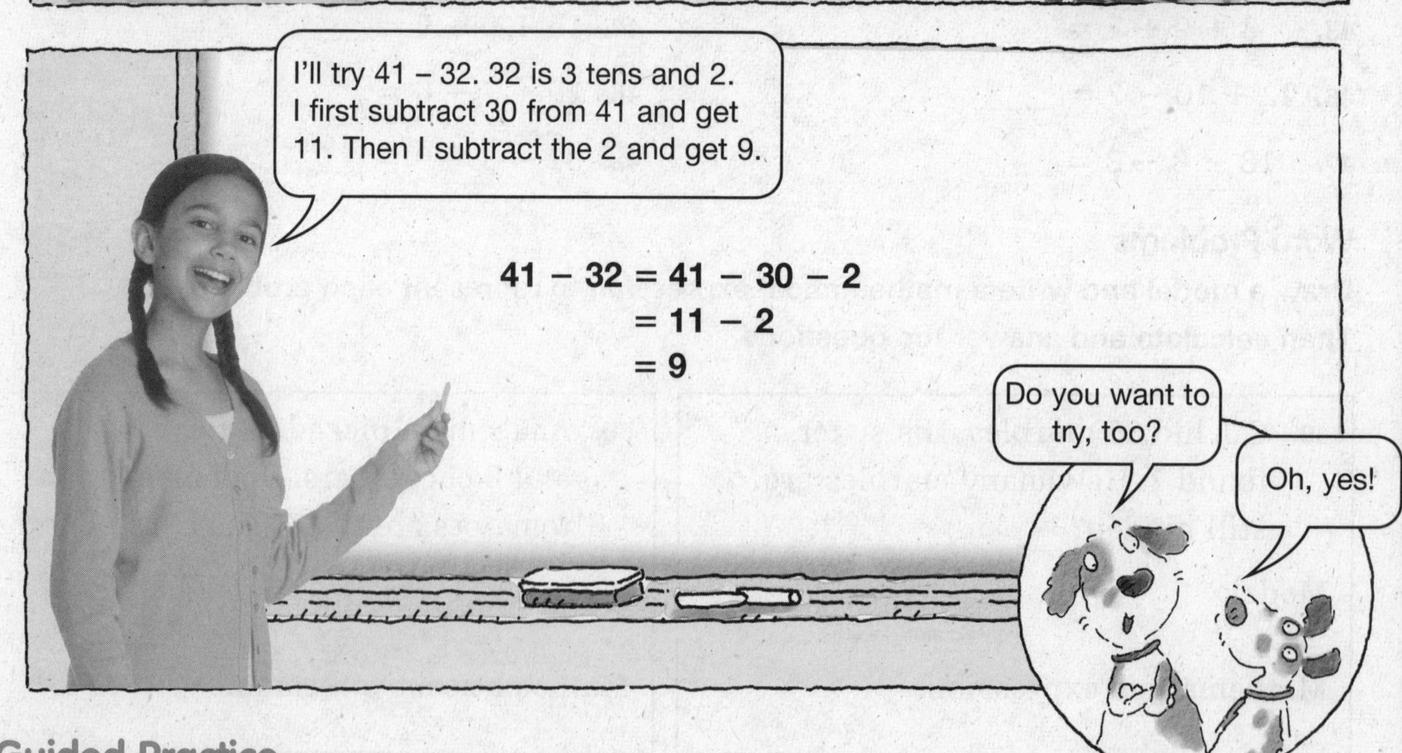
I'll try 41 – 32. 32 is 3 tens and 2. I first subtract 30 from 41 and get 11. Then I subtract the 2 and get 9.
41 − 32 = 41 − 30 − 2
= 11 − 2
= 9
Do you want to try, too?
Oh, yes!

Guided Practice

Try these calculations and fill in the answers.

A. 38 + 24 = ____ **B.** 92 − 13 = ____ **C.** 75 + 16 = ____ **D.** 64 − 25 = ____

Lesson 1–13 Exercises

Calculate without using your fingers and fill in the answers.

1. 29 + 12 = ____ **2.** 18 + 13 = ____ **3.** 15 + 16 = ____ **4.** 26 + 14 = ____

5. 38 + 13 = ____ **6.** 17 + 24 = ____ **7.** 18 + 15 = ____ **8.** 38 + 13 = ____

9. 11 + 19 = ____ **10.** 12 + 19 = ____ **11.** 13 + 19 = ____ **12.** 14 + 19 = ____

13. 23 + 18 = ____ **14.** 55 + 26 = ____ **15.** 42 + 29 = ____ **16.** 36 + 24 = ____

17. 21 − 11 = ____ **18.** 25 − 15 = ____ **19.** 33 − 13 = ____ **20.** 46 − 16 = ____

21. 74 − 24 = ____ **22.** 47 − 27 = ____ **23.** 48 − 38 = ____ **24.** 84 − 14 = ____

25. 43 − 15 = ____ **26.** 56 − 17 = ____ **27.** 36 − 28 = ____ **28.** 85 − 26 = ____

29. 32 − 27 = ____ **30.** 43 − 26 = ____ **31.** 54 − 29 = ____ **32.** 90 − 38 = ____

33. 60 + 24 = ____ **34.** 40 + 45 = ____ **35.** 50 + 29 = ____ **36.** 50 + 36 = ____

37. 80 − 11 = ____ **38.** 50 − 22 = ____ **39.** 90 − 9 = ____ **40.** 60 − 5 = ____

41. 12 + 4 + 3 = ____ **42.** 29 + 1 + 4 = ____

43. 11 + 9 + 5 = ____ **44.** 16 + 4 + 2 = ____

45. 22 + 12 − 2 = ____ **46.** 20 + 6 − 6 = ____

47. 12 − 2 − 3 = ____ **48.** 34 − 9 − 9 = ____

Word Problems

Draw a model and write a mathematical expression to represent each problem. Then calculate and answer the questions.

49. Juan had 59 books. Mary gave him 12 books. Now how many does Juan have? ____________

Model:

Mathematical expression:

50. Ping has 31 silkworms. She sees that 19 of them have spun cocoons. How many have not yet spun cocoons? ____________

Model:

Mathematical expression:

Reflection and Discussion

What is your strategy for calculating 64 − 25?

Warm-up Exercises

$33 - 22 =$ ____	$55 - 11 =$ ____	$77 - 44 =$ ____	$88 - 55 =$ ____
$29 + 2 =$ ____	$15 + 15 =$ ____	$16 + 16 =$ ____	$17 + 17 =$ ____

1-14 Unit 1 Review

Mathematical Conversation

You have learned a lot in this unit about addition and subtraction. Tell me, what has been most helpful to you?
I think it's cool that most addition and subtraction equations have four different versions. This means we only need to memorize a few arithmetic facts.

Ta-da! Look at my across-10 facts neighborhood.

11	12	13	14
2 9	3 9	4 9	5 9
3 8	4 8	5 8	6 8
4 7	5 7	6 7	7 7
5 6	6 6		

15	16	17	18
6 9	7 9	8 9	9 9
7 8	8 8		

Look carefully. You will find many interesting patterns in this neighborhood!

I will.

Unit 1 Review Exercises

Build your own across-10 facts neighborhood. Don't copy C.J.'s.

11
12
13
14
15
16
17
18

Build a within-10 facts neighborhood.

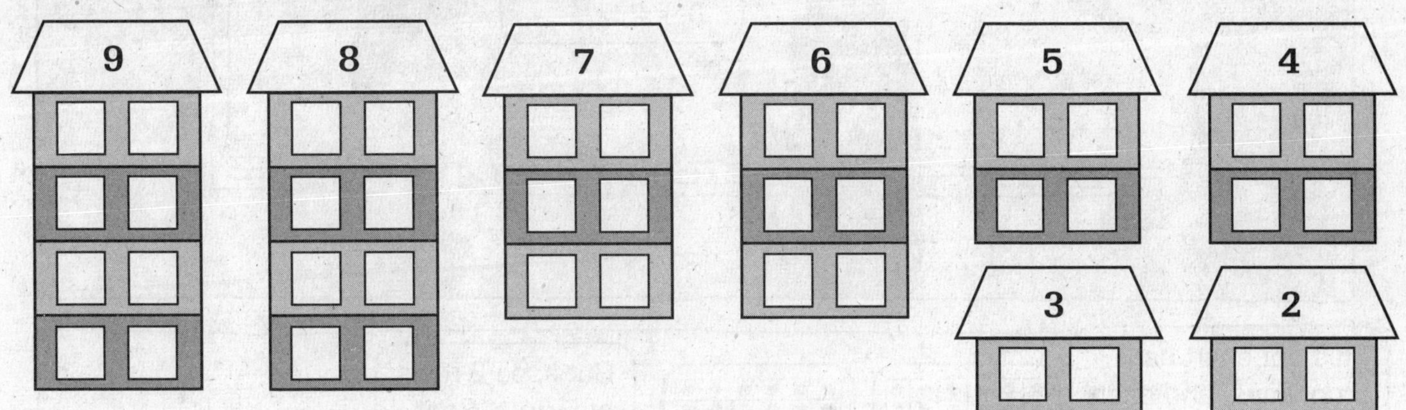

9
8
7
6
5
4
3
2

Calculate without using your fingers and fill in the answers.

1. ____ + 6 = 10 **2.** ____ + 5 = 10 **3.** ____ + 8 = 10

4. 10 − ____ = 9 **5.** 10 − ____ = 7 **6.** 10 − ____ = 6

7. ____ + 4 = 10 **8.** ____ + 6 = 10

9. 10 − ____ = 8 **10.** 10 − ____ = 5

11. 5 + 4 = ____ **12.** 7 + 8 = ____ **13.** 8 − 3 = ____ **14.** 12 − 6 = ____ **15.** 13 − 4 = ____

16. 20 + 20 = ____ **17.** 40 + 30 = ____ **18.** 28 + 10 = ____ **19.** 70 + 14 = ____ **20.** 56 + 30 = ____

21. 34 + 21 = ____ **22.** 51 + 32 = ____ **23.** 72 + 15 = ____ **24.** 38 + 21 = ____ **25.** 45 + 13 = ____

26. 5 + 24 + 5 = ____ **27.** 19 + 3 + 7 = ____ **28.** 3 + 18 + 7 = ____ **29.** 45 + 3 + 2 = ____

30. 24 + 10 − 4 = ____ **31.** 20 + 7 − 6 = ____ **32.** 38 − 8 − 30 = ____ **33.** 32 − 2 − 9 = ____

Warm-up Exercises

$2 + 2 =$ ____ $2 + 2 + 2 =$ ____ $2 + 2 + 2 + 2 =$ ____ $2 + 2 + 2 + 2 + 2 =$ ____

$3 + 3 =$ ____ $3 + 3 + 3 =$ ____ $3 + 3 + 3 + 3 =$ ____ $3 + 3 + 3 + 3 + 3 =$ ____

2-1 What does 6×2 mean?

Mathematical Conversation

Can you solve this problem?
2 + 2 + 2 + 2 + 2 + 2 = ?
Let me see.
2 + 2 = 4
4 + 2 = 6
6 + 2 = 8
8 + 2 = __
1, 2 . . ., 6. We have 6 twos here, 6 × 2 = 12!

This dot chart has 6 columns, and each column has 2 dots. That's how you get 6 × 2 = 12.
6 × 2 = 12
2 × 6 = 12
But I see 2 rows of 6 dots. So it should be 2 × 6 = 12.
Who is right, Lily or Danny?
Lily and Danny are both right. 6 × 2 = 2 × 6! They are seeing the same thing in different ways.

Guided Practice

Write two multiplication equations for each group of dots.

A. ●●● / ●●● **B.** ●●●● / ●●●● **C.** ●●●●● / ●●●●● **D.** ●●●●●● / ●●●●●● **E.** ●●●●●●●● / ●●●●●●●● **F.** ●●●●●●●● / ●●●●●●●●

____ ____ ____ ____ ____ ____

____ ____ ____ ____ ____ ____

Lesson 2–1 Exercises

Compare the two tables, line by line. How do we get the "2 Times" table from the "Times 2" table? Memorize the two tables.

"TIMES 2" TABLE	"2 TIMES" TABLE
Two twos make 4.	Two twos make 4.
Three twos make 6.	Two threes make 6.
Four twos make 8.	Two fours make 8.
Five twos make 10.	Two fives make 10.
Six twos make 12.	Two sixes make 12.
Seven twos make 14.	Two sevens make 14.
Eight twos make 16.	Two eights make 16.
Nine twos make 18.	Two nines make 18.

Investigate this multiplication table. Fill in the facts you learned today. Then lightly color the boxes.

2 × 2 =	2 × 3 =	2 × 4 =	2 × 5 =	2 × 6 =	2 × 7 =	2 × 8 =	2 × 9 =
3 × 2 =	3 × 3 =	3 × 4 =	3 × 5 =	3 × 6 =	3 × 7 =	3 × 8 =	3 × 9 =
4 × 2 =	4 × 3 =	4 × 4 =	4 × 5 =	4 × 6 =	4 × 7 =	4 × 8 =	4 × 9 =
5 × 2 =	5 × 3 =	5 × 4 =	5 × 5 =	5 × 6 =	5 × 7 =	5 × 8 =	5 × 9 =
6 × 2 =	6 × 3 =	6 × 4 =	6 × 5 =	6 × 6 =	6 × 7 =	6 × 8 =	6 × 9 =
7 × 2 =	7 × 3 =	7 × 4 =	7 × 5 =	7 × 6 =	7 × 7 =	7 × 8 =	7 × 9 =
8 × 2 =	8 × 3 =	8 × 4 =	8 × 5 =	8 × 6 =	8 × 7 =	8 × 8 =	8 × 9 =
9 × 2 =	9 × 3 =	9 × 4 =	9 × 5 =	9 × 6 =	9 × 7 =	9 × 8 =	9 × 9 =

Word Problems

Write a mathematical expression to solve each problem. Use the models to help you.

1. Ms. Park used 2 baskets to carry apples. She put 8 apples in each basket. How many apples did she have? ____________

?

Mathematical expression:

2. A bird has 2 wings. How many wings do 6 birds have? ____________

?

Mathematical expression:

Reflection and Discussion

What is the difference in meaning between 3 × 1 and 1 × 3? What does each one equal?

Warm-up Exercises

6 + 4 = ____	7 + 6 = ____	6 + 5 = ____	8 + 8 = ____
7 − 2 = ____	12 − 3 = ____	9 − 4 = ____	10 − 7 = ____

2-2 Why does $3 \times 5 = 5 \times 3$?

Mathematical Conversation

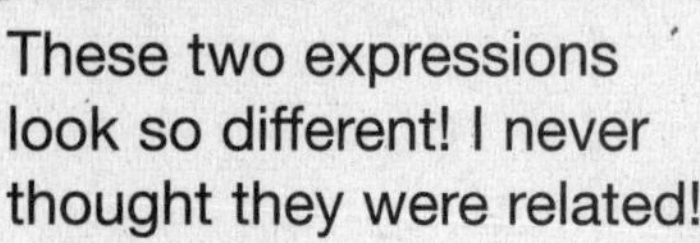
These two expressions look so different! I never thought they were related!
5 + 5 + 5 = ?
3 + 3 + 3 + 3 + 3 = ?
Here is the dot-chart that relates your two expressions.

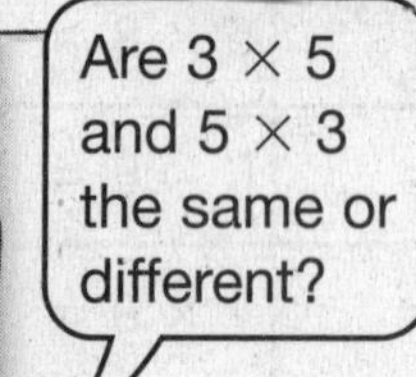
Are 3 × 5 and 5 × 3 the same or different?
They are different, because 3 × 5 means 3 fives, but 5 × 3 means 5 threes.
They are the same, because they have the same products.
With whom do you agree, Lily or Danny?

Guided Practice

Write two multiplication equations for each group of dots.

A. 

______

______

B. 

______

______

C. 

______

______

D. 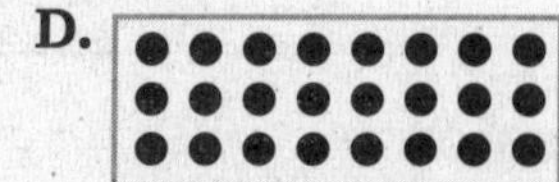

______

______

E. 

______

______

Lesson 2–2 Exercises

Compare the two tables, line by line. How do we get the "3 Times" table from the "Times 3" table? Memorize both tables.

"TIMES 3" TABLE	"3 TIMES" TABLE
Two threes make 6.	Three twos make 6.
Three threes make 9.	Three threes make 9.
Four threes make 12.	Three fours make 12.
Five threes make 15.	Three fives make 15.
Six threes make 18.	Three sixes make 18.
Seven threes make 21.	Three sevens make 21.
Eight threes make 24.	Three eights make 24.
Nine threes make 27.	Three nines make 27.

Fill in and shade the multiplication facts for 2 and 3. Use a different color for the facts you learned today.

2 × 2 =	2 × 3 =	2 × 4 =	2 × 5 =	2 × 6 =	2 × 7 =	2 × 8 =	2 × 9 =
3 × 2 =	3 × 3 =	3 × 4 =	3 × 5 =	3 × 6 =	3 × 7 =	3 × 8 =	3 × 9 =
4 × 2 =	4 × 3 =	4 × 4 =	4 × 5 =	4 × 6 =	4 × 7 =	4 × 8 =	4 × 9 =
5 × 2 =	5 × 3 =	5 × 4 =	5 × 5 =	5 × 6 =	5 × 7 =	5 × 8 =	5 × 9 =
6 × 2 =	6 × 3 =	6 × 4 =	6 × 5 =	6 × 6 =	6 × 7 =	6 × 8 =	6 × 9 =
7 × 2 =	7 × 3 =	7 × 4 =	7 × 5 =	7 × 6 =	7 × 7 =	7 × 8 =	7 × 9 =
8 × 2 =	8 × 3 =	8 × 4 =	8 × 5 =	8 × 6 =	8 × 7 =	8 × 8 =	8 × 9 =
9 × 2 =	9 × 3 =	9 × 4 =	9 × 5 =	9 × 6 =	9 × 7 =	9 × 8 =	9 × 9 =

Word Problems

Write a mathematical expression to solve each problem. Use the models to help you.

1. There are 3 wheels on a tricycle. How many wheels are there on 4 tricycles? ____________

?

Mathematical expression:

2. For a Thanksgiving food drive, each student brought 7 cans of food. How many cans did 3 students bring?

____

?

Mathematical expression:

Reflection and Discussion

If you calculate 3 × 4 and 4 × 3, will you get the same product? Why?

Warm-up Exercises

30 + 40 = ____	26 + 10 = ____	33 + 20 = ____	12 + 8 = ____
40 − 20 = ____	32 − 10 = ____	30 − 10 = ____	27 − 17 = ____

2-3 Can you make the times table for 4?

Mathematical Conversation

Can you make the times tables for 4 on your own?
Danny, do you want to work with me? Let's each make half.
I like that idea. You make the "4 Times" table and I'll write the "Times 4" table.

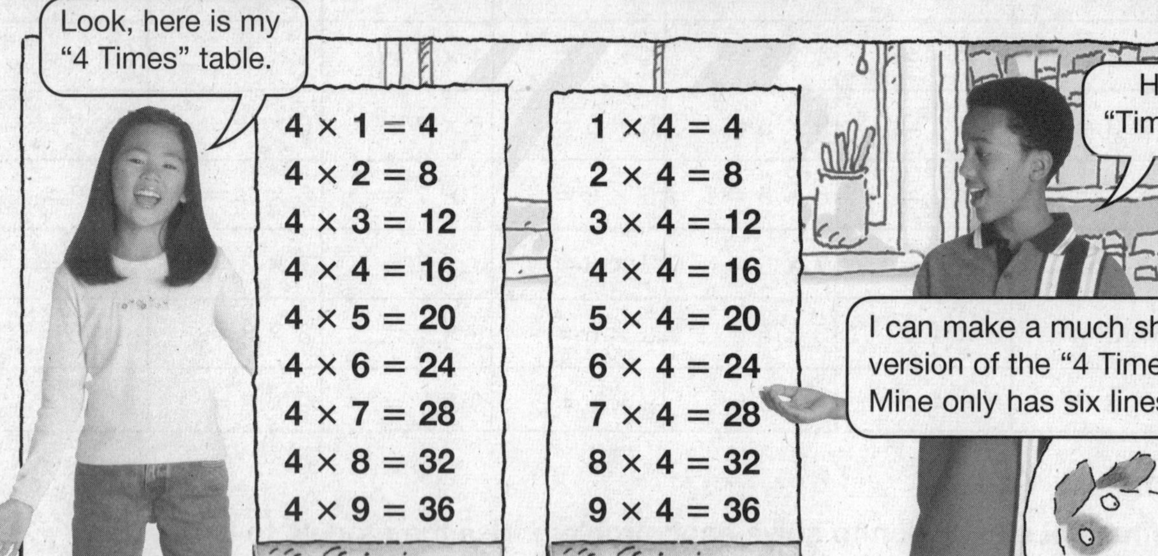
Look, here is my "4 Times" table.
4 × 1 = 4
4 × 2 = 8
4 × 3 = 12
4 × 4 = 16
4 × 5 = 20
4 × 6 = 24
4 × 7 = 28
4 × 8 = 32
4 × 9 = 36
1 × 4 = 4
2 × 4 = 8
3 × 4 = 12
4 × 4 = 16
5 × 4 = 20
6 × 4 = 24
7 × 4 = 28
8 × 4 = 32
9 × 4 = 36
Here is my "Times 4" table.
I can make a much shorter version of the "4 Times" table! Mine only has six lines!
Are yo sure?

Guided Practice

Write two multiplication equations for each group of dots.

A. 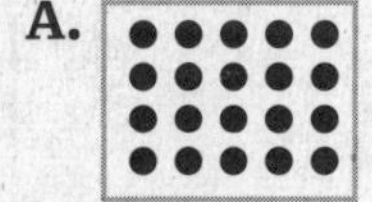

B. 

C. 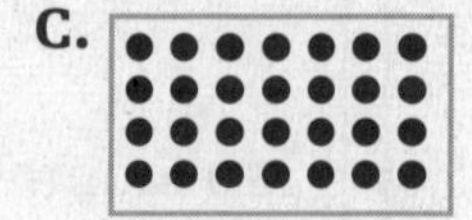

D. 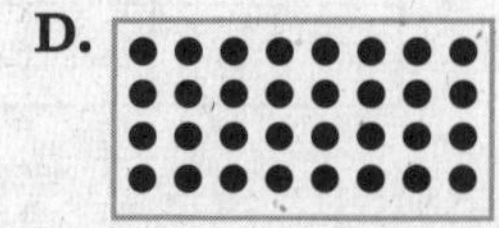

E. 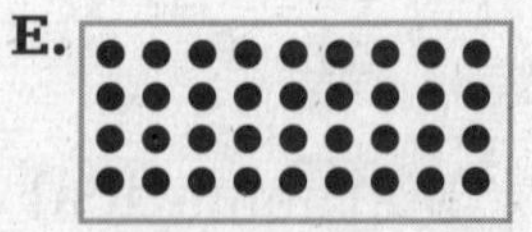

Lesson 2–3 Exercises

Compare the two tables, line by line. How do we get the "4 Times" table from the "Times 4" table? Memorize both tables.

"TIMES 4" TABLE	"4 TIMES" TABLE
Two fours make 8.	Four twos make 8.
Three fours make 12.	Four threes make 12.
Four fours make 16.	Four fours make 16.
Five fours make 20.	Four fives make 20.
Six fours make 24.	Four sixes make 24.
Seven fours make 28.	Four sevens make 28.
Eight fours make 32.	Four eights make 32.
Nine fours make 36.	Four nines make 36.

Fill in and shade the facts you have learned so far. Use a different color for the facts you learned today.

2 × 2 =	2 × 3 =	2 × 4 =	2 × 5 =	2 × 6 =	2 × 7 =	2 × 8 =	2 × 9 =
3 × 2 =	3 × 3 =	3 × 4 =	3 × 5 =	3 × 6 =	3 × 7 =	3 × 8 =	3 × 9 =
4 × 2 =	4 × 3 =	4 × 4 =	4 × 5 =	4 × 6 =	4 × 7 =	4 × 8 =	4 × 9 =
5 × 2 =	5 × 3 =	5 × 4 =	5 × 5 =	5 × 6 =	5 × 7 =	5 × 8 =	5 × 9 =
6 × 2 =	6 × 3 =	6 × 4 =	6 × 5 =	6 × 6 =	6 × 7 =	6 × 8 =	6 × 9 =
7 × 2 =	7 × 3 =	7 × 4 =	7 × 5 =	7 × 6 =	7 × 7 =	7 × 8 =	7 × 9 =
8 × 2 =	8 × 3 =	8 × 4 =	8 × 5 =	8 × 6 =	8 × 7 =	8 × 8 =	8 × 9 =
9 × 2 =	9 × 3 =	9 × 4 =	9 × 5 =	9 × 6 =	9 × 7 =	9 × 8 =	9 × 9 =

Word Problems

Write a mathematical expression to solve each problem. Use the models to help you.

1. A chair has 4 legs. How many legs do 4 chairs have? ______

?

Mathematical expression:

2. One movie ticket costs $7. Lily buys 4 tickets. How much does she pay?

?

______

Mathematical expression:

Reflection and Discussion

The models for the two word problems on this page look similar. Why then do the problems have different answers?

Warm-up Exercises

$6 + 9 =$ ____ $7 + 9 =$ ____ $8 + 9 =$ ____ $5 + 9 =$ ____

$13 - 9 =$ ____ $15 - 9 =$ ____ $16 - 9 =$ ____ $7 - 9 =$ ____

2-4 Can you find a pattern?

Mathematical Conversation

Today we are going to learn the times tables for 5.
We knew you would say that! We worked together again to make the tables.

Here is my "Times 5" table.

Look, here is my "5 Times" table.

Do you notice a pattern in the two tables? Can you explain it?

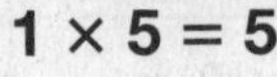

"Times 5" table	"5 Times" table
1 × 5 = 5	5 × 1 = 5
2 × 5 = 10	5 × 2 = 10
3 × 5 = 15	5 × 3 = 15
4 × 5 = 20	5 × 4 = 20
5 × 5 = 25	5 × 5 = 25
6 × 5 = 30	5 × 6 = 30
7 × 5 = 35	5 × 7 = 35
8 × 5 = 40	5 × 8 = 40
9 × 5 = 45	5 × 9 = 45

I see the pattern, but I want you to find it and explain it yourself.

Do I get any hints?

Guided Practice

Write two multiplications equations for each group of dots.

A. 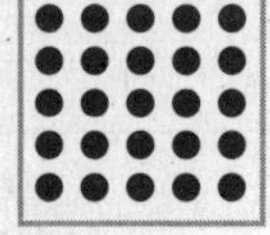

____

____

B. 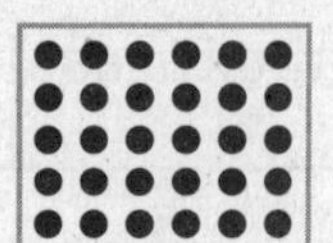

____

____

C. 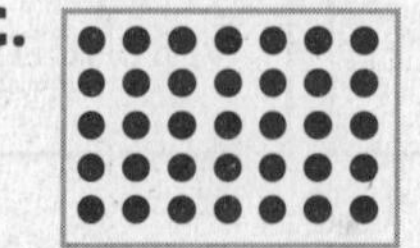

____

____

D. 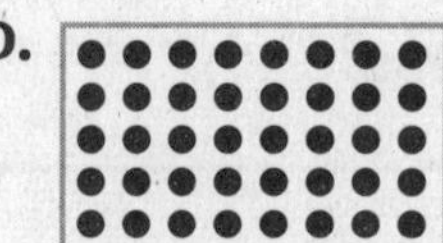

____

____

E. 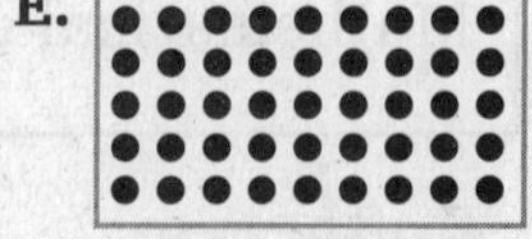

____

____

Lesson 2–4 Exercises

Compare the two tables, line by line. How do we get the "5 Times" table from the "Times 5" table? Memorize both tables.

"TIMES 5" TABLE	"5 TIMES" TABLE
Two fives make 10.	Five twos make 10.
Three fives make 15.	Five threes make 15.
Four fives make 20.	Five fours make 20.
Five fives make 25.	Five fives make 25.
Six fives make 30.	Five sixes make 30.
Seven fives make 35.	Five sevens make 35.
Eight fives make 40.	Five eights make 40.
Nines fives make 45.	Five nines make 45.

Fill in and shade the facts you have learned so far. Use a different color for the facts you learned today.

2 × 2 =	2 × 3 =	2 × 4 =	2 × 5 =	2 × 6 =	2 × 7 =	2 × 8 =	2 × 9 =
3 × 2 =	3 × 3 =	3 × 4 =	3 × 5 =	3 × 6 =	3 × 7 =	3 × 8 =	3 × 9 =
4 × 2 =	4 × 3 =	4 × 4 =	4 × 5 =	4 × 6 =	4 × 7 =	4 × 8 =	4 × 9 =
5 × 2 =	5 × 3 =	5 × 4 =	5 × 5 =	5 × 6 =	5 × 7 =	5 × 8 =	5 × 9 =
6 × 2 =	6 × 3 =	6 × 4 =	6 × 5 =	6 × 6 =	6 × 7 =	6 × 8 =	6 × 9 =
7 × 2 =	7 × 3 =	7 × 4 =	7 × 5 =	7 × 6 =	7 × 7 =	7 × 8 =	7 × 9 =
8 × 2 =	8 × 3 =	8 × 4 =	8 × 5 =	8 × 6 =	8 × 7 =	8 × 8 =	8 × 9 =
9 × 2 =	9 × 3 =	9 × 4 =	9 × 5 =	9 × 6 =	9 × 7 =	9 × 8 =	9 × 9 =

Word Problems

Write a mathematical expression to solve each problem. Use the models to help you.

1. One kind of star has 5 points. How many points do 6 of these stars have? ______

?

Mathematical expression:

2. Danny's mom needs 8 cups of flour to bake a cake. If she makes 5 cakes, how many cups of flour will she use? ______

?

Mathematical expression:

Reflection and Discussion

Without calculating 12 × 5, figure out what the digit in the ones place will be. How do you know?

Warm-up Exercises

2 × 4 = ____	3 × 2 = ____	4 × 5 = ____	2 × 6 = ____
4 × 2 = ____	2 × 3 = ____	5 × 4 = ____	6 × 2 = ____

2-5 Review, Reflection, and Quiz 3

Mathematical Conversation

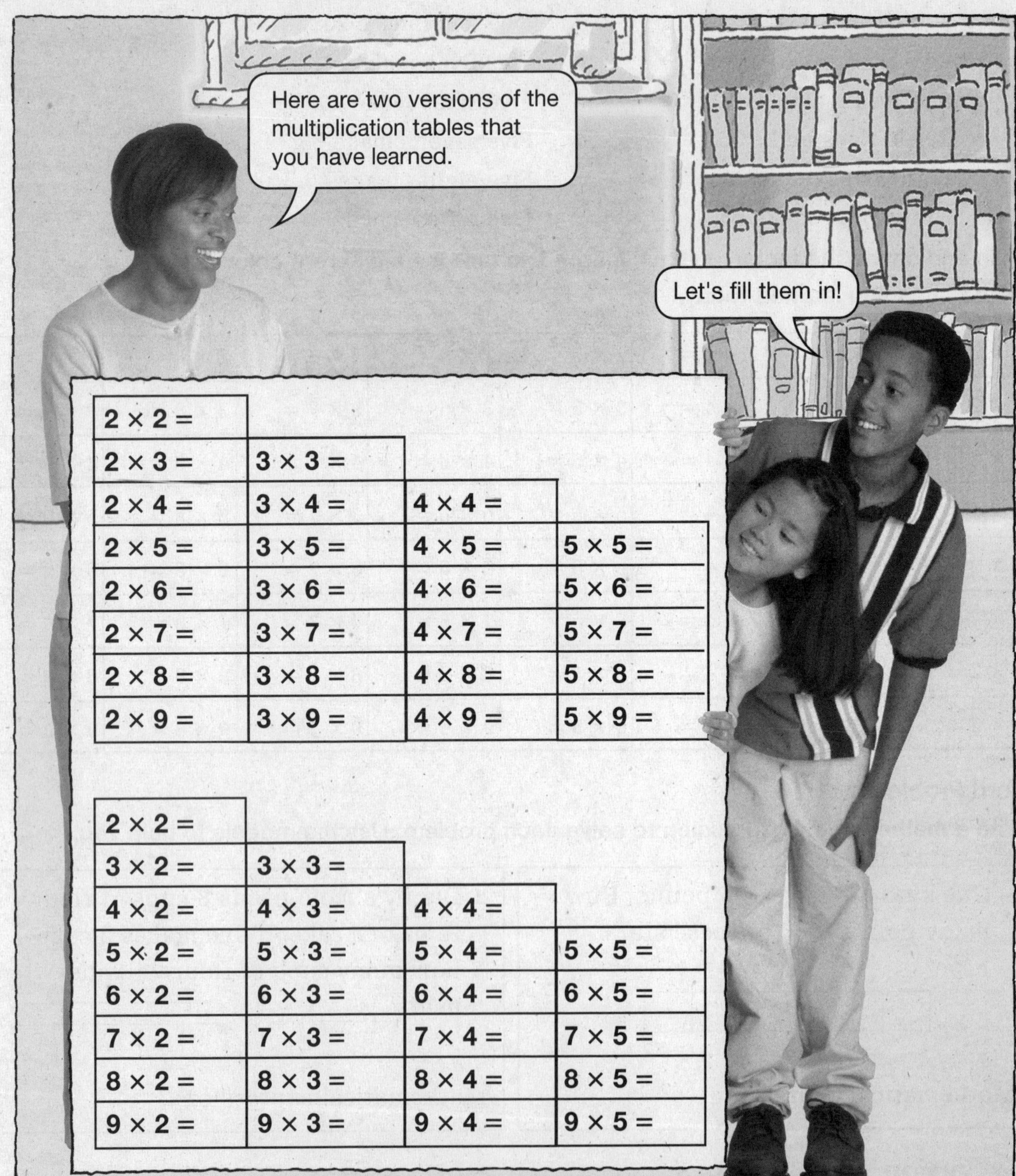

Here are two versions of the multiplication tables that you have learned.
Let's fill them in!

2 × 2 =			
2 × 3 =	3 × 3 =		
2 × 4 =	3 × 4 =	4 × 4 =	
2 × 5 =	3 × 5 =	4 × 5 =	5 × 5 =
2 × 6 =	3 × 6 =	4 × 6 =	5 × 6 =
2 × 7 =	3 × 7 =	4 × 7 =	5 × 7 =
2 × 8 =	3 × 8 =	4 × 8 =	5 × 8 =
2 × 9 =	3 × 9 =	4 × 9 =	5 × 9 =

2 × 2 =			
3 × 2 =	3 × 3 =		
4 × 2 =	4 × 3 =	4 × 4 =	
5 × 2 =	5 × 3 =	5 × 4 =	5 × 5 =
6 × 2 =	6 × 3 =	6 × 4 =	6 × 5 =
7 × 2 =	7 × 3 =	7 × 4 =	7 × 5 =
8 × 2 =	8 × 3 =	8 × 4 =	8 × 5 =
9 × 2 =	9 × 3 =	9 × 4 =	9 × 5 =

Score

Quiz 3

Calculate and fill in the answers.

1. 2 × 2 = ____ **2.** 2 × 3 = ____ **3.** 2 × 5 = ____ **4.** 2 × 7 = ____ **5.** 2 × 8 = ____

6. 3 × 2 = ____ **7.** 6 × 2 = ____ **8.** 4 × 2 = ____ **9.** 9 × 2 = ____ **10.** 5 × 2 = ____

11. 3 × 3 = ____ **12.** 3 × 5 = ____ **13.** 3 × 4 = ____ **14.** 3 × 8 = ____ **15.** 3 × 6 = ____

16. 7 × 3 = ____ **17.** 9 × 3 = ____ **18.** 4 × 3 = ____ **19.** 5 × 3 = ____ **20.** 8 × 3 = ____

21. 4 × 2 = ____ **22.** 4 × 4 = ____ **23.** 4 × 6 = ____ **24.** 4 × 8 = ____ **25.** 4 × 9 = ____

26. 5 × 4 = ____ **27.** 2 × 4 = ____ **28.** 6 × 4 = ____ **29.** 7 × 4 = ____ **30.** 9 × 4 = ____

31. 5 × 6 = ____ **32.** 5 × 7 = ____ **33.** 5 × 1 = ____ **34.** 5 × 9 = ____ **35.** 5 × 8 = ____

36. 7 × 5 = ____ **37.** 4 × 5 = ____ **38.** 5 × 5 = ____ **39.** 6 × 5 = ____ **40.** 7 × 5 = ____

Word Problem

Draw a model and write a mathematical expression to represent the problem. Then calculate and answer the question.

41. Ana's class has 4 math groups. Each math group has 5 students. How many students are there? ____________

Model:

Mathematical expression:

Challenge Yourself

42. 2 × 20 = ____ **43.** 3 × 30 = ____ **44.** 4 × 2 × 2 = ____ **45.** 3 × 3 × 3 = ____

Warm-up Exercises

$40 + 20 =$ ____ $30 + 20 =$ ____ $60 + 10 =$ ____ $50 + 50 =$ ____

$60 - 20 =$ ____ $50 - 30 =$ ____ $70 - 60 =$ ____ $100 - 50 =$ ____

2-6 What is the inverse of multiplication?

Mathematical Conversation

I think that today we are going to learn the times tables for 6. I worked out a short version—with only four lines!

6 × 6 = 36
6 × 7 = 42
6 × 8 = 48
6 × 9 = 54

That's great! I have a question, Lily. We learned that subtraction is the inverse of addition. Does multiplication have an inverse, too?

What's the inverse of multiplication? Interesting question! Let's use addition and subtraction to get some ideas . . .

If we have an addition equation with a missing addend before the equals sign, we can use subtraction to find the number.

I've got an idea. The inverse of multiplication may be the way to find a missing factor before the equals sign in a multiplication equation!

$3 +$ ____ $= 5$	____ $+ 1 = 6$
$5 - 3 = 2$	$6 - 1 = 5$

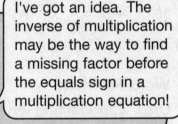

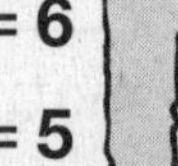

$2 \times$ ____ $= 10$	____ $\times 4 = 24$

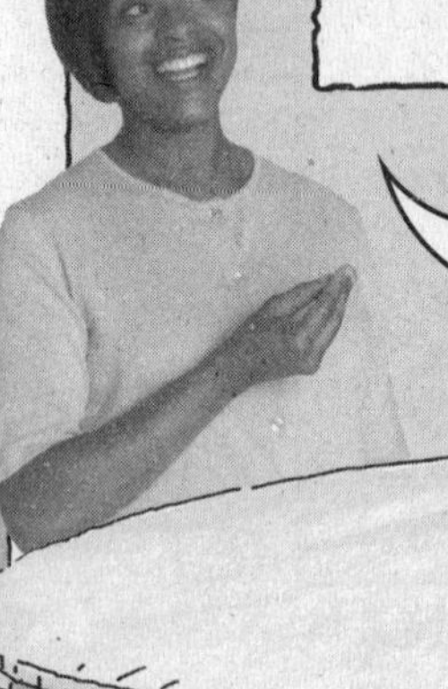

Good for you! The operation we use to find a missing factor in a multiplication is called division. For example, to find the missing factor in $6 \times$ ___ $= 42$, we do the division, $42 \div 6 = 7$.

We can use the multiplication tables to do division! Can you fill in this blank? ____ $\times 7 = 42$

Guided Practice

Complete each multiplication fact. Draw dot charts to represent the equations and then write related division equations.

A. $6 \times 6 =$ 36 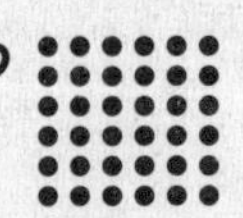 **B.** $6 \times 7 =$ **C.** $6 \times 8 =$ **D.** $6 \times 9 =$

36 ÷ 6 = 6 ____________ ____________ ____________

Lesson 2–6 Exercises

Compare the two tables, line by line. How do we get the "6 Times" table from the "Times 6" table? Memorize both tables.

"TIMES 6" TABLE	"6 TIMES" TABLE
Two sixes make 12.	Six twos make 12.
Three sixes make 18.	Six threes make 18.
Four sixes make 24.	Six fours make 24.
Five sixes make 30.	Six fives make 30.
Six sixes make 36.	Six sixes make 36.
Seven sixes make 42.	Six sevens make 42.
Eight sixes make 48.	Six eights make 48.
Nine sixes make 54.	Six nines make 54.

Fill in and shade the facts you have learned so far. Use a different color for facts you learned today.

2 × 2 =	2 × 3 =	2 × 4 =	2 × 5 =	2 × 6 =	2 × 7 =	2 × 8 =	2 × 9 =
3 × 2 =	3 × 3 =	3 × 4 =	3 × 5 =	3 × 6 =	3 × 7 =	3 × 8 =	3 × 9 =
4 × 2 =	4 × 3 =	4 × 4 =	4 × 5 =	4 × 6 =	4 × 7 =	4 × 8 =	4 × 9 =
5 × 2 =	5 × 3 =	5 × 4 =	5 × 5 =	5 × 6 =	5 × 7 =	5 × 8 =	5 × 9 =
6 × 2 =	6 × 3 =	6 × 4 =	6 × 5 =	6 × 6 =	6 × 7 =	6 × 8 =	6 × 9 =
7 × 2 =	7 × 3 =	7 × 4 =	7 × 5 =	7 × 6 =	7 × 7 =	7 × 8 =	7 × 9 =
8 × 2 =	8 × 3 =	8 × 4 =	8 × 5 =	8 × 6 =	8 × 7 =	8 × 8 =	8 × 9 =
9 × 2 =	9 × 3 =	9 × 4 =	9 × 5 =	9 × 6 =	9 × 7 =	9 × 8 =	9 × 9 =

Word Problems

Write a mathematical expression to solve each problem. Use the models to help you.

1. An ant has 6 legs. How many legs do 9 ants have? ________

6	6	6	6	6	6	6	6	6

?

Mathematical expression:

2. Maria has $48. A book costs $6. How many books can she buy? ________

6							

48

Mathematical expression:

Reflection and Discussion

Compare the two pairs of inverse operations: addition/subtraction and multiplication/division. What pattern do you see?

Warm-up Exercises

$40 + 5 =$ ____	$30 + 6 =$ ____	$60 + 4 =$ ____	$50 + 9 =$ ____
$60 - 2 =$ ____	$50 - 1 =$ ____	$70 - 10 =$ ____	$100 - 5 =$ ____

2-7 How are multiplication and division related?

Mathematical Conversation

This short version of the "7 Times" table has only three lines.
So it also means that:
Are there any other division equations you can get from Lily's "7 Times" table?
Let's see, there should be two more.
7 × 7 = 49
7 × 8 = 56
7 × 9 = 63
49 ÷ 7 = 7
56 ÷ 7 = 8
63 ÷ 7 = 9
56 ÷ 8 = 7
63 ÷ 9 = 7

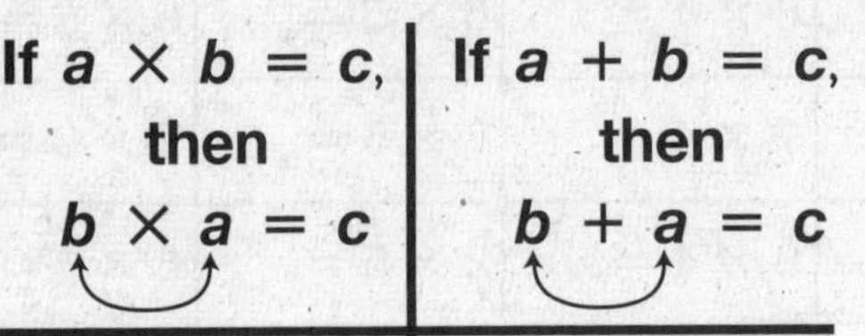
If $a \times b = c$, then $b \times a = c$
If $a + b = c$, then $b + a = c$
If $c \div b = a$, then $c \div a = b$
If $c - b = a$, then $c - a = b$

Here's what I notice. In multiplication and addition equations, the first two numbers can trade places. In division and subtraction equations, however, the last two numbers can trade places.

Do you notice that most multiplication equations have four different versions?

I know! There are two multiplication and two division versions.

Guided Practice

Complete each multiplication fact. Then write three other versions.

A. $7 \times 6 = 42$

____

____

____

B. $7 \times 8 =$

____

____

____

C. $7 \times 9 =$

____

____

____

Lesson 2–7 Exercises

Compare the two tables, line by line. How do we get the "7 times" table from the "times 7" table? Memorize both tables.

"TIMES 7" TABLE	"7 TIMES" TABLE
Two sevens make 14.	Seven twos make 14.
Three sevens make 21.	Seven threes make 21.
Four sevens make 28.	Seven fours make 28.
Five sevens make 35.	Seven fives make 35.
Six sevens make 42.	Seven sixes make 42.
Seven sevens make 49.	Seven sevens make 49.
Eight sevens make 56.	Seven eights make 56.
Nine sevens make 63.	Seven nines make 63.

Fill in and shade the facts you have learned so far. Use a different color for facts you learned today.

2 × 2 =	2 × 3 =	2 × 4 =	2 × 5 =	2 × 6 =	2 × 7 =	2 × 8 =	2 × 9 =
3 × 2 =	3 × 3 =	3 × 4 =	3 × 5 =	3 × 6 =	3 × 7 =	3 × 8 =	3 × 9 =
4 × 2 =	4 × 3 =	4 × 4 =	4 × 5 =	4 × 6 =	4 × 7 =	4 × 8 =	4 × 9 =
5 × 2 =	5 × 3 =	5 × 4 =	5 × 5 =	5 × 6 =	5 × 7 =	5 × 8 =	5 × 9 =
6 × 2 =	6 × 3 =	6 × 4 =	6 × 5 =	6 × 6 =	6 × 7 =	6 × 8 =	6 × 9 =
7 × 2 =	7 × 3 =	7 × 4 =	7 × 5 =	7 × 6 =	7 × 7 =	7 × 8 =	7 × 9 =
8 × 2 =	8 × 3 =	8 × 4 =	8 × 5 =	8 × 6 =	8 × 7 =	8 × 8 =	8 × 9 =
9 × 2 =	9 × 3 =	9 × 4 =	9 × 5 =	9 × 6 =	9 × 7 =	9 × 8 =	9 × 9 =

Word Problems

Write a mathematical expression to solve each problem. Use the models to help you.

1. A week has 7 days, so how many days do 5 weeks have? ________

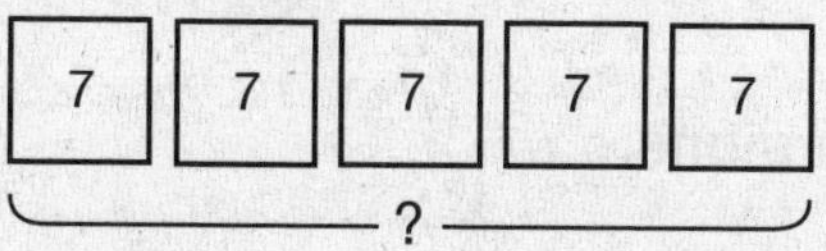

7
7
7
7
7
?

Mathematical expression:

2. A week has 7 days, so how many weeks does a February with 28 days have?

____

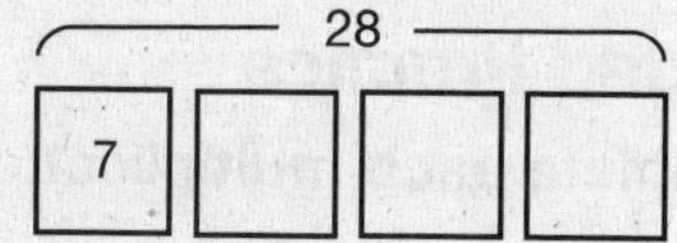

28
7

Mathematical expression:

Reflection and Discussion

How many division equations can you make from 7 × 7 = ? Why?

Warm-up Exercises

9 + 8 = ____	6 + 7 = ____	8 + 7 = ____	9 + 7 = ____
17 − 8 = ____	13 − 6 = ____	15 − 7 = ____	16 − 9 = ____

2-8 How many lines in the times table for 8?

Mathematical Conversation

Guess how many lines we have to memorize in the times table for 8.

I bet there are two.

That's because we started with the tables for small numbers. By now, we have learned a big part of the times tables for large numbers from the times tables for small numbers!

Hmm . . . what if we started by learning times tables in a different order? Say we started with tables for large numbers and ended with tables for small numbers. Then it would be the larger the number, the longer the table!

8 × 8 = 64
8 × 9 = 72

Cool! The larger the number, the shorter the table!

It is wise to start with small numbers!

I can see why!

Guided Practice

Complete each multiplication fact. Then write 3 other versions.

A. 8 × 3 = ____ **B.** 8 × 4 = ____ **C.** 8 × 5 = ____ **D.** 8 × 6 = ____ **E.** 8 × 7 = ____

Lesson 2–8 Exercises

Compare the two tables, line by line. How do we get the "8 Times" table from the "Times 8" table? Memorize both tables.

"TIMES 8" TABLE	**"8 TIMES" TABLE**
Two eights make 16.	Eight twos make 16.
Three eights make 24.	Eight threes make 24.
Four eights make 32.	Eight fours make 32.
Five eights make 40.	Eight fives make 40.
Six eights make 48.	Eight sixes make 48.
Seven eights make 56.	Eight sevens make 56.
Eight eights make 64.	Eight eights make 64.
Nine eights make 72.	Eight nines make 72.

Fill in and shade the facts you have learned so far. Use a different color for facts you learned today.

2 × 2 =	2 × 3 =	2 × 4 =	2 × 5 =	2 × 6 =	2 × 7 =	2 × 8 =	2 × 9 =
3 × 2 =	3 × 3 =	3 × 4 =	3 × 5 =	3 × 6 =	3 × 7 =	3 × 8 =	3 × 9 =
4 × 2 =	4 × 3 =	4 × 4 =	4 × 5 =	4 × 6 =	4 × 7 =	4 × 8 =	4 × 9 =
5 × 2 =	5 × 3 =	5 × 4 =	5 × 5 =	5 × 6 =	5 × 7 =	5 × 8 =	5 × 9 =
6 × 2 =	6 × 3 =	6 × 4 =	6 × 5 =	6 × 6 =	6 × 7 =	6 × 8 =	6 × 9 =
7 × 2 =	7 × 3 =	7 × 4 =	7 × 5 =	7 × 6 =	7 × 7 =	7 × 8 =	7 × 9 =
8 × 2 =	8 × 3 =	8 × 4 =	8 × 5 =	8 × 6 =	8 × 7 =	8 × 8 =	8 × 9 =
9 × 2 =	9 × 3 =	9 × 4 =	9 × 5 =	9 × 6 =	9 × 7 =	9 × 8 =	9 × 9 =

Word Problems

Write a mathematical expression to solve each problem. Use the models to help you.

1. An octopus has 8 tentacles. How many tentacles do 3 octopuses have?

______

8 8 8

?

Expression:

2. Ms. Park shares 48 sheets of origami paper equally among 8 students. How many sheets does each student receive? ______

48

?

Expression:

Reflection and Discussion

C.J. says "The larger the number, the shorter the table." Do you agree with that statement? Why?

Warm-up Exercises

9 + 9 = ____ 8 + 8 = ____ 7 + 7 = ____ 6 + 6 = ____

2 × 9 = ____ 2 × 8 = ____ 2 × 7 = ____ 2 × 6 = ____

2-9 Finally, the times table for 9!

Mathematical Conversation

Finally, the times table for 9! We will only have to memorize one line: 9 × 9 = 81!

That's true only if we know the earlier multiplication tables by heart.

Do you remember the patterns for adding and subtracting 9? Why don't you write out the whole times table for 9? See if you can find a pattern there, too.

Here is the whole times table for 9.

9 × 1 = 9	1 × 9 = 9
9 × 2 = 18	2 × 9 = 18
9 × 3 = 27	3 × 9 = 27
9 × 4 = 36	4 × 9 = 36
9 × 5 = 45	5 × 9 = 45
9 × 6 = 54	6 × 9 = 54
9 × 7 = 63	7 × 9 = 63
9 × 8 = 72	8 × 9 = 72
9 × 9 = 81	9 × 9 = 81

I see a pattern! When we multiply a number by 9, we put a zero after the number and subtract the number. For example:

9 × 1 equals 10 − 1, which is 9.
9 × 2 equals 20 − 2, which is 18.
9 × 3 equals 30 − 3, which is 27.

I like Lily's idea! But I think instead of saying "put a zero after the number" she might want to say "multiply the number by 10." Do you agree with me?

Oh, yes!

Guided Practice

Complete each multiplication fact. Then write three other versions.

A. 9 × 4 = ____ **B.** 9 × 5 = ____ **C.** 9 × 6 = ____ **D.** 9 × 7 = ____ **E.** 9 × 8 = ____

Lesson 2–9 Exercises

Compare the two tables, line by line. How do we get the "9 Times" table from the "Times 9" table? Memorize both tables.

"TIMES 9" TABLE	"9 TIMES" TABLE
Two nines make 18.	Nine twos make 18.
Three nines make 27.	Nine threes make 27.
Four nines 36.	Nine fours make 36.
Five nines 45.	Nine fives make 45.
Six nines make 54.	Nine sixes make 54.
Seven nines make 63.	Nine sevens make 63.
Eight nines make 72.	Nine eights make 72.
Nine nines make 81.	Nine nines make 81.

Complete the facts below. Then lightly color the boxes of the facts you learned today.

2 × 2 =	2 × 3 =	2 × 4 =	2 × 5 =	2 × 6 =	2 × 7 =	2 × 8 =	2 × 9 =
3 × 2 =	3 × 3 =	3 × 4 =	3 × 5 =	3 × 6 =	3 × 7 =	3 × 8 =	3 × 9 =
4 × 2 =	4 × 3 =	4 × 4 =	4 × 5 =	4 × 6 =	4 × 7 =	4 × 8 =	4 × 9 =
5 × 2 =	5 × 3 =	5 × 4 =	5 × 5 =	5 × 6 =	5 × 7 =	5 × 8 =	5 × 9 =
6 × 2 =	6 × 3 =	6 × 4 =	6 × 5 =	6 × 6 =	6 × 7 =	6 × 8 =	6 × 9 =
7 × 2 =	7 × 3 =	7 × 4 =	7 × 5 =	7 × 6 =	7 × 7 =	7 × 8 =	7 × 9 =
8 × 2 =	8 × 3 =	8 × 4 =	8 × 5 =	8 × 6 =	8 × 7 =	8 × 8 =	8 × 9 =
9 × 2 =	9 × 3 =	9 × 4 =	9 × 5 =	9 × 6 =	9 × 7 =	9 × 8 =	9 × 9 =

Word Problems

Write a mathematical expression to solve each problem. Use the models to help you.

1. There are 9 books in a complete set of "Little House" books. How many books are there in 6 complete sets of "Little House" books? ________

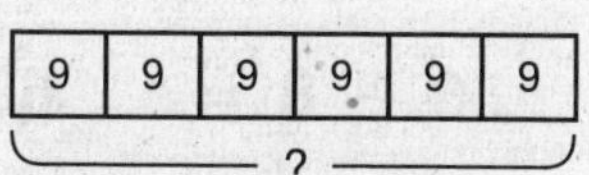
9
9
9
9
9
9
?

Mathematical expression:

2. Danny arranged 18 chairs in 2 rows. He put the same number of chairs in each row. How many chairs were there in each row? ________

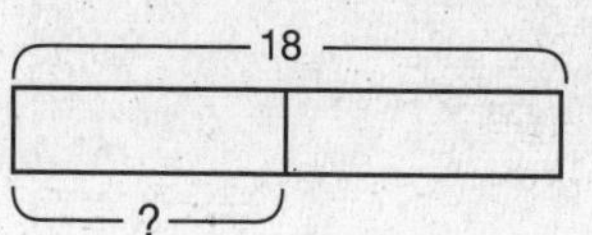
18
?

Mathematical expression:

Reflection and Discussion

Can you explain the pattern that Ana found for multiplying by 9?

Warm-up Exercises

2 + 4 = ____	3 + 3 = ____	4 + 1 = ____	2 + 2 = ____
4 − 2 = ____	5 − 2 = ____	3 − 1 = ____	4 − 2 = ____

2-10 Review, Reflection, and Quiz 4

Mathematical Conversation

Today we are going to review multiplication tables by doing division.
Cool! Let's try!

2 ÷ 2 =	3 ÷ 3 =	4 ÷ 4 =	5 ÷ 5 =
4 ÷ 2 =	6 ÷ 3 =	8 ÷ 4 =	10 ÷ 5 =
6 ÷ 2 =	9 ÷ 3 =	12 ÷ 4 =	15 ÷ 5 =
8 ÷ 2 =	12 ÷ 3 =	16 ÷ 4 =	20 ÷ 5 =
10 ÷ 2 =	15 ÷ 3 =	20 ÷ 4 =	25 ÷ 5 =
12 ÷ 2 =	18 ÷ 3 =	24 ÷ 4 =	30 ÷ 5 =
14 ÷ 2 =	21 ÷ 3 =	28 ÷ 4 =	35 ÷ 5 =
16 ÷ 2 =	24 ÷ 3 =	32 ÷ 4 =	40 ÷ 5 =

6 ÷ 6 =	7 ÷ 7 =	8 ÷ 8 =	9 ÷ 9 =
12 ÷ 6 =	14 ÷ 7 =	16 ÷ 8 =	18 ÷ 9 =
18 ÷ 6 =	21 ÷ 7 =	24 ÷ 8 =	27 ÷ 9 =
24 ÷ 6 =	28 ÷ 7 =	32 ÷ 8 =	36 ÷ 9 =
30 ÷ 6 =	35 ÷ 7 =	40 ÷ 8 =	45 ÷ 9 =
36 ÷ 6 =	42 ÷ 7 =	48 ÷ 8 =	54 ÷ 9 =
42 ÷ 6 =	49 ÷ 7 =	56 ÷ 8 =	63 ÷ 9 =
48 ÷ 6 =	56 ÷ 7 =	64 ÷ 8 =	72 ÷ 9 =

Quiz 4

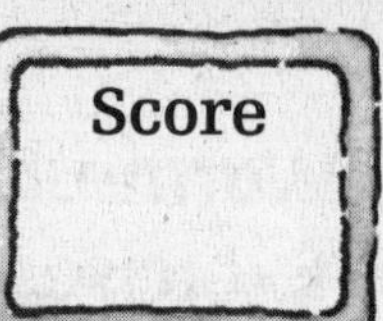
Score

Calculate and fill in the answers.

1. 6 × 6 = ____ **2.** 6 × 3 = ____ **3.** 6 × 5 = ____ **4.** 6 × 7 = ____ **5.** 6 × 8 = ____

6. 3 × 6 = ____ **7.** 2 × 6 = ____ **8.** 4 × 6 = ____ **9.** 9 × 6 = ____ **10.** 5 × 6 = ____

11. 7 × 7 = ____ **12.** 7 × 5 = ____ **13.** 7 × 4 = ____ **14.** 7 × 8 = ____ **15.** 7 × 6 = ____

16. 3 × 7 = ____ **17.** 2 × 7 = ____ **18.** 4 × 7 = ____ **19.** 5 × 7 = ____ **20.** 8 × 7 = ____

21. 8 × 8 = ____ **22.** 8 × 4 = ____ **23.** 8 × 6 = ____ **24.** 8 × 8 = ____ **25.** 8 × 9 = ____

26. 5 × 8 = ____ **27.** 2 × 8 = ____ **28.** 5 × 8 = ____ **29.** 4 × 9 = ____ **30.** 1 × 8 = ____

31. 9 × 9 = ____ **32.** 9 × 7 = ____ **33.** 9 × 5 = ____ **34.** 9 × 6 = ____ **35.** 9 × 8 = ____

36. 7 × 9 = ____ **37.** 4 × 9 = ____ **38.** 2 × 9 = ____ **39.** 3 × 9 = ____ **40.** 6 × 9 = ____

Word Problem

Draw a model and write a mathematical expression to represent the problem. Then calculate and answer the question.

41. Ms. Park wants to divide her class of 28 students into 7 equal groups to work on a science project. How many students will be in each group? ____________

Model:

Mathematical Expression:

Challenge Yourself

42. 20 ÷ 2 = ____ **43.** 60 ÷ 3 = ____ **44.** 8 ÷ 2 ÷ 2 = ____ **45.** 27 ÷ 3 ÷ 3 = ____

Warm-up Exercises

$40 + 20 =$ ____ $30 + 40 =$ ____ $60 + 20 =$ ____ $50 + 50 =$ ____

$50 - 10 =$ ____ $80 - 40 =$ ____ $40 - 20 =$ ____ $100 - 20 =$ ____

2-11 Why is multiplying by 10 so easy?

Mathematical Conversation

We have already learned the multiplication tables for 2 through 9.
I wonder what the times table for 10 would look like. We had three lines for the 7 times table, two lines for the 8 times table, and only one line for the 9 times table. So I guess we will have no lines for the times table for ten.
You are probably right, Danny! We may not need a table for 10. Think about how many students there are in 3 groups with 10 students in each group. Can you solve the problem without a new times table?

That's 30 students! 3 × 10 = 30.
How about 3 groups with 20 students in each group? Hmm . . . There will be 60 students! 3 × 20 = 60.
To multiply a number by 10, put a zero on the end of the number. To multiply a number by a multiple of ten, you multiply that number by the digit in the tens place and then put a zero at the end of the product.

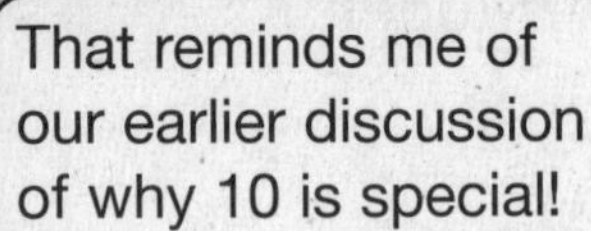
That reminds me of our earlier discussion of why 10 is special!

Guided Practice

Try these on your own and fill in the answers.

A. $20 \times 2 =$ ____ **B.** $30 \times 3 =$ ____ **C.** $30 \div 3 =$ ____ **D.** $40 \div 2 =$ ____

Lesson 2–11 Exercises

Recite the multiplication tables from 2 to 9. Calculate these in your mind and fill in the answers.

1. $20 \times 3 =$ ____	**2.** $10 \times 6 =$ ____	**3.** $30 \times 3 =$ ____	**4.** $20 \times 4 =$ ____
5. $3 \times 20 =$ ____	**6.** $6 \times 10 =$ ____	**7.** $3 \times 30 =$ ____	**8.** $4 \times 20 =$ ____
9. $30 \div 3 =$ ____	**10.** $40 \div 2 =$ ____	**11.** $50 \div 5 =$ ____	**12.** $60 \div 6 =$ ____
13. $20 \div 2 =$ ____	**14.** $60 \div 2 =$ ____	**15.** $70 \div 7 =$ ____	**16.** $100 \div 5 =$ ____
17. $7 \times 3 =$ ____	**18.** $6 \times 6 =$ ____	**19.** $9 \times 5 =$ ____	**20.** $7 \times 7 =$ ____
21. $8 \times 6 =$ ____	**22.** $8 \times 7 =$ ____	**23.** $5 \times 9 =$ ____	**24.** $8 \times 8 =$ ____
25. $35 \div 5 =$ ____	**26.** $14 \div 7 =$ ____	**27.** $36 \div 9 =$ ____	**28.** $30 \div 6 =$ ____
29. $42 \div 7 =$ ____	**30.** $42 \div 6 =$ ____	**31.** $54 \div 6 =$ ____	**32.** $72 \div 8 =$ ____
33. $50 \times 2 =$ ____	**34.** $50 \times 3 =$ ____	**35.** $40 \times 3 =$ ____	**36.** $30 \times 6 =$ ____
37. $100 \div 2 =$ ____	**38.** $150 \div 3 =$ ____	**39.** $120 \div 3 =$ ____	**40.** $180 \div 3 =$ ____
41. $3 + 7 + 5 =$ ____	**42.** $9 + 3 + 1 =$ ____	**43.** $20 - 10 - 2 =$ ____	**44.** $30 - 7 - 6 =$ ____
45. $9 + 9 - 7 =$ ____	**46.** $15 - 5 + 9 =$ ____	**47.** $18 + 2 - 3 =$ ____	**48.** $32 - 3 + 4 =$ ____

Word Problems

Write a mathematical expression to solve each problem. Use the models to help you.

49. April, June, and September each have 30 days. How many days do the 3 months have altogether?

____

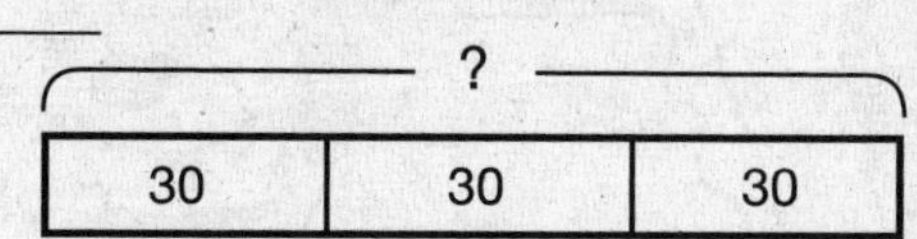

?
30
30
30

Mathematical expression:

50. If 30 apples are shared equally among 3 people, how many apples will each person receive? ____

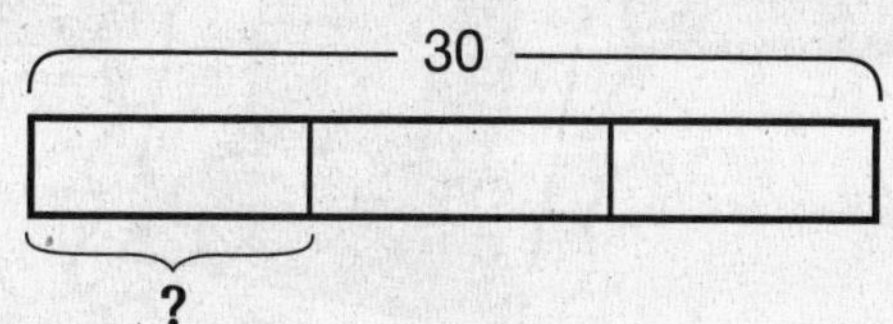

30
?

Mathematical expression:

Reflection and Discussion

Since you know that $20 \times 2 = 40$, how can you calculate 20×20?

Warm-up Exercises

$22 + 22 =$ ____ $31 + 42 =$ ____ $30 + 25 =$ ____ $25 + 21 =$ ____

$55 - 11 =$ ____ $88 - 40 =$ ____ $28 - 10 =$ ____ $100 - 30 =$ ____

2-12 Can you calculate 21 × 3?

Mathematical Conversation

Look! I filled up 21 rows of my stamp album. Each row holds 3 stamps. How many stamps do I have in my stamp album?
21 × 3 = 63. I can't believe that I can do multiplication with a 2-digit number without pencil and paper!
You can probably do multiplication with a 3-digit number, too. Try this: 120 × 2 = ?
240!
Cool! I think I can do that, too!
Good for you!

Guided Practice

Try these on your own.

A. $13 \times 2 =$ ____ **B.** $22 \times 3 =$ ____ **C.** $33 \div 3 =$ ____ **D.** $84 \div 2 =$ ____

Lesson 2–12 Exercises

Recite the multiplication tables from 2 to 9. Calculate these in your mind and fill in the answers.

1. $12 \times 3 =$ ____	**2.** $22 \times 2 =$ ____	**3.** $31 \times 3 =$ ____	**4.** $34 \times 2 =$ ____
5. $12 \times 4 =$ ____	**6.** $22 \times 4 =$ ____	**7.** $21 \times 3 =$ ____	**8.** $42 \times 2 =$ ____
9. $39 \div 3 =$ ____	**10.** $44 \div 2 =$ ____	**11.** $55 \div 5 =$ ____	**12.** $63 \div 3 =$ ____
13. $86 \div 2 =$ ____	**14.** $66 \div 3 =$ ____	**15.** $77 \div 7 =$ ____	**16.** $28 \div 2 =$ ____
17. $4 \times 7 =$ ____	**18.** $5 \times 5 =$ ____	**19.** $9 \times 4 =$ ____	**20.** $7 \times 9 =$ ____
21. $8 \times 5 =$ ____	**22.** $8 \times 3 =$ ____	**23.** $6 \times 9 =$ ____	**24.** $3 \times 9 =$ ____
25. $20 \div 5 =$ ____	**26.** $21 \div 7 =$ ____	**27.** $36 \div 9 =$ ____	**28.** $16 \div 4 =$ ____
29. $14 \div 7 =$ ____	**30.** $40 \div 5 =$ ____	**31.** $36 \div 6 =$ ____	**32.** $16 \div 8 =$ ____
33. $60 \times 2 =$ ____	**34.** $40 \times 4 =$ ____	**35.** $30 \times 7 =$ ____	**36.** $60 \times 6 =$ ____
37. $100 \div 5 =$ ____	**38.** $150 \div 3 =$ ____	**39.** $120 \div 3 =$ ____	**40.** $180 \div 6 =$ ____
41. $5 + 7 + 5 =$ ____	**42.** $12 + 3 + 1 =$ ____	**43.** $35 - 4 - 1 =$ ____	**44.** $48 - 5 - 8 =$ ____
45. $12 + 8 - 8 =$ ____	**46.** $24 - 5 + 6 =$ ____	**47.** $40 + 4 - 6 =$ ____	**48.** $77 - 7 + 9 =$ ____

Word Problems

Write a mathematical expression to solve each problem. Use the models to help you.

49. January, March, and July each have 31 days. How many days do the 3 months have altogether? ________

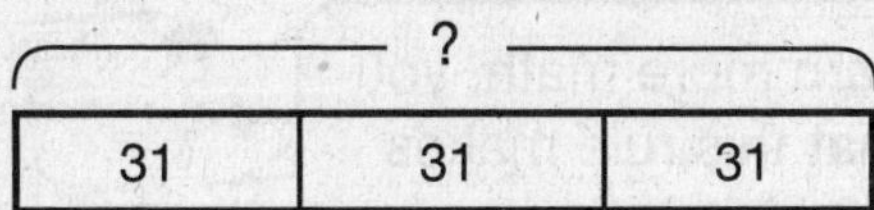
?
31
31
31

Mathematical expression:

50. A big box contains 48 tennis balls. A small box contains a dozen (12) balls. How many small boxes are there in a large box? ________

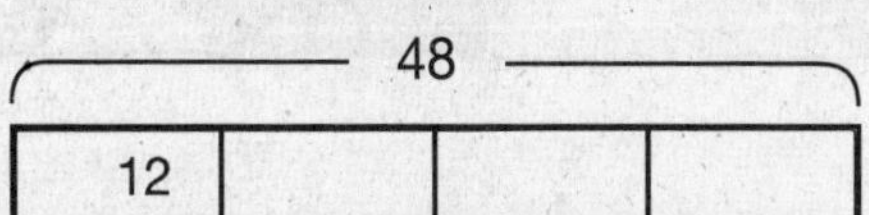
48
12

Mathematical expression:

Reflection and Discussion

Can you calculate $84 \div 21$ without using paper and pencil or a calculator?

Warm-up Exercises

5 + 5 − 2 = ____ 6 + 4 + 8 = ____ 9 + 4 − 4 = ____ 15 − 3 + 3 = ____

10 − 2 + 1 = ____ 7 − 6 + 1 = ____ 8 − 8 + 8 = ____ 24 + 12 − 4 = ____

2-13 Multiplication and division vs. addition and subtraction . . .

I understand what you've written except for one word. Addition and subtraction are inverses of each other. So are multiplication and division. But why does this say multiplication and division versus addition and subtraction?
Multiplication and Division versus Addition and Subtraction
I can't figure it out either.
Well, when we do a computation, multiplication and division take priority over addition and subtraction. For example, when calculating 3 + 2 × 4, we do 2 × 4 first. Then we add the product, 8, to 3. The result is 11.

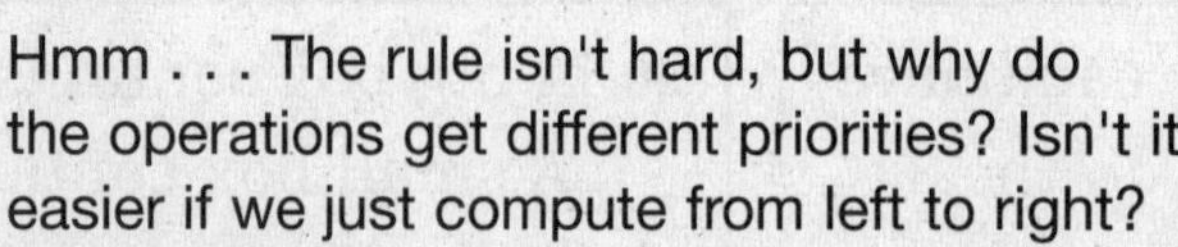

Hmm . . . The rule isn't hard, but why do the operations get different priorities? Isn't it easier if we just compute from left to right?
As you learn more math, you will see that this rule makes complicated operations much easier.

Guided Practice

Try these on your own.

A. 3 + 3 × 2 = ____ **B.** 10 + 5 × 3 = ____ **C.** 15 + 3 ÷ 3 = ____ **D.** 28 − 25 ÷ 5 = ____

Lesson 2–13 Exercises

Recite the multiplication tables from 2 to 9. Calculate these in your mind and fill in the answers.

1. $4 \times 3 + 8 =$ ___	**2.** $5 \times 5 + 5 =$ ___	**3.** $7 \times 7 + 1 =$ ___	**4.** $3 \times 8 + 4 =$ ___
5. $8 + 4 \times 3 =$ ___	**6.** $5 + 5 \times 5 =$ ___	**7.** $1 + 7 \times 7 =$ ___	**8.** $4 + 3 \times 8 =$ ___
9. $7 \times 2 - 2 =$ ___	**10.** $15 \div 5 - 1 =$ ___	**11.** $40 \div 8 - 4 =$ ___	**12.** $8 \times 8 + 4 =$ ___
13. $7 - 2 \times 2 =$ ___	**14.** $15 - 5 \div 1 =$ ___	**15.** $40 - 8 \div 4 =$ ___	**16.** $8 + 8 \times 4 =$ ___
17. $2 \times 7 \div 2 =$ ___	**18.** $5 \times 6 \div 3 =$ ___	**19.** $9 \times 2 \div 6 =$ ___	**20.** $4 \times 6 \div 3 =$ ___
21. $8 \div 4 \times 8 =$ ___	**22.** $9 \div 3 \times 6 =$ ___	**23.** $6 \div 2 \times 5 =$ ___	**24.** $16 \div 2 \times 5 =$ ___
25. $7 + 7 - 4 =$ ___	**26.** $20 + 20 - 2 =$ ___	**27.** $8 + 7 - 6 =$ ___	**28.** $18 + 2 - 5 =$ ___
29. $9 - 7 + 2 =$ ___	**30.** $12 - 10 + 6 =$ ___	**31.** $8 - 7 + 6 =$ ___	**32.** $12 - 6 + 7 =$ ___

Word Problems

Write a mathematical expression to solve each problem. Use the models to help you.

33. A box contains 40 erasers in five different colors. There are the same number of erasers in each color. How many erasers of each color are there? ________

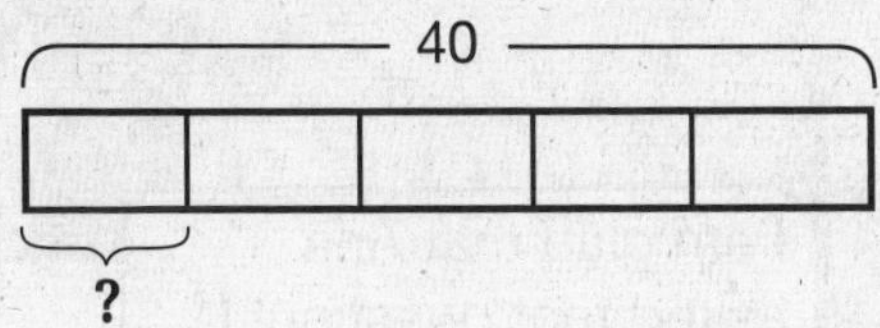

40
?

Mathematical expression:

34. A box contains 40 erasers. There are 8 erasers of each color. How many different colors are there?

____

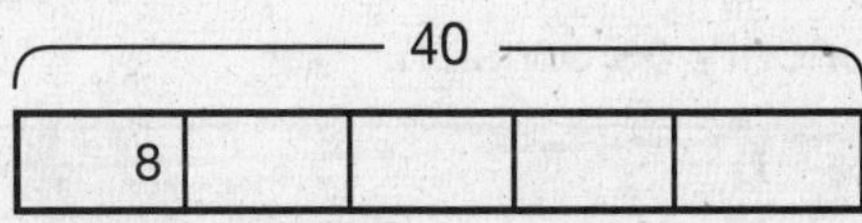

40
8

Mathematical expression:

Reflection and Discussion

Both word problems on this page use the same three numbers: 5, 8, and 40. Make up another word problem that uses these three numbers. You may write a division problem or a multiplication problem.

Warm-up Exercises

$2 + 3 \times 2 =$ ____ $3 + 5 \times 2 =$ ____ $9 - 9 \div 3 =$ ____ $12 - 10 \div 2 =$ ____

$14 - 2 =$ ____ $25 - 5 =$ ____ $73 - 3 =$ ____ $54 - 4 =$ ____

2-14 Unit 2 Review

Mathematical Conversation

Tell me, what did you learn in this unit?
We learned multiplication tables very well.
And we learned about order of operations. We know that multiplication and division have higher priority than addition and subtraction in multistep computations.
Speaking of priority, does addition have higher priority than subtraction?
No. If two operations are inverses, one doesn't take priority over the other. In other words, addition has the same priority as subtraction, and multiplication has the same priority as division.
I am glad that Ana asked that question! I was a bit confused, too.

Lesson 2–14 Exercises

Fill in this multiplication table.

2 × 2 =	2 × 3 =	2 × 4 =	2 × 5 =	2 × 6 =	2 × 7 =	2 × 8 =	2 × 9 =
3 × 2 =	3 × 3 =	3 × 4 =	3 × 5 =	3 × 6 =	3 × 7 =	3 × 8 =	3 × 9 =
4 × 2 =	4 × 3 =	4 × 4 =	4 × 5 =	4 × 6 =	4 × 7 =	4 × 8 =	4 × 9 =
5 × 2 =	5 × 3 =	5 × 4 =	5 × 5 =	5 × 6 =	5 × 7 =	5 × 8 =	5 × 9 =
6 × 2 =	6 × 3 =	6 × 4 =	6 × 5 =	6 × 6 =	6 × 7 =	6 × 8 =	6 × 9 =
7 × 2 =	7 × 3 =	7 × 4 =	7 × 5 =	7 × 6 =	7 × 7 =	7 × 8 =	7 × 9 =
8 × 2 =	8 × 3 =	8 × 4 =	8 × 5 =	8 × 6 =	8 × 7 =	8 × 8 =	8 × 9 =
9 × 2 =	9 × 3 =	9 × 4 =	9 × 5 =	9 × 6 =	9 × 7 =	9 × 8 =	9 × 9 =

Calculate and fill in the answers.

10 ÷ 2 = ____

20 ÷ 4 = ____ 24 ÷ 4 = ____

30 ÷ 5 = ____ 36 ÷ 6 = ____ 40 ÷ 5 = ____

21 ÷ 7 = ____ 16 ÷ 4 = ____ 24 ÷ 8 = ____ 12 ÷ 6 = ____

18 ÷ 3 = ____ 14 ÷ 2 = ____ 15 ÷ 3 = ____

18 ÷ 9 = ____ 45 ÷ 9 = ____

25 ÷ 5 = ____

Warm-up Exercises

$2 \times 2 =$ ____ $2 \times 4 =$ ____ $2 \times 6 =$ ____ $2 \times 8 =$ ____

$2 \times 3 =$ ____ $2 \times 5 =$ ____ $2 \times 7 =$ ____ $2 \times 9 =$ ____

3-1 Why does "place" have a value?

Mathematical Conversation

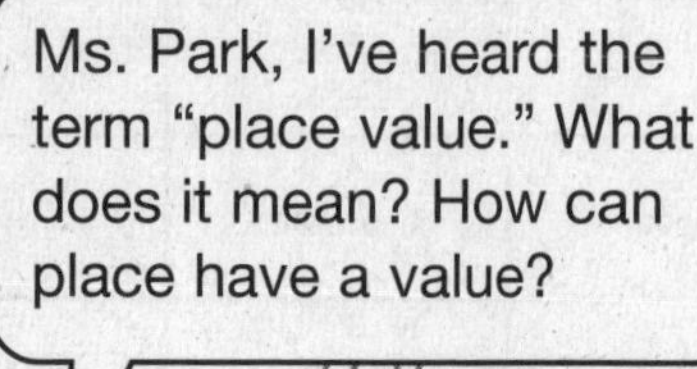

Ms. Park, I've heard the term "place value." What does it mean? How can place have a value?

Take a look at these cartoons. They will give you an answer.

Who can count faster?

1, 2, 3, 4, 5, 6, 7, 8, 9, 10
1, 2, 3, 4, 5, 6, 7, 8, 9, 10

1, 2, 3, 4, 5, 6, 7
. . .21, 22, 23

10, 20, 30, 40, 50, 60, 70, 80, 90, 100!
. . .72, 73, 74

I know why the girl on the left won. She made groups of 10 so that the big pile was easier to manage!

This idea started long ago, in ancient history. When people had to count many objects, they grouped the objects. People have 10 fingers, so the size of groups was often 10.

I see! So when they recorded the amount, I bet they put the number of groups next to the number of single pieces! That's how each place in a number got a different value! Of course, a group of 10 apples has a greater value than just one apple!

Do you remember that 10 is the special organizer of our numeral system?

Of course I do!

Lesson 3–1 Exercises

Rewrite these expressions in columns. Use place value to line up the numbers. Then calculate and fill in the answers.

1. 3,200 + 32 = ____ **2.** 2,500 + 25 = ____ **3.** 71 + 7,100 = ____ **4.** 16 + 1,600 = ____

5. 3,200 + 320 = ____ **6.** 2,500 + 250 = ____ **7.** 710 + 7,100 = ____ **8.** 160 + 1,600 = ____

9. 8,585 − 32 = ____ **10.** 5,555 − 14 = ____ **11.** 9,500 − 400 = ____ **12.** 7,840 − 320 = ____

13. 8,585 − 320 = ____ **14.** 5,555 − 140 = ____ **15.** 9,500 − 4,000 = ____ **16.** 7,840 − 3,200 = ____

Calculate these in your mind and fill in the answers.

17. 33 × 2 = ____ **18.** 40 × 4 = ____ **19.** 50 × 5 = ____ **20.** 60 × 6 = ____

21. 80 ÷ 2 = ____ **22.** 120 ÷ 3 = ____ **23.** 240 ÷ 8 = ____ **24.** 280 ÷ 7 = ____

25. 4 + 7 + 3 = ____ **26.** 20 − 6 − 4 = ____ **27.** 15 − 5 + 5 = ____ **28.** 52 − 3 + 4 = ____

Word Problems

Draw a model and write a mathematical expression to represent these problems. Then calculate and answer the questions.

29. Ms. Park packed 50 bottles equally into 5 boxes. How many bottles did she pack in each box? ____________

Model:

Mathematical expression:

30. Last week Danny recycled 30 cans. Ana recycled 42 cans. How many cans did they recycle? ____________

Model:

Mathematical expression:

Reflection and Discussion

Do you think it is a good idea to have 10 as a special organizer in our numeral system? Why? Are there times when other numbers are used as organizers?

Warm-up Exercises

3 × 20 = ____	3 × 40 = ____	3 × 60 = ____	3 × 80 = ____
3 × 30 = ____	3 × 50 = ____	3 × 70 = ____	3 × 90 = ____

3-2 What happens when you go right?

Mathematical Conversation

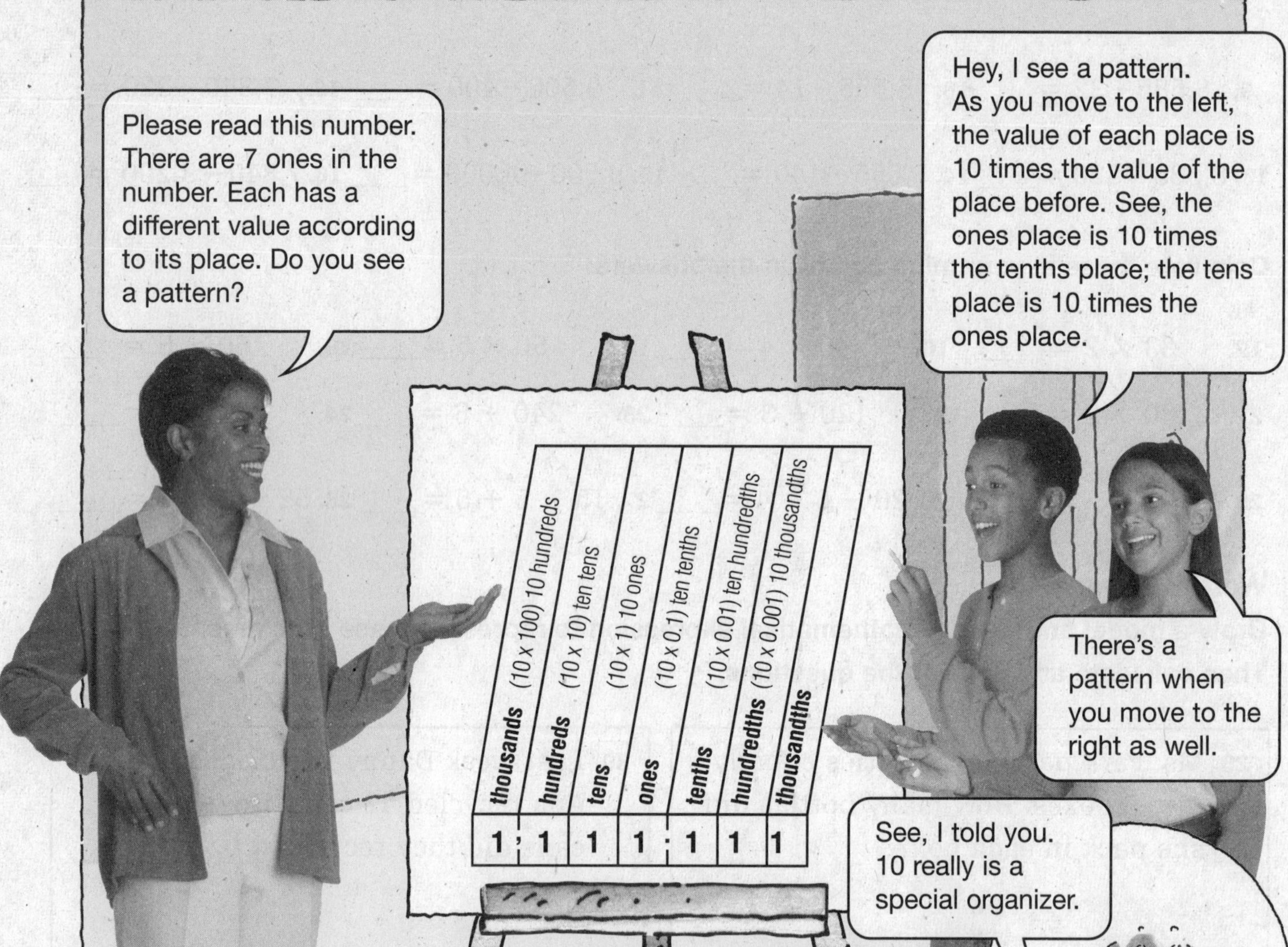
Please read this number. There are 7 ones in the number. Each has a different value according to its place. Do you see a pattern?
Hey, I see a pattern. As you move to the left, the value of each place is 10 times the value of the place before. See, the ones place is 10 times the tenths place; the tens place is 10 times the ones place.
thousands (10 x 100) 10 hundreds
hundreds (10 x 10) ten tens
tens (10 x 1) 10 ones
ones (10 x 0.1) ten tenths
tenths (10 x 0.01) ten hundredths
hundredths (10 x 0.001) 10 thousandths
thousandths
1,1 1 1.1 1 1
There's a pattern when you move to the right as well.
See, I told you. 10 really is a special organizer.

Guided Practice

Rewrite these expressions in columns. Then calculate and fill in the answers.

A. 345.9 − 23.5 = ____ **B.** 527 + 6.05 = ____

Fill in the blanks with >, <, or =.

C. 1 ____ 0.999 **D.** 1.2 ____ 2.1

E. 1.03 ____ 1.003 **F.** 9.7 ____ 9.7

Lesson 3–2 Exercises

Rewrite these expressions in columns. Use place value to line up the numbers. Then calculate and fill in the answers.

1. $1.2 + 3.5 =$ ____ **2.** $6.4 + 0.3 =$ ____ **3.** $7.1 + 1.8 =$ ____ **4.** $1.6 + 5.2 =$ ____

5. $12.5 + 2.4 =$ ____ **6.** $3.3 + 33.3 =$ ____ **7.** $45.6 + 0.22 =$ ____ **8.** $20 + 0.2 =$ ____

9. $4.5 - 3.2 =$ ____ **10.** $5.56 - 1.42 =$ ____ **11.** $95.6 - 12 =$ ____ **12.** $0.4 - 0.2 =$ ____

13. $8.5 - 1.1 =$ ____ **14.** $54.8 - 2.5 =$ ____ **15.** $188.9 - 52 =$ ____ **16.** $7.84 - 0.4 =$ ____

Calculate these in your mind and fill in the answers.

17. $27 + 8 =$ ____ **18.** $66 + 6 =$ ____ **19.** $86 + 5 =$ ____ **20.** $48 + 8 =$ ____

21. $32 - 5 =$ ____ **22.** $74 - 5 =$ ____ **23.** $55 - 8 =$ ____ **24.** $81 - 7 =$ ____

25. $5 + 6 + 5 =$ ____ **26.** $40 - 8 - 2 =$ ____ **27.** $24 - 8 + 7 =$ ____ **28.** $35 - 6 + 7 =$ ____

Fill in the blanks with >, <, or =.

29. 1 ____ 1.1 **30.** 9.5 ____ 9.05 **31.** 18.8 ____ 188 **32.** 0.004 ____ 0.0005

Word Problems

Draw models and write mathematical expressions to represent these problems. Then calculate and answer the questions.

33. Danny bought 5.6 pounds of apples and 1.2 pounds of oranges. How many pounds of fruit did Danny buy? ____________

Model:

Mathematical expression:

34. Ana needs 2.5 cups of white flour and 1.5 cups of rye to make bread. How much more white than rye does she need? ____________

Model:

Mathematical expression:

Reflection and Discussion To decide how great a number is, which is more important to know: where the digits are placed, or what the digits are?

Warm-up Exercises

$4 \times 9 =$ ____	$4 \times 7 =$ ____	$4 \times 5 =$ ____	$4 \times 30 =$ ____
$4 \times 8 =$ ____	$4 \times 6 =$ ____	$4 \times 40 =$ ____	$4 \times 20 =$ ____

3-3 Where should I put the 1?

Mathematical Conversation

5 + 7 = 12
Where should I write the 1?

If you use the real names for numbers, it's easy! The 1 means 1 ten, so you can put it in the tens column. You "store" the 1 near the 2, then add it when you work in the tens column.

625 + 117 =

$$\begin{array}{r} 625 \\ +\ 117 \\ \hline \end{array}$$

OK. Then I get 4 in the tens place and 7 in the hundreds place.

625 + 117 = 742
1
625
+ 117
742

Let me change one digit in the problem to make it more challenging.

625 + 187 =

$$\begin{array}{r} {\scriptstyle 1\,1}\ \\ 625 \\ +\ 187 \\ \hline \end{array}$$

I bet this time we have to store a 1 in the hundreds column.

So this time the 1 is 1 hundred.

Look at the change I made. Can you calculate this?

62.5 + 18.7 = ?

Guided Practice

Rewrite these expressions in columns. Then calculate and fill in the answers.

A. 355 + 126 = ____ **B.** 473 + 272 = ____ **C.** 56.2 + 1.9 = ____ **D.** 341.8 + 100.4 = ____

Lesson 3–3 Exercises

Rewrite these problems in columns. Use place value to line up the numbers. Then calculate and fill in the answers.

1. $36 + 25 =$ ____ **2.** $456 + 216 =$ ____ **3.** $877 + 415 =$ ____ **4.** $122 + 78 =$ ____

5. $77 + 14 =$ ____ **6.** $738 + 181 =$ ____ **7.** $433 + 286 =$ ____ **8.** $345 + 165 =$ ____

9. $7.5 + 2.6 =$ ____ **10.** $0.17 + 0.05 =$ ____ **11.** $8.36 + 1.16 =$ ____ **12.** $4.55 + 2.17 =$ ____

13. $3{,}006 + 179 =$ ____ **14.** $1{,}368 + 2{,}581 =$ ____ **15.** $7{,}182 + 2{,}047 =$ ____ **16.** $30.06 + 1.79 =$ ____

Calculate these in your mind and fill in the answers.

17. $123 \times 3 =$ ____ **18.** $400 \times 4 =$ ____ **19.** $60 \times 5 =$ ____ **20.** $70 \times 6 =$ ____

21. $100 \div 2 =$ ____ **22.** $160 \div 4 =$ ____ **23.** $240 \div 6 =$ ____ **24.** $350 \div 7 =$ ____

25. $3 + 3 + 3 =$ ____ **26.** $5 + 5 + 5 =$ ____ **27.** $4 + 4 + 4 =$ ____ **28.** $2 + 2 + 2 =$ ____

29. $9 + 9 + 9 =$ ____ **30.** $6 + 6 + 6 =$ ____ **31.** $7 + 7 + 7 =$ ____ **32.** $8 + 8 + 8 =$ ____

Word Problems

Draw a model and write a mathematical expression to represent these problems. Then calculate and answer the questions.

33. The school is 1.5 miles north of Danny's home. The library is 2.7 miles north of the school. How many miles north of Danny's home is the library? ________

Model:

Mathematical expression:

34. Ana spent 0.5 hour doing math homework and 0.8 hour doing English homework. How many hours did she spend on homework?

____

Model:

Mathematical expression:

Reflection and Discussion

Without doing the problems, decide which calculation would be easier: 3.5 + 0.6 or 3.5 + 0.06. Why is it easier?

Warm-up Exercises

5 × 3 = ____	5 × 7 = ____	4 × 5 = ____	8 × 5 = ____
5 × 5 = ____	5 × 9 = ____	6 × 5 = ____	2 × 5 = ____

3-4 Help! There aren't enough ones to do subtraction!

Mathematical Conversation

Help! There aren't enough ones to subtract 8!
62 − 18 =
62
− 18
Wait a minute! In the last lesson, when we added and had too many ones, we composed a ten. Why don't you decompose one of the tens? That will give you 12 ones. You can subtract 8 from 12.

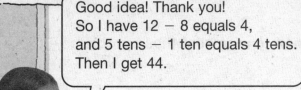

Good idea! Thank you!
So I have 12 − 8 equals 4,
and 5 tens − 1 ten equals 4 tens.
Then I get 44.
62 − 18 = 44
5 12
~~6~~~~2~~
− 18
44
Actually, I know some other ways to do that computation.
I know other ways to regroup, too!
Really?

Guided Practice

Rewrite these expressions in columns. Then calculate and fill in the answers.

A. 355 − 126 = ____ **B.** 423 − 262 = ____ **C.** 56.2 − 1.9 = ____ **D.** 341.1 − 200.3 = ____

Lesson 3–4 Exercises

Rewrite these expressions in columns. Line up the numbers carefully. Then calculate and fill in the answers.

1. $184 - 75 =$ ____ 2. $984 - 335 =$ ____ 3. $450 - 255 =$ ____ 4. $333 - 206 =$ ____

5. $549 - 146 =$ ____ 6. $832 - 7 =$ ____ 7. $453 - 146 =$ ____ 8. $218 - 120 =$ ____

9. $3.5 - 1.7 =$ ____ 10. $55.7 - 18.2 =$ ____ 11. $8.3 - 1.6 =$ ____ 12. $3.22 - 0.6 =$ ____

13. $8.8 - 6.9 =$ ____ 14. $1.2 - 0.8 =$ ____ 15. $12.8 - 1.9 =$ ____ 16. $1.4 - 1.7 =$ ____

17. $2{,}340 - 1{,}006 =$ ____ 18. $4{,}928 - 1{,}845 =$ ____ 19. $6{,}694 - 2{,}275 =$ ____

Calculate these in your mind and fill in the answers.

20. $8 + 6 =$ ____ 21. $7 + 8 =$ ____ 22. $5 + 8 =$ ____ 23. $6 + 8 =$ ____

24. $13 - 5 =$ ____ 25. $15 - 7 =$ ____ 26. $12 - 5 =$ ____ 27. $13 - 8 =$ ____

28. $18 - 4 - 4 =$ ____ 29. $19 - 4 - 5 =$ ____ 30. $28 - 2 - 6 =$ ____ 31. $59 - 6 - 3 =$ ____

32. $16 - 5 - 1 =$ ____ 33. $17 - 6 - 1 =$ ____ 34. $74 - 2 - 12 =$ ____ 35. $87 - 3 - 4 =$ ____

Word Problems

Draw models and write mathematical expressions to represent these problems. Then calculate and answer the questions.

36. Maria spent 3.5 hours reading two books. Reading the first book took 2.6 hours. How long did the second book take? ________

Model:

Mathematical expression:

37. An elephant is 3.2 meters high. A camel is 1.7 meters high. How much higher is the elephant than the camel? ________

Model:

Mathematical expression:

Reflection and Discussion

How would you calculate $1 - 0.0001$?

Warm-up Exercises

$4 + 4 + 4 =$ ____ $8 + 8 + 8 =$ ____ $7 + 7 + 7 =$ ____ $6 + 6 + 6 =$ ____

$3 \times 4 =$ ____ $3 \times 8 =$ ____ $3 \times 7 =$ ____ $3 \times 6 =$ ____

3-5 Review, Reflection, and Quiz 5

Mathematical Conversation

Please use what you have learned about place value in this unit to explain why the third inequality sign has a different direction.
9 > 1
0.9 > 0.1
0.009 < 0.01
Umm . . . 9 should be greater than 1.
But the place makes the difference!
But how can a number with 9 in it be less than a number with 1 in it?

Score

Quiz 5

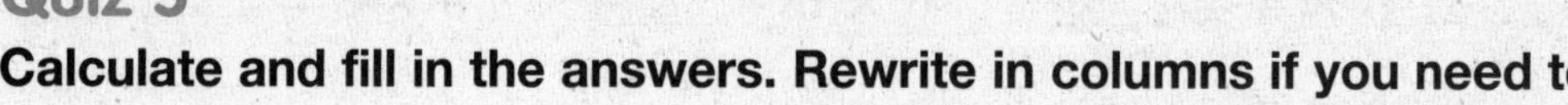

Calculate and fill in the answers. Rewrite in columns if you need to.

1. $104 + 75 =$ ____ **2.** $623 + 4 =$ ____ **3.** $984 + 12 =$ ____ **4.** $456 + 225 =$ ____

5. $813 + 209 =$ ____ **6.** $368 + 29 =$ ____ **7.** $584 - 222 =$ ____ **8.** $458 - 230 =$ ____

9 . $854 - 312 =$ ____ **10.** $430 - 205 =$ ____ **11.** $956 - 207 =$ ____ **12.** $512 - 104 =$ ____

13. $32.7 + 44.2 =$ ____ **14.** $4.3 + 1.8 =$ ____ **15.** $7.12 + 0.6 =$ ____ **16.** $3.6 - 0.7 =$ ____

17 $8.8 - 0.3 =$ ____ **18.** $7.5 - 0.9 =$ ____ **19.** $12.8 - 2.7 =$ ____ **20.** $1.2 - 0.6 =$ ____

Fill in the blanks with >, <, or =.

21. 1 ____ 0.1 **22.**6.4 ____ 6.04 **23.**232 ____ 332 **24.**0.001 ____ 0.0009

Word Problem

Draw a model and write a mathematical expression to represent this problem. Then calculate and answer the question.

25. Derek took 0.3 hour to do the first part of a math quiz and 0.7 hour to do the rest. How many hours did Derek take to finish the whole quiz? ________________

Model:

Mathematical expression:

Challenge Yourself

26. $2{,}250 + 21 =$ ____ **27.** $3{,}773 + 23 =$ ____ **28.** $4{,}510 + 104 =$ ____ **29.** $421.5 + 23.4 =$ ____

Warm-up Exercises

6 × 2 = ____	6 × 4 = ____	6 × 6 = ____	6 × 8 = ____
6 × 3 = ____	6 × 5 = ____	6 × 7 = ____	6 × 9 = ____

3-6 If you know how 312 x 3 works, then . . .

Mathematical Conversation

Here is one way to calculate 312 x 3. Do you know how it works?
I know! We multiply each digit in 312 by 3. Start from the ones place of 312: 3 times 2 is 6; that's 6 ones. Next, 3 times 1 is 3; that's 3 tens. Then we multiply 3 times 3 to get 9 hundreds.
312
× 3
936

Multiplication with a 4-digit number works the same way.
That's right. Place value is very important when we work with multidigit numbers.
3,124 × 2 = 6,248
3,124
× 2
6,248
This is really cool!

Guided Practice

Rewrite these expressions in columns. Then calculate and fill in the answers.

A. 434 × 2 = ____ **B.** 3,323 × 2 = ____ **C.** 232 × 3 = ____ **D.** 2,212 × 4 = ____

Lesson 3–6 Exercises

Rewrite these expressions in columns. Then calculate and fill in the answers. Check your answers with a calculator.

1. $121 \times 2 =$ ____ 2. $323 \times 3 =$ ____ 3. $422 \times 4 =$ ____ 4. $333 \times 2 =$ ____

5. $121 \times 4 =$ ____ 6. $323 \times 2 =$ ____ 7. $222 \times 3 =$ ____ 8. $333 \times 3 =$ ____

9. $122 \times 3 =$ ____ 10. $1.22 \times 3 =$ ____ 11. $1{,}220 \times 3 =$ ____ 12. $22 \times 3 =$ ____

13. $12.2 \times 3 =$ ____ 14. $0.122 \times 3 =$ ____ 15. $12{,}200 \times 3 =$ ____ 16. $2.2 \times 3 =$ ____

Calculate these in your mind and fill in the answers.

17. $56 + 14 =$ ____ 18. $38 + 6 =$ ____ 19. $17 + 18 =$ ____ 20. $25 + 26 =$ ____

21. $80 - 2 =$ ____ 22. $60 - 5 =$ ____ 23. $50 - 8 =$ ____ 24. $100 - 9 =$ ____

25. $15 + 15 + 5 =$ ____ 26. $23 + 23 + 4 =$ ____ 27. $77 - 2 - 7 =$ ____ 28. $86 - 4 - 6 =$ ____

29. $30 + 30 - 30 =$ ____ 30. $60 - 5 + 15 =$ ____ 31. $58 + 2 - 8 =$ ____ 32. $44 - 14 + 4 =$ ____

Word Problems

Draw a model and write a mathematical expression to represent these problems. Then calculate and answer the questions.

33. A large bag of rice contains 12 pounds. C.J.'s mom bought 3 bags. How much rice did she buy?

____

Model:

Mathematical expression:

34. Two buses can carry 84 people. If each bus can carry the same number of people, how many people can each bus carry?

____

Model:

Mathematical expression:

Reflection and Discussion

Can you calculate 821×4? (Bonus problem)

Warm-up Exercises

7 × 2 = ____	7 × 4 = ____	7 × 6 = ____	7 × 8 = ____
7 × 3 = ____	7 × 5 = ____	7 × 7 = ____	7 × 9 = ____

3-7 Where will the bonus problem lead us?

Mathematical Conversation

This is the bonus problem you had yesterday. Do you know why it's a bonus problem?

$821 \times 4 = 3{,}284$

$$\begin{array}{r} 821 \\ \times\ 4 \\ \hline 3{,}284 \end{array}$$

Look at the hundreds place! When you calculate 8 x 4, you get 32, which is a 2-digit number.

Now let me make a small change. I will switch the 8 in the hundreds place with the 2 in the tens place. Will you still be able to find a place to write the 32?

Let's see, 32 tens . . . I know! We can do what we did with addition. We can store the 3 above the hundreds place, and then add it to the product of 4 times 2.

$281 \times 4 =$

$$\begin{array}{r} {\scriptstyle 3} \\ 281 \\ \times\ 4 \\ \hline 1{,}124 \end{array}$$

Good idea, Ana.

We can use what we already know to help us learn new things!

Wow! this time they stored a 3!

Guided Practice

Rewrite these expressions in columns. Then calculate and fill in the answers.

A. 124 × 4 = ____ **B.** 321 × 6 = ____ **C.** 542 × 3 = ____ **D.** 2,232 × 4 = ____

Lesson 3–7 Exercises

Rewrite these expressions in columns. Then calculate and fill in the answers.

1. $332 \times 4 =$ ____ 2. $561 \times 7 =$ ____ 3. $332 \times 2 =$ ____ 4. $5{,}611 \times 7 =$ ____

5. $242 \times 8 =$ ____ 6. $333 \times 9 =$ ____ 7. $242 \times 4 =$ ____ 8. $313 \times 9 =$ ____

9. $715 \times 3 =$ ____ 10. $352 \times 8 =$ ____ 11. $533 \times 4 =$ ____ 12. $333 \times 2 =$ ____

Calculate these in your mind and fill in answers.

13. $65 + 20 =$ ____ 14. $34 + 8 =$ ____ 15. $25 + 7 =$ ____ 16. $18 + 26 =$ ____

17. $90 - 9 =$ ____ 18. $80 - 8 =$ ____ 19. $70 - 7 =$ ____ 20. $100 - 1 =$ ____

21. $45 + 5 + 45 =$ ____ 22. $26 + 18 + 4 =$ ____ 23. $34 - 2 - 3 =$ ____ 24. $73 - 6 - 3 =$ ____

25. $24 + 68 - 68 =$ ____ 26. $92 - 12 + 15 =$ ____ 27. $89 + 9 - 8 =$ ____ 28. $54 + 9 - 4 =$ ____

Word Problems

Draw a model and write a mathematical expression to represent these problems. Then calculate and answer the questions.

29. The 9 classes in C.J.'s school donated books to the school library. Each class donated 35 books. How many library books were donated?

____

Model:

Mathematical expression:

30. For a paper folding project, 9 children made paper cranes. Each child made 12 cranes. How many cranes did the children make?

____

Model:

Mathematical expression:

Reflection and Discussion

Compare the across-ten addition in 214×7 and $214 + 7$. Is the across-ten addition in multiplication like that in addition?

Warm-up Exercises

8 × 2 = ____ 8 × 4 = ____ 8 × 6 = ____ 8 × 8 = ____

8 × 3 = ____ 8 × 5 = ____ 8 × 7 = ____ 8 × 9 = ____

3-8 Hey, there's a zero in between!

Mathematical Conversation

Do you see anything special about this computation?
Well, there's a 0 between the hundreds place and the ones place.
Let me do it! . . .
Look at this Danny. It's easier than the 3-digit multiplication we did before.
405 × 9 =
405
× 9
3,645

How about this one?
I need a 0 in the hundreds place.
4,005 × 9 =
4,005
× 9
36,045

Guided Practice

Rewrite these expressions in columns. Then calculate and fill in the answers.

A. 203 × 6 = ____ **B.** 102 × 4 = ____ **C.** 1,002 × 3 = ____ **D.** 2,005 × 7 = ____

Lesson 3–8 Exercises

Rewrite these expressions in columns. Then calculate and fill in the answers.

1. $203 \times 3 =$ ____ **2.** $703 \times 5 =$ ____ **3.** $804 \times 3 =$ ____ **4.** $804 \times 6 =$ ____

5. $126 \times 6 =$ ____ **6.** $202 \times 8 =$ ____ **7.** $805 \times 7 =$ ____ **8.** $303 \times 3 =$ ____

9. $126 \times 3 =$ ____ **10.** $202 \times 4 =$ ____ **11.** $805 \times 3 =$ ____ **12.** $303 \times 9 =$ ____

Calculate these in your mind and fill in the answers.

13. $36 + 20 =$ ____ **14.** $46 + 8 =$ ____ **15.** $75 + 5 =$ ____ **16.** $28 + 22 =$ ____

17. $80 - 7 =$ ____ **18.** $70 - 9 =$ ____ **19.** $61 - 7 =$ ____ **20.** $100 - 6 =$ ____

21. $28 + 15 + 2 =$ ____ **22.** $26 + 35 + 5 =$ ____ **23.** $21 - 9 - 1 =$ ____ **24.** $64 - 6 - 4 =$ ____

25. $42 + 8 - 2 =$ ____ **26.** $70 - 52 + 52 =$ ____ **27.** $91 + 9 - 1 =$ ____ **28.** $32 + 4 + 4 =$ ____

Word Problems

Draw a model and write a mathematical expression to represent these problems. Then calculate and answer the questions.

29. Danny keeps 201 baseball cards in each box. If he has 4 boxes of cards, how many cards does he have? ________

Model:

Mathematical expression:

30. Ana collected 103 leaves for a mural and C.J. collected 105 leaves. How many leaves did Ana and C.J. collect? ________

Model:

Mathematical expression:

Reflection and Discussion

Can you calculate 603 × 3 in your head?

Warm-up Exercises

9 × 2 = ____	9 × 3 = ____	9 × 4 = ____	9 × 5 = ____
9 × 6 = ____	9 × 7 = ____	9 × 8 = ____	9 × 9 = ____

3-9 Unit 3 Review

Mathematical Conversation

Ms. Park, we will have a test tomorrow, right?
Yes, tomorrow is the last day for this unit.
I am very proud of myself. Now I can do advanced calculations. I can calculate with multidigit numbers and with decimals!
I have a challenge for you. Can you fill in the blanks? Here is a hint: You may need to use decimals for some of these.
1,295 = ______ tenths
1,295 = ______ ones
1,295 = ______ tens
1,295 = ______ hundreds
1,295 = ______ thousands
That's five ways to think about the same number!

Lesson 3–9 Exercises

Fill in the blanks with >, <, or =.

1. 4,120 ______ 3,900 **2.** 10 ______ 101 **3.** 403 ______ 304

4. 1.2 ______ 2 **5.** 0.5 ______ 0.07 **6.** 10.8 ______ 1.08

Calculate and fill in the answers. Rewrite in columns if you need to.

7. 761 + 127 = ______

8. 404 + 175 = ______

9. 1,623 + 3,405 = ______

10. 8.13 + 10.6 = ______

11. 3.6 + 3.09 = ______

12. 8.3 + 0.7 = ______

13. 983 − 143 = ______

14. 184 − 15 = ______

15. 8,854 − 5,312 = ______

16. 4.13 − 2.02 = ______

17. 51.24 − 1.12 = ______

18. 0.43 − 0.24 = ______

19. 412 × 2 = ______

20. 131 × 5 = ______

21. 432 × 4 = ______

22. 712 × 6 = ______

23. 82 × 3 = ______

24. 25 × 7 = ______

25. 112 × 8 = ______

Warm-up Exercises

$8 + 8 =$ ____ $8 + 7 =$ ____ $7 + 8 =$ ____ $9 + 8 =$ ____

$16 - 7 =$ ____ $16 - 9 =$ ____ $16 - 6 =$ ____ $15 - 7 =$ ____

4-1 Letters in an equation?

Mathematical Conversation

Lily, do you understand this poster? Why are there letters in this equation?

Hmm . . . I think "l" stands for the length of the rectangle, and "w" stands for its width. "$l + l + w + w$" means add the two lengths and the two widths. But what does "P" mean?

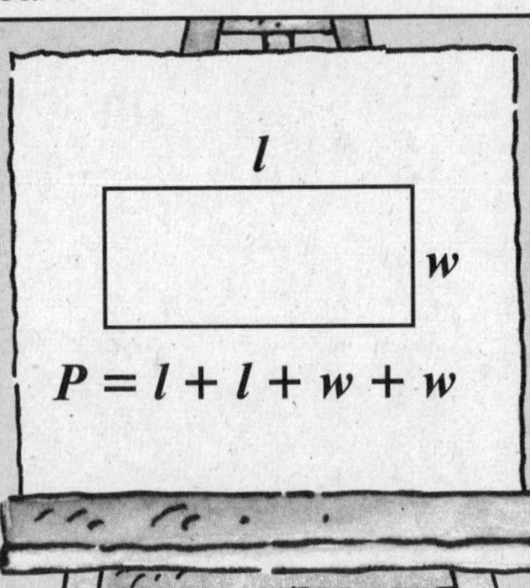

l
w
P = l + l + w + w

"P" stands for perimeter. Perimeter is the distance around a shape. Does the equation make sense to you now?

I remember seeing letters in my sister's algebra book: $x + 8 = 10$. That's another equation with letters!

I think that equation means some number plus 8 equals 10.

Yes, you are right! In mathematics, "x" stands for an unknown number. As you learn more mathematics, you will find out more about the power of numbers.

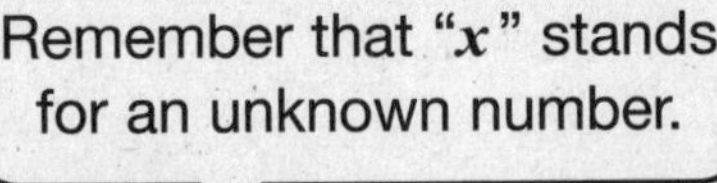

Remember that "x" stands for an unknown number.

Got it!

Guided Practice

Find the number that x represents and fill in the answers.

A. $x + 5 = 15$ **B.** $20 - x = 17$ **C.** $x \times 4 = 24$ **D.** $42 \div x = 6$

$x =$ ____ $x =$ ____ $x =$ ____ $x =$ ____

Lesson 4–1 Exercises

Find the number that x represents and fill in the answers.

1. $x + 15 = 25$ $x =$ ____

2. $70 - x = 60$ $x =$ ____

3. $x \times 6 = 18$ $x =$ ____

4. $35 \div x = 7$ $x =$ ____

5. $28 + x = 37$ $x =$ ____

6. $41 - 2 = x$ $x =$ ____

7. $9 \times x = 27$ $x =$ ____

8. $20 \div x = 5$ $x =$ ____

9. $x + 7 = 42$ $x =$ ____

10. $22 - x = 16$ $x =$ ____

11. $x \times 5 = 40$ $x =$ ____

12. $40 \div x = 10$ $x =$ ____

13. $69 + x = 72$ $x =$ ____

14. $35 - 6 = x$ $x =$ ____

15. $7 \times x = 28$ $x =$ ____

16. $49 \div x = 7$ $x =$ ____

Calculate these in your mind and fill in the answers.

17. $36 + 6 =$ ____ **18.** $47 + 4 =$ ____ **19.** $15 + 15 =$ ____ **20.** $28 + 5 =$ ____

21. $80 - 9 =$ ____ **22.** $70 - 3 =$ ____ **23.** $61 - 8 =$ ____ **24.** $100 - 60 =$ ____

25. $17 + 9 =$ ____ **26.** $38 + 9 =$ ____ **27.** $23 + 9 =$ ____ **28.** $45 + 9 =$ ____

29. $17 - 9 =$ ____ **30.** $38 - 3 =$ ____ **31.** $23 - 8 =$ ____ **32.** $45 - 9 =$ ____

These equations use two letters. Find the number that x represents and fill in the answers.

33. $x + y = 32$ and $y = 20$ $x =$ ____

34. $x - y = 32$ and $y = 2$ $x =$ ____

35. $x \times y = 32$ and $y = 4$ $x =$ ____

36. $x \div y = 32$ and $y = 2$ $x =$ ____

Reflection and Discussion

If $x + y = 10$, how many different pairs of x and y could there be? What are they? What happens if you include decimal numbers?

Warm-up Exercises

68 + 4 = ____ 85 + 6 = ____ 54 + 7 = ____ 26 + 9 = ____

63 − 5 = ____ 55 − 8 = ____ 73 − 5 = ____ 40 − 6 = ____

4-2 How can the Commutative Law help?

Mathematical Conversation

Have you heard of the Commutative Law? These equations show what it means for addition and multiplication.

The Commutative Law has already helped us! Because $a + b = b + a$, we only needed to memorize half of the addition facts. Because $a \times b = b \times a$, we only needed to memorize half of the times tables!

$$a + b = b + a$$
$$a \times b = b \times a$$

Yes! If I know that 8 + 7 = 15, then I know that 7 + 8 = 15. If I know that 8 × 7 = 56, then I know that 7 × 8 = 56, too.

The Commutative Law also applies when we have more than two numbers. For example, the Commutative Law makes these calculations easier: 25 + 68 + 5 and 5 × 45 × 2.

And here's how it works for the multiplication problem.

I see! Here's how it works for the first one.

$$\begin{aligned} 25 + 68 + 5 &= 25 + 5 + 68 \\ &= 30 + 68 \\ &= 98 \end{aligned}$$

$$\begin{aligned} 5 \times 45 \times 2 &= 5 \times 2 \times 45 \\ &= 10 \times 45 \\ &= 450 \end{aligned}$$

Get ready for algebra!
No problem!

Guided Practice

Use the Commutative Law to do these calculations and fill in the answers.

A. 97 + 86 + 3 = ____ **B.** 50 + 38 + 50 = ____

C. 5 × 86 × 2 = ____ **D.** 2 × 47 × 50 = ____

Lesson 4–2 Exercises

Use the Commutative Law to help do these calculations and fill in the answers.

1. 199 + 85 + 1 = ____
2. 450 + 76 + 50 = ____
3. 80 + 90 + 20 = ____
4. 75 + 88 + 25 = ____
5. 26 + 48 + 24 = ____
6. 170 + 59 + 30 = ____
7. 2 × 4 × 5 = ____
8. 2 × 9 × 3 = ____
9. 3 × 8 × 3 = ____
10. 5 × 7 × 2 = ____
11. 50 × 7 × 2 = ____
12. 28 × 9 × 0 = ____

Use the Commutative Law to write another version of each mathematical expression.

13. 7 + 33 = ______
14. 6 + 78 = ______
15. 9 + 52 = ______
16. 22 + 29 = ______
17. 3 × 7 = ______
18. 4 × 9 = ______
19. 5 × 8 = ______
20. 6 × 100 = ______

Calculate these in your mind and fill in the answers.

21. 34 + 12 = ____
22. 58 + 4 = ____
23. 72 + 11 = ____
24. 45 + 45 = ____
25. 40 − 7 = ____
26. 34 − 5 = ____
27. 28 − 14 = ____
28. 60 − 9 = ____
29. 22 + 33 = ____
30. 69 + 8 = ____
31. 42 + 52 = ____
32. 37 + 6 = ____
33. 73 − 7 = ____
34. 84 − 9 = ____
35. 50 − 8 = ____
36. 25 − 6 = ____

Word Problems

Draw a model and write a mathematical expression to represent these problems. Then calculate and answer the questions.

37. On a field trip, one adult is needed for every 4 students. How many adults are needed for a class of 24 students? __________

Model:

Mathematical expression:

38. On a field trip, one adult is needed for every 4 students. How many adults are needed for a class of 25 students? __________

Model:

Mathematical expression:

Reflection and Discussion

Calculate 198 + 85 + 2 with and without using the Commutative Law. Which way is easier? Why?

Warm-up Exercises

$6 \times 6 =$ ____	$6 \times 7 =$ ____	$6 \times 8 =$ ____	$6 \times 9 =$ ____
$7 \times 7 =$ ____	$7 \times 8 =$ ____	$7 \times 9 =$ ____	$8 \times 8 =$ ____

4-3 What is the Associative Law?

Mathematical Conversation

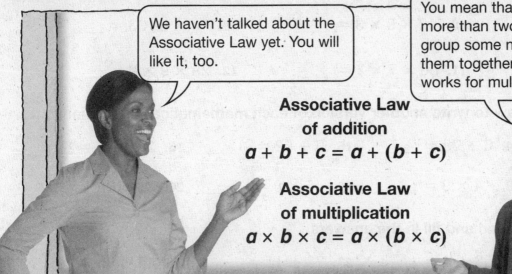

We haven't talked about the Associative Law yet. You will like it, too.

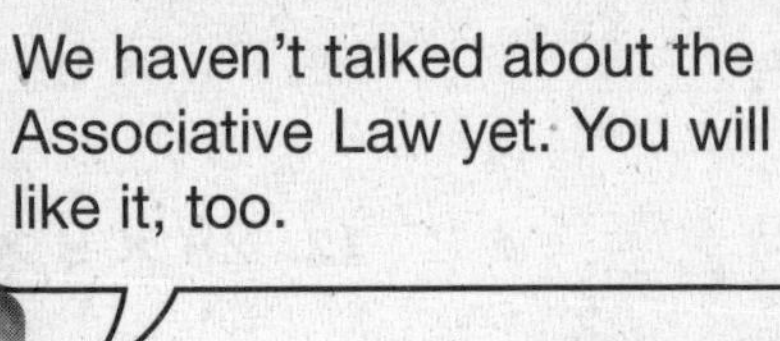

You mean that if we're adding more than two numbers, we can group some numbers and add them together first? And this works for multiplication, too?

Associative Law of addition

$$a + b + c = a + (b + c)$$

Associative Law of multiplication

$$a \times b \times c = a \times (b \times c)$$

Yes!

I will try it for multiplication.

$$a + b + c = a + (b + c) = b + c + a$$

Let me try it for addition. It works!

$$4 + 3 + 2 = 4 + (3 + 2) = 4 + 5 = 9$$

$$4 \times 3 \times 2 = 4 \times (3 \times 2) = 4 \times 6 = 24$$

The Associative Law can also help with computation!

Wow!

Guided Practice

Use the Commutative and Associative Laws to do these calculations.

A. $53 + 88 + 12 =$ ____________ **B.** $47 + 36 + 53 =$ ____________

C. $24 \times 4 \times 5 =$ ____________ **D.** $5 \times 62 \times 2 =$ ____________

Lesson 4–3 Exercises

Make the following calculations using the Associative Law and fill in the answers.

1. 356 + 80 + 20 = ____
2. 278 + 70 + 30 = ____
3. 88 + 90 + 10 = ____
4. 75 + 8 + 2 = ____
5. 26 + 9 + 1 = ____
6. 177 + 5 + 5 = ____
7. 35 × 5 × 2 = ____
8. 94 × 5 × 2 = ____
9. 3 × 50 × 2 = ____
10. 67 × 2 × 5 = ____
11. 57 × 2 × 5 = ____
12. 14 × 20 × 5 = ____

Use the Associative Law to write another version of each mathematical expression.

13. 7 + 33 + 67 = ________
14. 6 + 78 + 22 = ________
15. 9 + 52 + 48 = ________
16. 15 × 2 × 5 = ________
17. 99 × 5 × 2 = ________
18. 27 × 5 × 2 = ________

Calculate these in your mind and fill in the answers.

19. 120 + 120 = ____
20. 230 + 230 = ____
21. 400 + 400 = ____
22. 420 + 420 = ____
23. 400 − 200 = ____
24. 340 − 40 = ____
25. 280 − 70 = ____
26. 600 − 90 = ____
27. 29 + 7 = ____
28. 96 + 5 = ____
29. 45 + 7 = ____
30. 73 + 8 = ____
31. 75 − 8 = ____
32. 83 − 5 = ____
33. 30 − 21 = ____
34. 45 − 6 = ____

Word Problems

Draw a model and write a mathematical expression to represent these problems. Then calculate and answer the questions.

35. Lily has 8 red marbles, 19 blue marbles, and 2 golden marbles. How many marbles does she have?

____

Model:

Mathematical expression:

36. Danny has 30 books on his bookshelf and 12 books on his desk. How many more books are there on his shelf than on his desk? ________

Model:

Mathematical expression:

Reflection and Discussion

Calculate 356 + 80 + 20 with and without using the Associative Law. Which way is easier? Why?

Warm-up Exercises

$9 \times 2 =$ ____ $9 \times 3 =$ ____ $9 \times 4 =$ ____ $9 \times 5 =$ ____

$9 \times 6 =$ ____ $9 \times 7 =$ ____ $9 \times 8 =$ ____ $9 \times 9 =$ ____

4-4 Are there numbers less than 0?

Mathematical Conversation

I spent every penny to buy a present for my mom. Now I have 0 dollars. Nobody can have less money than I do.
I do! I had 5 dollars. My favorite car model costs 7 dollars. I borrowed 2 dollars from my brother to buy it. Now I owe him 2 dollars.
We say that Danny now has $^-2$ dollars. This means we are dealing with a negative number. A negative number is less than 0.

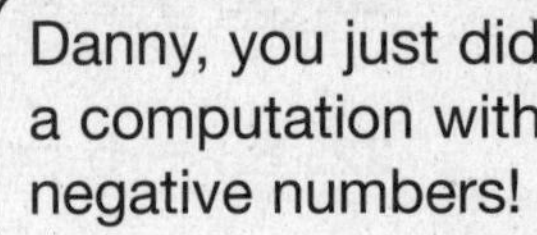

Tomorrow I will earn 2 dollars by mowing the lawn. I will return the 2 dollars to my brother. Then I will have 0 dollars—that's more than what I have now. If I can earn 3 dollars, then I will have 1 dollar, which is more than 0 dollars!
Danny, you just did a computation with negative numbers!

$5 - 7 = {^-2} \quad 2 + (^-2) = 0 \quad 3 + (^-2) = 1$

What pattern do you see in these equations?

Guided Practice

Calculate and fill in the answers.

A. $3 + (^-3) =$ ____ **B.** $4 + (^-6) =$ ____ **C.** $3 - 10 =$ ____

D. $9 + (^-9) =$ ____ **E.** $6 + (^-4) =$ ____ **F.** $20 - 30 =$ ____

Lesson 4–4 Exercises

Calculate and fill in the answers.

1. $1 + (^{-}1) =$ ____ **2.** $5 + (^{-}5) =$ ____ **3.** $10 + (^{-}10) =$ ____

4. $12 + (^{-}12) =$ ____ **5.** $30 + (^{-}30) =$ ____ **6.** $100 + (^{-}100) =$ ____

7. $1 + (^{-}3) =$ ____ **8.** $5 + (^{-}7) =$ ____ **9.** $10 + (^{-}17) =$ ____

10. $12 + (^{-}14) =$ ____ **11.** $30 + (^{-}35) =$ ____ **12.** $100 + (^{-}102) =$ ____

13. $4 + (^{-}1) =$ ____ **14.** $15 + (^{-}5) =$ ____ **15.** $14 + (^{-}10) =$ ____

16. $14 + (^{-}12) =$ ____ **17.** $33 + (^{-}30) =$ ____ **18.** $105 + (^{-}100) =$ ____

19. $9 - 5 =$ ____ **20.** $12 - 8 =$ ____ **21.** $10 - 7 =$ ____

22. $12 - 4 =$ ____ **23.** $32 - 25 =$ ____ **24.** $100 - 5 =$ ____

25. $1 - 5 =$ ____ **26.** $9 - 10 =$ ____ **27.** $5 - 10 =$ ____

28. $2 - 4 =$ ____ **29.** $6 - 12 =$ ____ **30.** $2 - 100 =$ ____

31. $90 + (^{-}100) =$ ____ **32.** $230 + (^{-}250) =$ ____ **33.** $400 + (^{-}600) =$ ____

34. $200 - 400 =$ ____ **35.** $40 - 340 =$ ____ **36.** $10 - 270 =$ ____

37. $25 + 7 =$ ____ **38.** $96 + 6 =$ ____ **39.** $47 + 13 =$ ____

40. $84 - 8 =$ ____ **41.** $33 - 5 =$ ____ **42.** $80 - 72 =$ ____

Reflection and Discussion

Danny has no money. He borrowed 5 dollars from his sister and spent it all on lunch. How much money does he owe his sister? How much money does he have?

Warm-up Exercises

$9 \times 2 =$ ____ $9 \times 3 =$ ____ $9 \times 4 =$ ____ $9 \times 5 =$ ____

$9 \times 6 =$ ____ $9 \times 7 =$ ____ $9 \times 8 =$ ____ $9 \times 9 =$ ____

4-5 Unit 4 Review

Mathematical Conversation

In this unit, the equations with letters impressed me the most. They are different from what we have seen before.

Look at Danny's two examples carefully and tell me the differences between them.

I see two differences. First, there is a letter in the top one and there are only numbers in the bottom one. Second, the top one has something on both sides of the equals sign, and the bottom one has nothing after the equals sign.

$3 + x = 5$

$3 + 2 =$

Good, Lily. Equations can be written using letters to stand for unknown numbers. What else do you remember learning in this unit?

We learned about the Commutative and Associative Laws. But the Commutative Law was not totally new to us. We had used it before.

We also learned about negative numbers. They are cool!

Are negative numbers new to you?

Yup!

Lesson 4–5 Exercises

Find the number that x represents and fill in the answers.

1. $x + 10 = 30$

$x =$ ____

2. $80 - x = 10$

$x =$ ____

3. $x \times 8 = 24$

$x =$ ____

4. $28 \div x = 4$

$x =$ ____

5. $x + y = 15$ and $y = 5$

$x =$ ____

6. $x - y = 12$ and $y = 10$

$x =$ ____

7. $x \times y = 42$ and $y = 7$

$x =$ ____

Calculate and fill in the answers.

8. $8 + 78 + 2 =$ ____

9. $25 + 37 + 25 =$ ____

10. $80 + 59 + 20 =$ ____

11. $2 \times 8 \times 5 =$ ____

12. $2 \times 8 \times 3 =$ ____

13. $38 + 8 + 2 =$ ____

14. $78 + 9 + 1 =$ ____

15. $139 + 5 + 5 =$ ____

16. $42 \times 5 \times 2 =$ ____

17. $32 \times 5 \times 2 =$ ____

18. $3 + (^{-}2) =$ ____

19. $12 + (^{-}3) =$ ____

20. $25 + (^{-}10) =$ ____

21. $18 + (^{-}8) =$ ____

22. $5 - 7 =$ ____

23. $4 - 10 =$ ____

24. $7 - 10 =$ ____

25. $7 - 9 =$ ____

Warm-up Exercises

11 + 7 = ____	11 + 5 = ____	11 + 3 = ____	11 + 1 = ____
7 + 11 = ____	5 + 11 = ____	3 + 11 = ____	1 + 11 = ____

5-1 How many 1-digit numbers are there?

Mathematical Conversation

C.J., I have a question for you. How many 1-digit numbers are there in the numeral system?

Easy! 1, 2, 3, 4, 5, 6, 7, 8, 9; nine 1-digit numbers!

Are you sure? What about 0? Isn't 0 a 1-digit number, too?

You're right. I forgot 0! So, there are ten 1-digit numbers, 1, 2, 3, 4, 5, 6, 7, 8, 9, and 0.

I noticed that 0 is a very interesting number. When you add 0 to any number or subtract 0 from any number, nothing changes—the number stays the same.

Zero means nothing, so when you add 0, that means you're adding nothing; and when you subtract 0, that means you're subtracting nothing.

Zero is interesting but tricky. You will learn more about it during the next few days.

The sum of any number and zero is equal to that number.

Any number minus zero is equal to that number.

Lesson 5-1 Exercises

Calculate and fill in the answers.

1. 725 + 0 = ____
2. 658 + 0 = ____
3. 1,287 + 0 = ____
4. 1,649 + 0 = ____
5. 0 + 725 = ____
6. 0 + 658 = ____
7. 0 + 1,287 = ____
8. 0 + 1,649 = ____
9. 856 − 0 = ____
10. 447 − 0 = ____
11. 9,191 − 0 = ____
12. 7,236 − 0 = ____
13. 373 − 0 = ____
14. 585 − 0 = ____
15. 8,541 − 0 = ____
16. 8,242 − 0 = ____
17. 31 + 29 = ____
18. 48 + 22 = ____
19. 55 + 25 = ____
20. 46 + 44 = ____
21. 352 − 352 = ____
22. 948 − 948 = ____
23. 735 − 735 = ____
24. 470 − 470 = ____
25. 9 × 2 = ____
26. 8 × 4 = ____
27. 7 × 5 = ____
28. 6 × 6 = ____
29. 14 ÷ 2 = ____
30. 27 ÷ 3 = ____
31. 24 ÷ 8 = ____
32. 49 ÷ 7 = ____
33. 4 + 8 + 2 = ____
34. 19 + 9 + 1 = ____
35. 35 − 3 − 2 = ____
36. 46 − 4 − 2 = ____
37. 9 + 9 − 9 = ____
38. 15 − 7 + 7 = ____
39. 18 + 0 − 2 = ____
40. 52 − 0 + 4 = ____

Word Problems

Draw a model and write a mathematical expression to represent these problems. Then calculate and answer the questions.

41. Ms. Park had 50 empty bottles. She recycled all of the bottles. How many bottles does she have now? ____________

Model:

Mathematical expression:

42. Lily went fishing today. She caught 5 fish in the morning, but none in the afternoon. How many fish did she catch in all? ____________

Model:

Mathematical expression:

Reflection and Discussion

Is it true that "any number minus zero equals that number"? Is it also true that "any number minus itself equals that number"?

Warm-up Exercises

$3 \times 2 =$ ____	$3 \times 1 =$ ____	$1 \times 3 =$ ____	$2 \times 3 =$ ____
$3 \times 5 =$ ____	$3 \times 7 =$ ____	$3 \times 9 =$ ____	$9 \times 3 =$ ____

5-2 What if you multiply by 0?

Mathematical Conversation

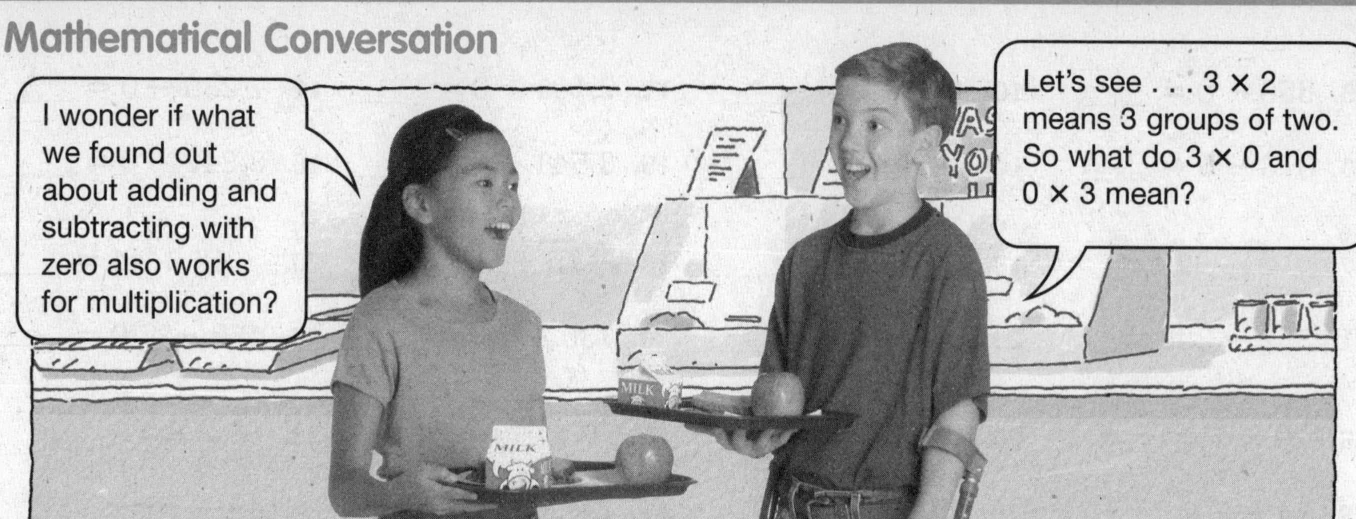
I wonder if what we found out about adding and subtracting with zero also works for multiplication?
Let's see . . . 3 × 2 means 3 groups of two. So what do 3 × 0 and 0 × 3 mean?

Hm . . . 3 × 0 means 3 groups of 0 objects, and 0 × 3 means 0 groups of 3 objects. Aha! I see!

"3 groups of 0 objects and 0 groups of 3 objects." Oh! So 3 groups of 0 things is 0 things, and 0 groups of 3 things is also 0 things! Both 3 × 0 and 0 × 3 are 0!

It means that any number multiplied by zero equals zero. Multiplication with zero is even easier than addition and subtraction with zero!

Just wait. Tomorrow you'll see that zero can be tricky!

$a \times 0 = 0$

$0 \times a = 0$

Lesson 5–2 Exercises

Calculate and fill in the answers.

1. 239 × 0 = ____ 2. 576 × 0 = ____ 3. 7,182 × 0 = ____ 4. 1,060 × 0 = ____

5. 0 × 239 = ____ 6. 0 × 576 = ____ 7. 0 × 7,182 = ____ 8. 0 × 1,060 = ____

9. 855 + 0 = ____ 10. 0 + 108 = ____ 11. 9,521 + 0 = ____ 12. 0 + 3,298 = ____

13. 509 − 0 = ____ 14. 898 − 0 = ____ 15. 929 − 929 = ____ 16. 784 − 784 = ____

17. 526 + 24 = ____ 18. 468 + 32 = ____ 19. 7,335 + 35 = ____ 20. 4,876 + 124 = ____

21. 526 − 26 = ____ 22. 468 − 48 = ____ 23. 7,335 − 35 = ____ 24. 4,876 − 176 = ____

25. 13 × 2 = ____ 26. 22 × 4 = ____ 27. 11 × 5 = ____ 28. 24 × 2 = ____

29. 44 ÷ 2 = ____ 30. 99 ÷ 3 = ____ 31. 88 ÷ 8 = ____ 32. 14 ÷ 7 = ____

33. 23 + 23 + 23 = __ 34. 32 + 32 + 32 = __ 35. 89 − 12 − 12 = __ 36. 76 − 13 − 12 = __

37. 20 + 20 − 10 = __ 38. 50 − 20 + 30 = __ 39. 182 + 8 − 90 = __ 40. 521 − 21 + 4 = __

Word Problems

Draw a model and write a mathematical expression to represent these problems. Then calculate and answer the questions.

41. Ms. Park bought 50 stamps. Today she bought 50 more. How many stamps does she have? ________

Model:

Mathematical expression:

42. C.J. planned to collect 30 postcards. He now has 32 postcards. How many more postcards did he collect than he planned to?

____

Model:

Mathematical expression:

Reflection and Discussion

Which do you think is easier: Calculating 1,389 + 0 or calculating 1,389 × 0? Why?

Warm-up Exercises

$4 \times 5 =$ ____ $5 \times 4 =$ ____ $4 \times 7 =$ ____ $4 \times 9 =$ ____

$20 \div 4 =$ ____ $20 \div 5 =$ ____ $28 \div 4 =$ ____ $36 \div 9 =$ ____

5-3 Is 0 really a tricky number?

Mathematical Conversation

Let's try to figure out what happens when zero is divided by a number.
OK. We can turn 3 × 2 = 6 into 6 ÷ 3 = 2 or 6 ÷ 2 = 3. We also know that 3 × 0 = 0 and 0 × 2 = 0. So 0 ÷ 3 = 0, and 0 ÷ 2 = 0. So zero divided by any number is zero!
Cool! How about dividing by zero? What happens if you divide by zero?
Mathematicians say that division by zero is undefined. They warn us not to divide by zero. What do you think?
"Don't divide by zero?" Hm! Let's see . . . Go back to 6 ÷ 3 = 2. We know that a multiplication version for 6 ÷ 3 = 2 is 3 × 2 = 6. So a multiplication version for 6 ÷ 0 = ? would be 0 × ? = 6. That's impossible, because we know that any number multiplied by 0 is 0.
So that's why mathematicians say that dividing by zero is undefined! That makes sense!
0 ÷ a = 0
Don't try to divide by zero!

Lesson 5–3 Exercises

Calculate and fill in the answers.

1. $0 \div 439 =$ ____ **2.** $0 \div 745 =$ ____ **3.** $0 \div 7{,}194 =$ ____ **4.** $0 \div 1{,}200 =$ ____

5. $0 \div 320 =$ ____ **6.** $0 \div 568 =$ ____ **7.** $0 \div 8{,}326 =$ ____ **8.** $0 \div 3{,}600 =$ ____

9. $0 \times 923 =$ ____ **10.** $565 \times 0 =$ ____ **11.** $4{,}762 \times 0 =$ ____ **12.** $7{,}557 \times 0 =$ ____

13. $923 \times 0 =$ ____ **14.** $0 \times 565 =$ ____ **15.** $0 \times 4{,}762 =$ ____ **16.** $0 \times 7{,}557 =$ ____

17. $395 + 0 =$ ____ **18.** $428 + 0 =$ ____ **19.** $3{,}751 + 0 =$ ____ **20.** $6{,}487 + 0 =$ ____

21. $395 - 0 =$ ____ **22.** $428 - 0 =$ ____ **23.** $3{,}751 - 0 =$ ____ **24.** $6{,}487 - 0 =$ ____

25. $9 \times 9 =$ ____ **26.** $8 \times 8 =$ ____ **27.** $7 \times 7 =$ ____ **28.** $6 \times 6 =$ ____

29. $81 \div 9 =$ ____ **30.** $64 \div 8 =$ ____ **31.** $49 \div 7 =$ ____ **32.** $36 \div 6 =$ ____

33. $9 + 7 \times 3 =$ ____ **34.** $15 + 5 \times 3 =$ ____ **35.** $24 - 6 \times 4 =$ ____ **36.** $30 - 4 \times 5 =$ ____

37. $17 + 9 \div 3 =$ ____ **38.** $25 - 10 \div 2 =$ ____ **39.** $18 + 4 \div 2 =$ ____ **40.** $52 - 6 \div 3 =$ ____

Word Problems

Draw a model and write a mathematical expression to represent these problems. Then calculate and answer the questions.

41. Ms. Park brought 3 cans of food for a food drive. C.J. brought 3 cans, too. Lily brought 5 cans. How many cans did the three of them bring?

____

Model:

Mathematical expression:

42. There were 16 cherries on the table. C.J. ate 2 and Lily ate 3. How many cherries are left?

____

Model:

Mathematical expression:

Reflection and Discussion

Make up a story for "$6 \div 3 =$ ____." Then replace the 3 in the expression with 0. Does your story still make sense?

Warm-up Exercises

$9 + 0 =$ ____ $9 + 10 =$ ____ $9 + 100 =$ ____ $0 + 100 =$ ____

$9 \times 0 =$ ____ $9 \times 10 =$ ____ $9 \times 100 =$ ____ $0 \times 100 =$ ____

5-4 Can zero change a number?

Mathematical Conversation

Ms. Park, I found something else about zero that is tricky.
What did you find?
I found that even though zero means nothing, putting zeros after a number will change it. If you put a zero after 5, it becomes 50. If you put two zeros after 5, it becomes 500. If you put three zeros after 5 . . .
It becomes 5,000! I know what you're saying. Every time you put a zero after a number, the number gets 10 times larger.

However, adding zeros to a number does not always change the value of the number. For example, putting a zero before 5 makes it 05. 05 is still 5!
Do you mean that writing zeros after a number changes the value of the number, but writing zeros before a number doesn't?

Actually, if you put zeros after a decimal, you don't change its value either. For example, if you put a zero after 0.5, you get 0.50. The value of 0.5 and 0.50 is the same.

Hm! I bet this is related to place value.

Yes. Putting a zero after a whole number will change the place value of the original digits.

I see!

Lesson 5-4 Exercises

Calculate and fill in the answers.

1. $2 + 20 =$ ____	**2.** $4 + 40 =$ ____	**3.** $7 + 70 =$ ____	**4.** $6 + 60 =$ ____
5. $2 + 200 =$ ____	**6.** $4 + 400 =$ ____	**7.** $7 + 7{,}000 =$ ____	**8.** $6 + 6{,}000 =$ ____
9. $20 - 2 =$ ____	**10.** $40 - 4 =$ ____	**11.** $70 - 7 =$ ____	**12.** $60 - 6 =$ ____
13. $200 - 2 =$ ____	**14.** $400 - 4 =$ ____	**15.** $7{,}000 - 7 =$ ____	**16.** $6{,}000 - 6 =$ ____
17. $107 + 103 =$ ____	**18.** $909 + 11 =$ ____	**19.** $5{,}795 + 5 =$ ____	**20.** $6{,}487 + 3 =$ ____
21. $9{,}526 - 526 =$ ____	**22.** $4{,}968 - 968 =$ ____	**23.** $7{,}535 - 535 =$ ____	**24.** $4{,}687 - 687 =$ ____
25. $4 \times 9 =$ ____	**26.** $5 \times 9 =$ ____	**27.** $6 \times 9 =$ ____	**28.** $7 \times 9 =$ ____
29. $40 \div 8 =$ ____	**30.** $56 \div 8 =$ ____	**31.** $48 \div 8 =$ ____	**32.** $32 \div 8 =$ ____
33. $12 + 4 \times 3 =$ ____	**34.** $10 + 5 \times 2 =$ ____	**35.** $9 - 3 \times 3 =$ ____	**36.** $15 - 5 \times 3 =$ ____
37. $9 + 9 \div 9 =$ ____	**38.** $18 - 8 \div 8 =$ ____	**39.** $81 + 7 \div 7 =$ ____	**40.** $25 - 4 \div 4 =$ ____

Word Problems

Draw a model and write a mathematical expression to represent these problems. Then calculate and answer the questions.

41. C.J.'s basketball team had 14 members when school started. They got 3 new members in late September and 2 new members in October. Now how many members do they have? __________

Model:

Mathematical expression:

42. Lily had 30 books. She donated 3 books to the library. Then she got 5 new books from her mother. How many books does Lily have now?

____

Model:

Mathematical expression:

Reflection and Discussion

What is the difference between adding zero to a number and adding a zero after a number?

Warm-up Exercises

$22 \times 2 =$ ____	$22 \times 3 =$ ____	$22 \times 4 =$ ____	$22 \times 0 =$ ____
$20 \times 2 =$ ____	$20 \times 3 =$ ____	$20 \times 4 =$ ____	$20 \times 0 =$ ____

5-5 Review, Reflection, and Quiz 6

Mathematical Conversation

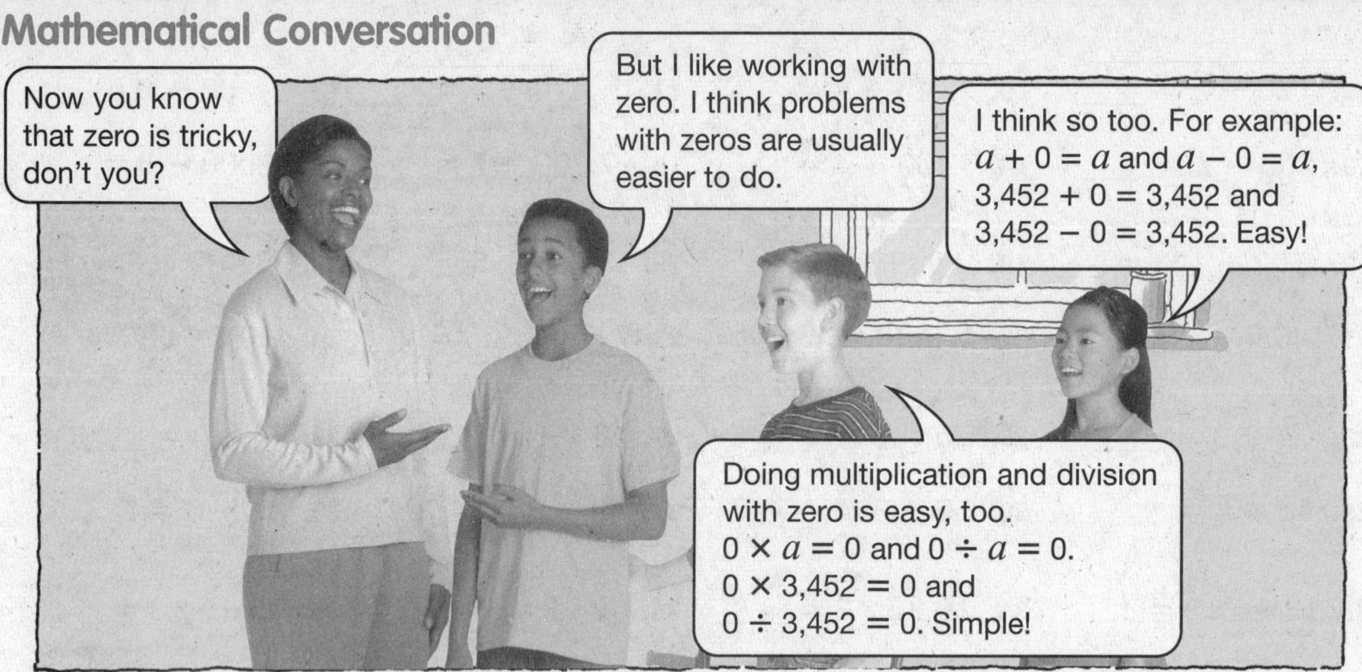
Now you know that zero is tricky, don't you?
But I like working with zero. I think problems with zeros are usually easier to do.
I think so too. For example: $a + 0 = a$ and $a - 0 = a$, 3,452 + 0 = 3,452 and 3,452 − 0 = 3,452. Easy!
Doing multiplication and division with zero is easy, too. $0 \times a = 0$ and $0 \div a = 0$. 0 × 3,452 = 0 and 0 ÷ 3,452 = 0. Simple!

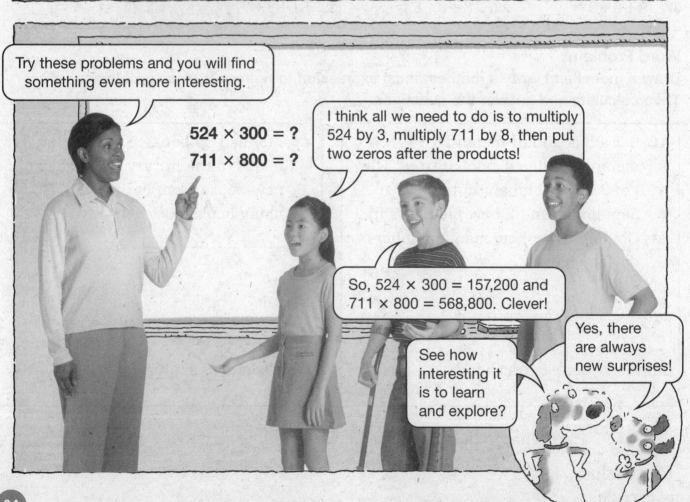

Try these problems and you will find something even more interesting.

524 × 300 = ?

711 × 800 = ?

I think all we need to do is to multiply 524 by 3, multiply 711 by 8, then put two zeros after the products!

So, 524 × 300 = 157,200 and 711 × 800 = 568,800. Clever!

See how interesting it is to learn and explore?

Yes, there are always new surprises!

Quiz 6

Score

Calculate and fill in the answers.

1. 25 + 0 = ____ **2.** 79 + 0 = ____ **3.** 0 + 45 = ____

4. 5 − 0 = ____ **5.** 67 − 0 = ____ **6.** 617 − 0 = ____

7. 0 + 338 = ____ **8.** 0 + 0 = ____

9. 26 − 0 = ____ **10.** 0 − 0 = ____

11. 15 × 0 = ____ **12.** 164 × 0 = ____ **13.** 490 × 0 = ____

14. 7 ÷ 0 = ____ **15.** 28 ÷ 0 = ____ **16.** 124 ÷ 0 = ____

17. 5,352 × 0 = ____ **18.** 0 × 0 = ____

19. 6 ÷ 6 = ____ **20.** 15 ÷ 15 = ____

21. 5 + ____ = 5 **22.** 16 + ____ = 16 **23.** 10 + ____ = 17

24. 5 − ____ = 5 **25.** 16 − ____ = 16 **26.** 17 − ____ = 10

27. ____ + 20 = 20 **28.** 32 + ____ = 35

29. ____ − 20 = 20 **30.** 32 − ____ = 16

Calculate and fill in the answers. Then write the other versions for each equation.

31. 50 + 0 = ____ **32.** 14 + 0 = ____ **33.** 9 − 9 = ____ **34.** 72 − 72 = ____

__________ __________ __________ __________

__________ __________ __________ __________

__________ __________ __________ __________

Challenge Yourself

35. 3 × 300 = ____ **36.** 21 × 40 = ____ **37.** 144 × 200 = ____

38. 4 × 80 = ____ **39.** 71 × 500 = ____

Warm-up Exercises

$2 \times 3 + 4 =$ ____ $4 \times 3 + 8 =$ ____ $5 \times 5 + 5 =$ ____ $6 \times 7 + 2 =$ ____

$4 + 2 \times 3 =$ ____ $8 + 4 \times 3 =$ ____ $5 + 5 \times 5 =$ ____ $2 + 6 \times 7 =$ ____

6-1 Why and how do we measure?

Mathematical Conversation

Homework for today

Dear students,

In the envelope you will find a piece of string and a paper shape. Compare the length of your string and the area of your shape with those of one of your classmates. But you are not allowed to talk in person; you may only talk by phone. Good luck!

Know what? It's easy to compare the strings. Measure them with a ruler! Mine is 6.5 inches long; how about yours?

Mine is longer than yours. It is 7.5 inches.

OK. Then what about the area of the shapes? We can't measure that with a ruler, can we?

Let's see . . . I've got an idea! Let's cut out little squares, all the same size, say, 1-inch long on a side. Then we cover our shape with the small squares. The shape that takes more little squares will be bigger!

Great idea! Let's do it! . . . It took 16 little squares to cover my rectangle.

I've got a square! I used 16 small squares to cover it, too! So, my square and your rectangle have the same area!

Each small square that they are using has the same area—called a square inch. The area of a figure can be measured in square inches. Does that make sense to you?

Oh, yes!

Guided Practice

If each little square represents one square inch, what are the areas of these figures?

A. 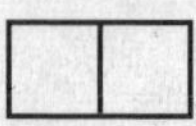

____ square inches

B. 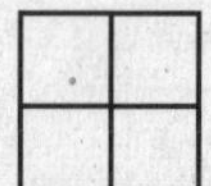

____ square inches

C. 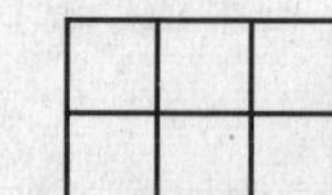

____ square inches

D. 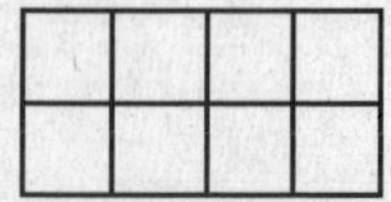

____ square inche

Basic Geometry Terms

Study these figures and their names. Discuss with your class.

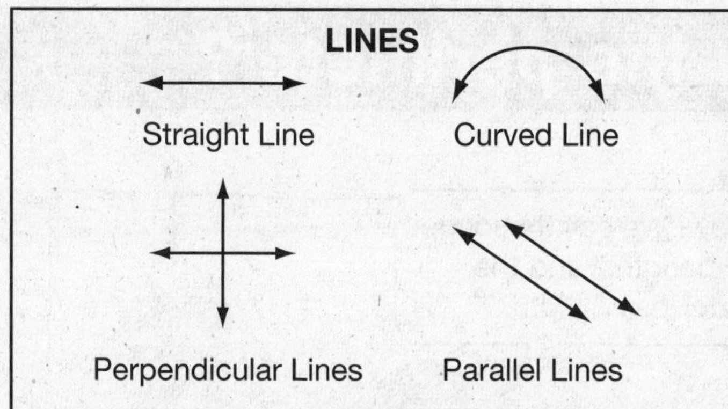
LINES
Straight Line
Curved Line
Perpendicular Lines
Parallel Lines

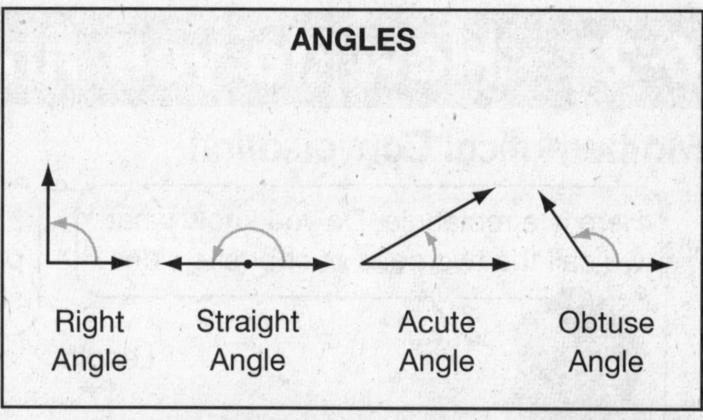
ANGLES
Right Angle
Straight Angle
Acute Angle
Obtuse Angle

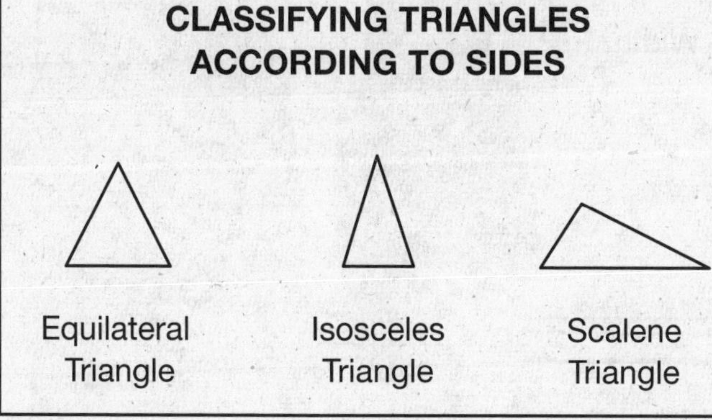
CLASSIFYING TRIANGLES ACCORDING TO SIDES
Equilateral Triangle
Isosceles Triangle
Scalene Triangle

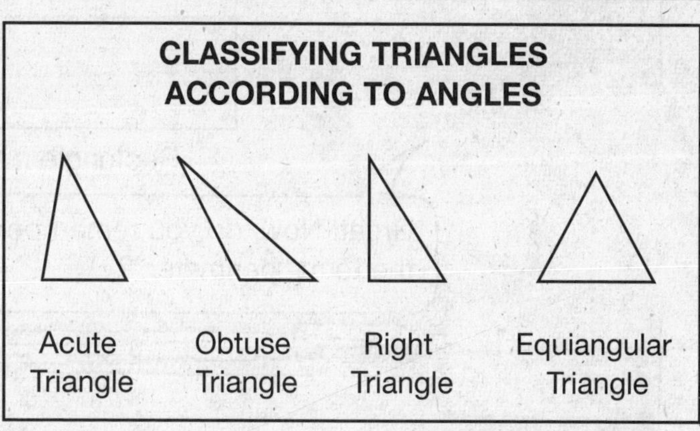
CLASSIFYING TRIANGLES ACCORDING TO ANGLES
Acute Triangle
Obtuse Triangle
Right Triangle
Equiangular Triangle

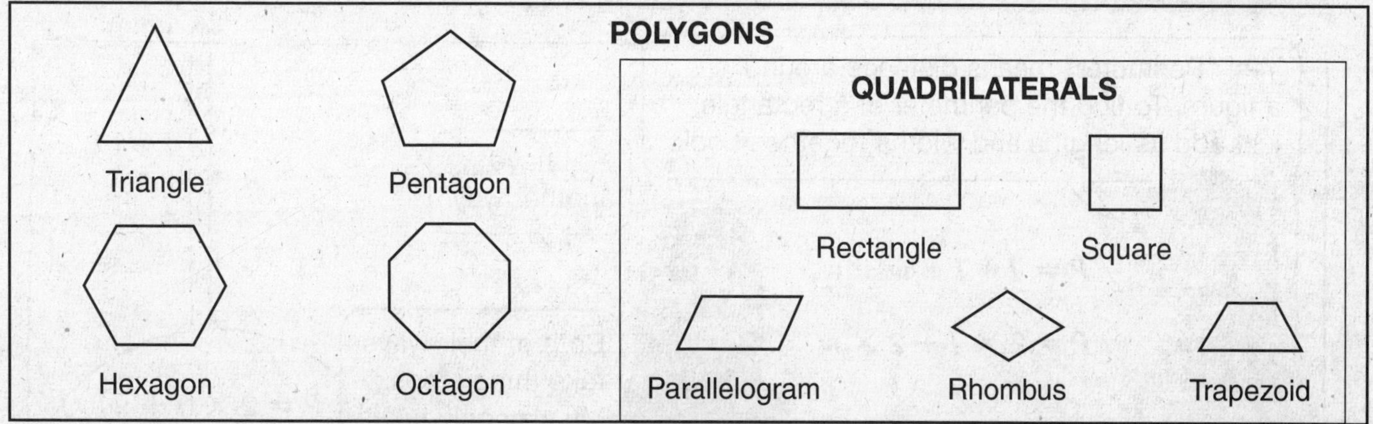
POLYGONS
Triangle
Pentagon
Hexagon
Octagon
QUADRILATERALS
Rectangle
Square
Parallelogram
Rhombus
Trapezoid

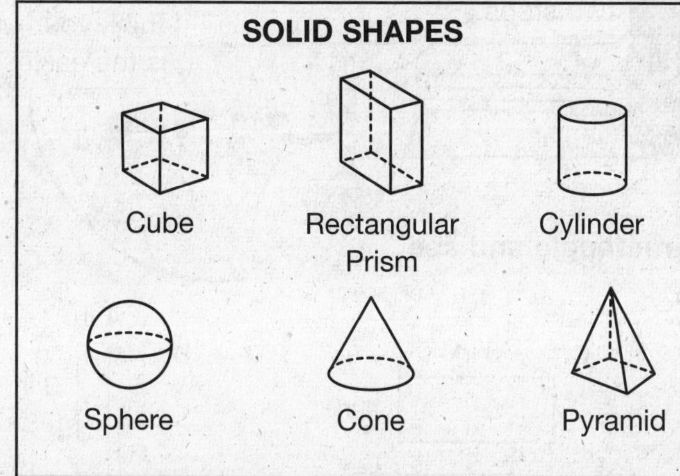
SOLID SHAPES
Cube
Rectangular Prism
Cylinder
Sphere
Cone
Pyramid

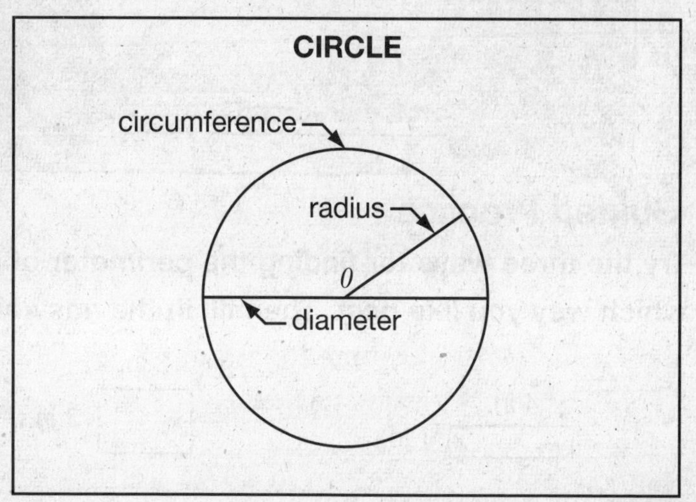
CIRCLE
circumference
radius
0
diameter

Warm-up Exercises

$3 \times 3 + 1 =$ ____ $4 \times 5 - 5 =$ ____ $5 \times 3 + 10 =$ ____ $7 \times 7 - 9 =$ ____

$4 + 3 \times 3 =$ ____ $5 + 4 \times 5 =$ ____ $2 + 5 \times 3 =$ ____ $9 + 7 \times 7 =$ ____

6-2 How do you find the perimeter?

Mathematical Conversation

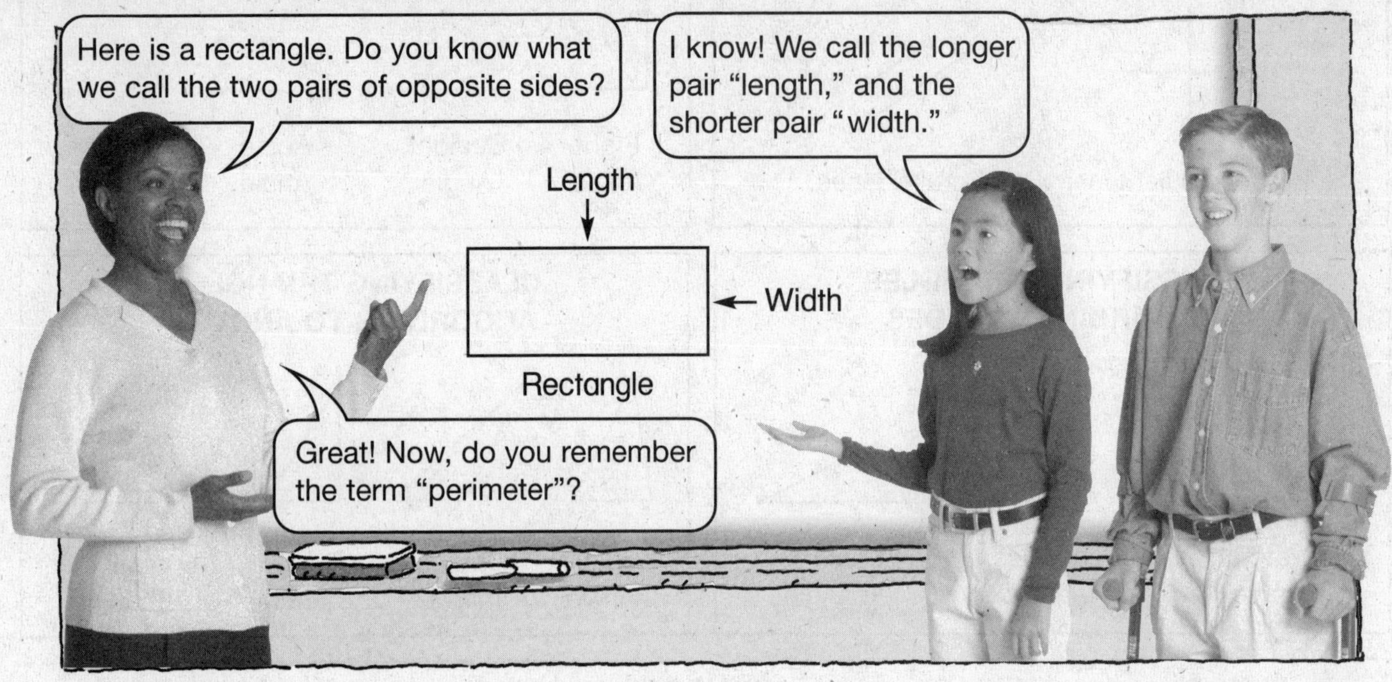

Here is a rectangle. Do you know what we call the two pairs of opposite sides?
I know! We call the longer pair "length," and the shorter pair "width."
Length
Width
Rectangle
Great! Now, do you remember the term "perimeter"?

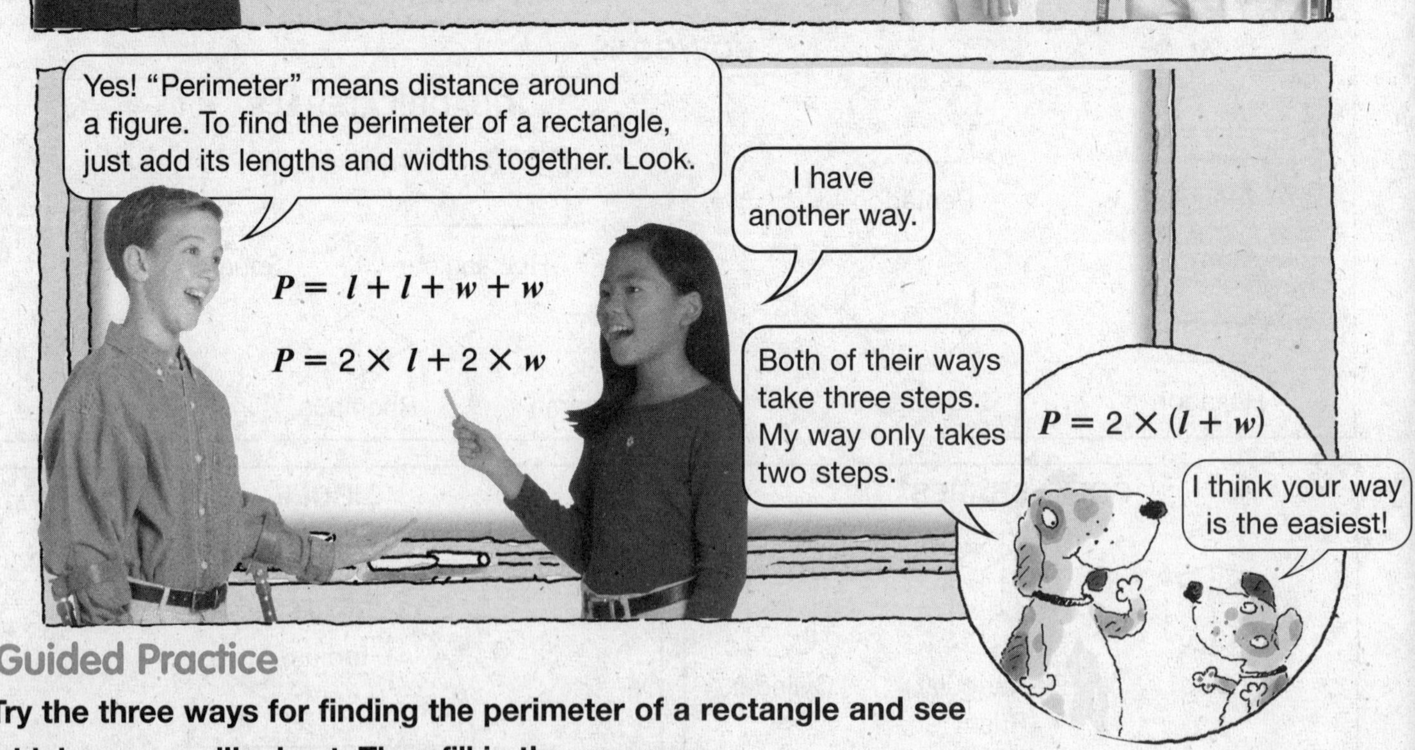

Yes! "Perimeter" means distance around a figure. To find the perimeter of a rectangle, just add its lengths and widths together. Look.
I have another way.
P = l + l + w + w
P = 2 × l + 2 × w
Both of their ways take three steps. My way only takes two steps.
P = 2 × (l + w)
I think your way is the easiest!

Guided Practice

Try the three ways for finding the perimeter of a rectangle and see which way you like best. Then fill in the answers.

A. 4 in. by 1 in.

$P =$ ____ inches

B. 3 in. by 2 in.

$P =$ ____ inches

C. 5 in. by 2 in.

$P =$ ____ inches

D. 1 in. by 3 in.

$P =$ ____ inches

Lesson 6-2 Exercises

Calculate the perimeter of these rectangles using two different formulas. Write the equations.

7 in.

5 in.

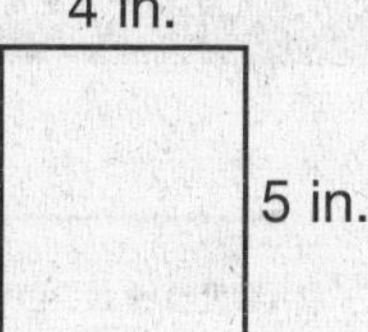
4 in.
5 in.

Formulas for the perimeter of a rectangle:

$P = l + l + w + w$

$P = 2 \times l + 2 \times w$

$P = 2 \times (l + w)$

1. ______________

____

____

2. ______________

____

____

9 in.

4 in.

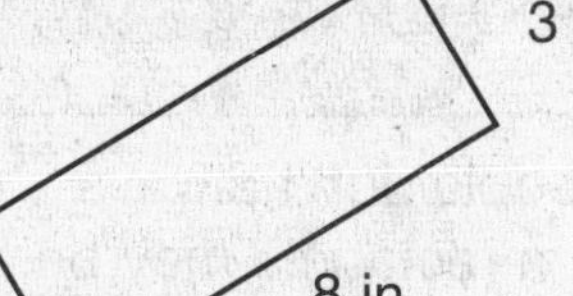
3 in.
8 in.

6 in.

1 in.

3. ______________

____

____

4. ______________

____

____

5. ______________

____

____

Calculate these in your mind and fill in the answers.

6. 17 + 7 = ____ **7.** 28 + 12 = ____ **8.** 79 + 3 = ____ **9.** 16 + 13 = ____

10. 9 − 5 = ____ **11.** 24 − 4 = ____ **12.** 45 − 6 = ____ **13.** 81 − 7 = ____

14. 27 + 8 = ____ **15.** 66 + 6 = ____ **16.** 86 + 5 = ____ **17.** 48 + 8 = ____

18. 32 − 2 = ____ **19.** 74 − 5 = ____ **20.** 55 − 15 = ____ **21.** 81 − 6 = ____

22. 9 × 9 = ____ **23.** 9 × 8 = ____ **24.** 9 × 7 = ____ **25.** 9 × 6 = ____

26. 45 ÷ 9 = ____ **27.** 18 ÷ 9 = ____ **28.** 27 ÷ 9 = ____ **29.** 36 ÷ 9 = ____

Reflection and Discussion

Tell your classmates the way you like best to find the perimeter of a rectangle. Explain why you like it best.

Warm-up Exercises

$3 \times 6 - 2 =$ ____ $4 \times 7 - 8 =$ ____ $8 \times 2 + 4 =$ ____ $9 \times 4 - 1 =$ ____

$2 + 3 \times 6 =$ ____ $2 + 4 \times 7 =$ ____ $10 + 8 \times 2 =$ ____ $4 + 9 \times 4 =$ ____

6-3 How do you find the area of a rectangle?

Mathematical Conversation

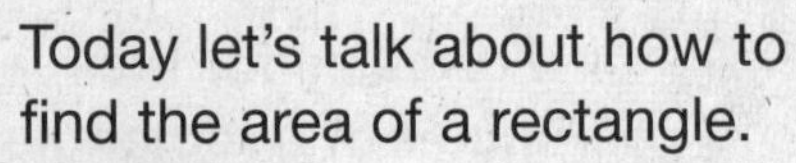

Today let's talk about how to find the area of a rectangle.

We already know that! For our homework for the first lesson, I covered a rectangle with square-inch pieces and found its area!
Good for you! But, think about this: people don't always have lots of little squares handy. Also, a rectangle may be very large, such as a basketball court. It would be very hard to cover a basketball court with square-inch pieces.
I think finding the area without using square-inch pieces would be difficult!

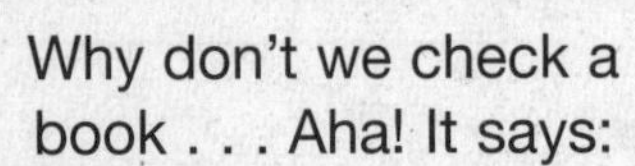

Why don't we check a book . . . Aha! It says:
Hmm . . . this makes sense! I covered my rectangle with 8 columns and 2 rows of square-inch pieces. 8 × 2 = 16. This is just what I got!
If you measure with inches, the area will be in square inches; if you measure with feet, the area will be in square feet; if you measure with yards, the area will be in square yards, and so on . . .
Got you!

Area of a rectangle = length × width

or

$A = l \times w$

Guided Practice

Try the two ways for finding the area of a rectangle: draw squares and and use the area formula. Then fill in the answers.

A. 4 in. by 1 in.

$A =$ ____ square inches

B. 3 in. by 2 in.

$A =$ ____ square inches

Lesson 6–3 Exercises

Find the area of each rectangle. Use the formula shown to write mathematical equations. The result will be in square inches.

7 in.
5 in.

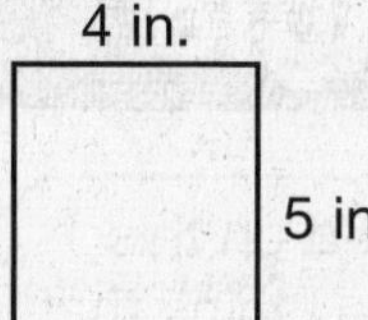
4 in.
5 in.

Formula for the area of a rectangle:

$$A = l \times w$$

1. ______________________

____

2. ______________________

____

9 in.

4 in.

3 in.

8 in.

6 in.

1 in.

3. ______________________

____

4. ______________________

____

5. ______________________

____

Calculate these in your mind and fill in the answers.

6. $22 + 12 =$ ____ **7.** $30 + 20 =$ ____ **8.** $55 + 11 =$ ____ **9.** $9 + 8 =$ ____

10. $15 - 5 =$ ____ **11.** $16 - 9 =$ ____ **12.** $17 - 8 =$ ____ **13.** $13 - 7 =$ ____

14. $40 + 17 =$ ____ **15.** $12 + 30 =$ ____ **16.** $34 + 10 =$ ____ **17.** $24 + 50 =$ ____

18. $22 - 11 =$ ____ **19.** $38 - 6 =$ ____ **20.** $49 - 2 =$ ____ **21.** $49 - 7 =$ ____

22. $8 \times 9 =$ ____ **23.** $8 \times 8 =$ ____ **24.** $8 \times 7 =$ ____ **25.** $8 \times 6 =$ ____

26. $40 \div 8 =$ ____ **27.** $16 \div 8 =$ ____ **28.** $32 \div 8 =$ ____ **29.** $24 \div 8 =$ ____

Reflection and Discussion

Can the two factors trade places in the formula for area so that the formula looks like this: $A = w \times l$? Explain.

Warm-up Exercises

$2 \times 2 + 6 =$ ____ $4 \times 4 - 6 =$ ____ $6 \times 6 - 6 =$ ____ $8 \times 8 - 4 =$ ____

$1 + 3 \times 3 =$ ____ $5 + 5 \times 5 =$ ____ $1 + 7 \times 7 =$ ____ $9 + 9 \times 9 =$ ____

6-4 From a rectangle . . . where?

Mathematical Conversation

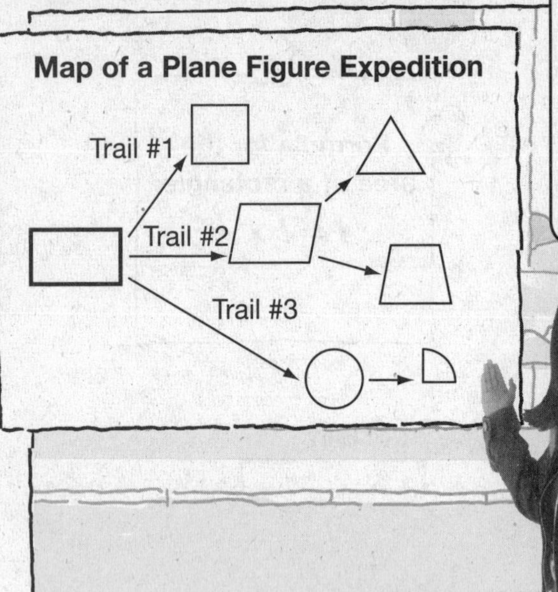

Map of a Plane Figure Expedition
Trail #1
Trail #2
Trail #3

Based on this map, I think that the rectangle is the base camp and you can go to other figures from there . . .

I see why a rectangle can lead to a square. Keep shrinking the length of a rectangle. When the length is the same as the width, the rectangle turns into a square!

Wait a minute! If the four sides of the rectangle are the same, how can you tell which are length and which are width?

We don't need to identify them; we just call them the "sides" of a square.

Hmm. Now I know how to find the perimeter of a square. It should be:

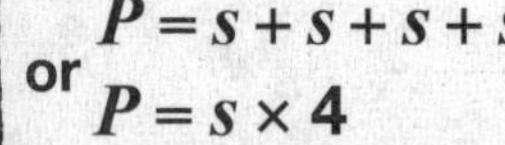

$P = s + s + s + s$
or
$P = s \times 4$

That means the formula for the area of a square is:

$A = s \times s$

Expeditions are fun!

You bet!

Guided Practice

Find the perimeter and area of each square. Then fill in the answers.

A.

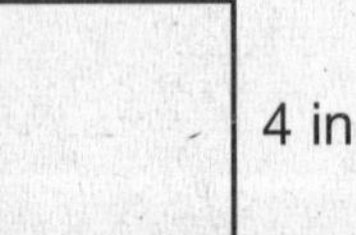

4 in.

$P =$ ____ inches

$A =$ ____ square inches

B.

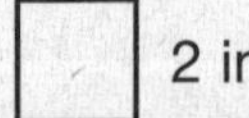

2 in.

$P =$ ____ inches

$A =$ ____ square inches

C.

1 in.

$P =$ ____ inches

$A =$ ____ square inche

Lesson 6–4 Exercises

Find the perimeter and area of each square and fill in the answers. Remember to use inches for perimeter measurements and square inches for area measurements.

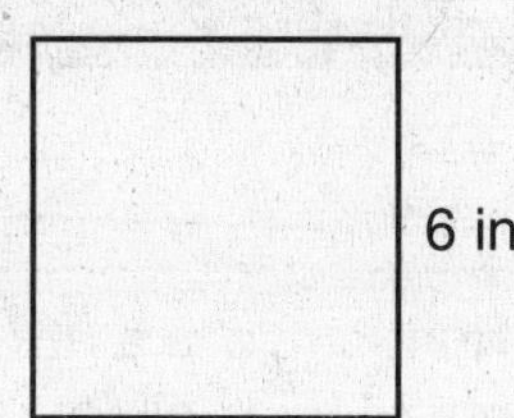
6 in.

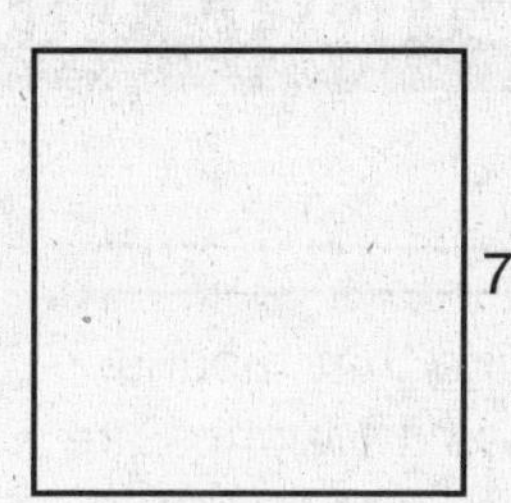
7 in.

Formula for the perimeter of a square:

$P = s \times 4$

Formula for the area of a square:

$A = s \times s$

1. ______ ______

2. ______ ______

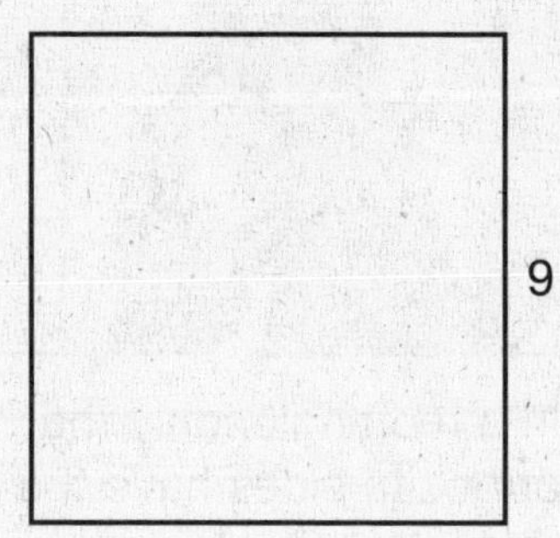
9 in.

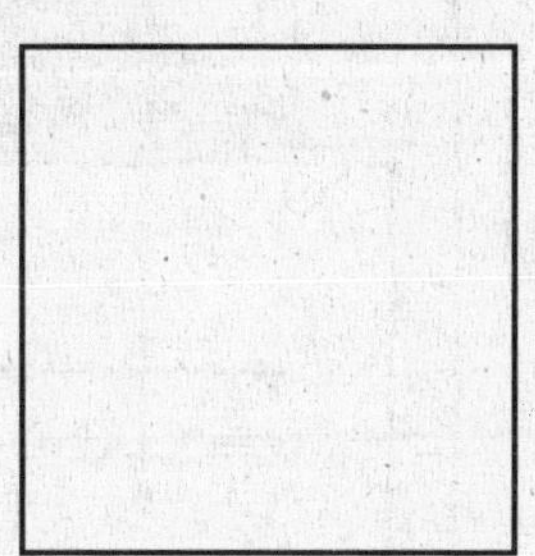
8 in.

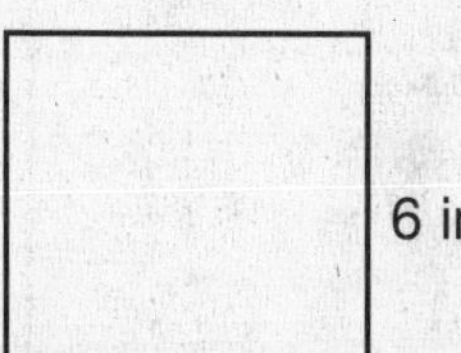
6 in.

3. ______ ______

4. ______ ______

5. ______ ______

Calculate these in your mind and fill in the answers.

6. 13 + 13 = ____	**7.** 18 + 2 = ____	**8.** 24 + 24 = ____	**9.** 22 + 22 = ____
10. 12 − 6 = ____	**11.** 12 − 7 = ____	**12.** 12 − 8 = ____	**13.** 12 − 9 = ____
14. 40 + 17 = ____	**15.** 12 + 30 = ____	**16.** 34 + 10 = ____	**17.** 24 + 50 = ____
18. 22 − 11 = ____	**19.** 38 − 6 = ____	**20.** 49 − 2 = ____	**21.** 49 − 7 = ____
22. 7 × 6 = ____	**23.** 7 × 7 = ____	**24.** 7 × 8 = ____	**25.** 7 × 9 = ____
26. 14 ÷ 7 = ____	**27.** 21 ÷ 7 = ____	**28.** 35 ÷ 7 = ____	**29.** 28 ÷ 7 = ____

Reflection and Discussion

Which do you think is easier, calculating measurements of rectangles or of squares? Why?

Warm-up Exercises

$3 \times 3 + 1 =$ ____ $4 \times 4 + 2 =$ ____ $5 \times 6 + 8 =$ ____ $6 \times 6 + 4 =$ ____

$3 + 3 \times 1 =$ ____ $4 + 4 \times 2 =$ ____ $5 + 6 \times 8 =$ ____ $6 + 6 \times 4 =$ ____

6-5 Review, Reflection, and Quiz 6

Mathematical Conversation

I copied this from my older brother's geometry book. Why is there a little square in each figure?

A little square like that means that the two lines it touches are perpendicular to each other. In other words, the lines form a right angle.

I see. A right angle is a 90° angle, right? I think all four corners of a rectangle or a square are right angles.

Yes. That is how rectangles and squares are similar. But how are they different?

In a rectangle, only the opposite sides have the same length. In a square, all four sides have the same length!

Perpendicular lines

I know! We call the long pair of opposite sides of a rectangle "length," and the short pair "width." All the sides of a square are called "side"!

Very good. Now please fill in the answers.

Geometry formulas

To find the perimeter of a rectangle: $P =$ ____________

To find the perimeter of a square: $P =$ ____________

To find the area of a rectangle: $A =$ ____________

To find the area of a square: $A =$ ____________

Quiz 6

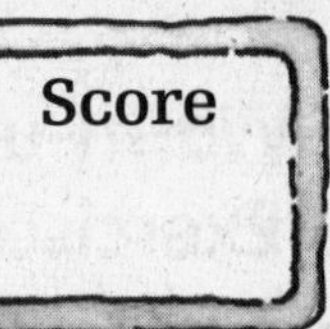
Score

Draw a rectangle with a length of 3 inches and width of 1.5 inches. Find the perimeter and area of the rectangle. Show your work.

Draw a square with sides that are 2 inches long. Find the perimeter and area of the square. Show your work.

Write the name of each figure on the line below it.

POLYGONS

__________ __________

__________ __________

QUADRILATERALS

__________ __________

__________ __________ __________

Warm-up Exercises

$3 \div 3 + 1 =$ ____ $4 \div 2 - 2 =$ ____ $6 \div 3 + 10 =$ ____ $7 \div 7 + 9 =$ ____

$4 + 3 \div 3 =$ ____ $5 + 4 \div 2 =$ ____ $3 + 6 \div 3 =$ ____ $9 + 7 \div 7 =$ ____

6-6 Where does Trail #2 go?

Mathematical Conversation

Trail #2 goes from a rectangle to a parallelogram. Here is a paper parallelogram. Can you change it into a rectangle by cutting it apart and rearranging the pieces?
Here's how I changed a parallelogram into a rectangle.
Here's how I did it.

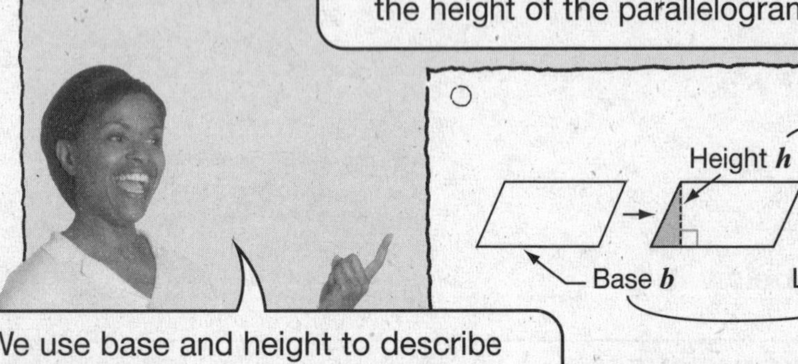
Look. The base of the parallelogram = the length of the rectangle and the height of the parallelogram = the width of the rectangle, so . . .
Height h
Width w
Base b
Length l
We use base and height to describe the parts of a parallelogram. Study this chart carefully. How are the base and height of a parallelogram related to the length and width of a rectangle?
. . . the area of a rectangle = length × width or A = l × w and the area of a parallelogram = base × height or A = b × h.
Did you understand what Lily said?
Umm . . .

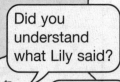

Guided Practice

Find the areas of these parallelograms and fill in the answers.

A.

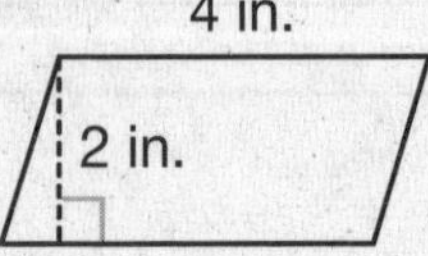
4 in.
2 in.

$A =$ ____ square inches

B.

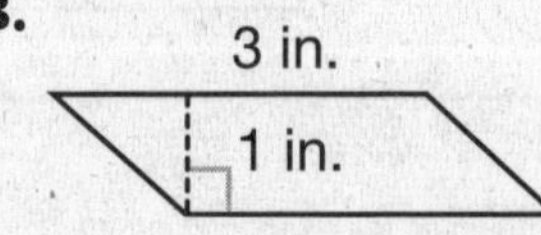
3 in.
1 in.

$A =$ ____ square inches

C.

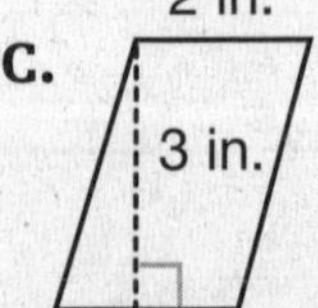
2 in.
3 in.

$A =$ ____ square inches

Lesson 6–6 Exercises

Find the areas of these figures and fill in the answers. The results will be in square inches.

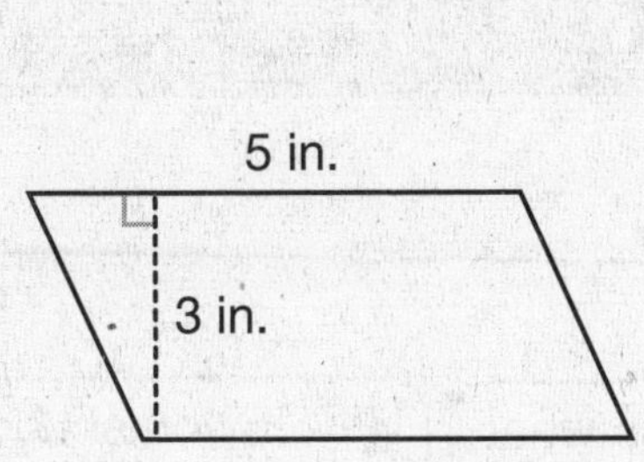

5 in.
3 in.

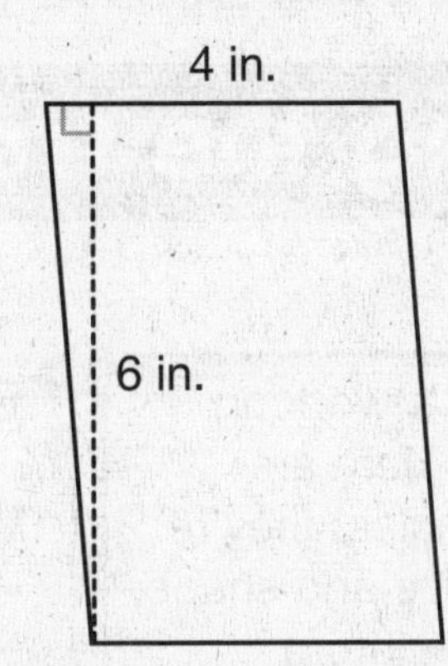

4 in.
6 in.

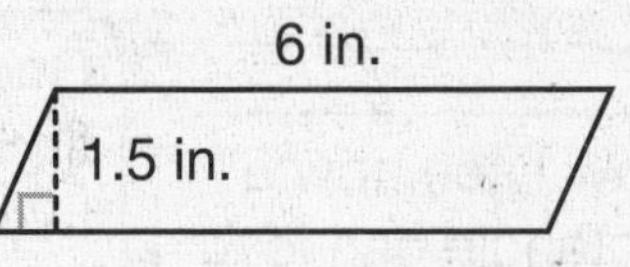

6 in.
1.5 in.

1. $A =$ ____ square inches **2.** $A =$ ____ square inches **3.** $A =$ ____ square inches

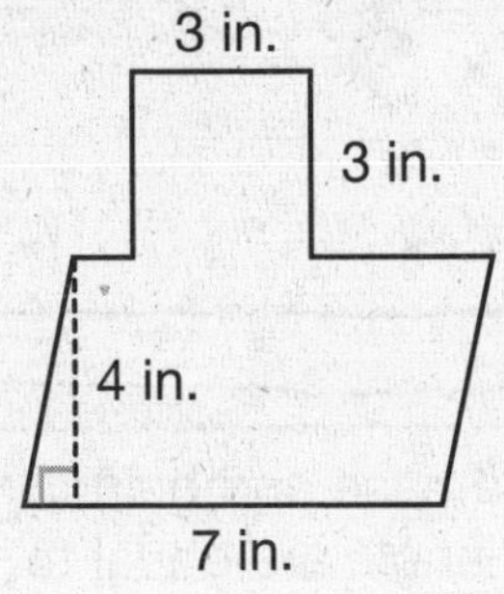

3 in.
3 in.
4 in.
7 in.

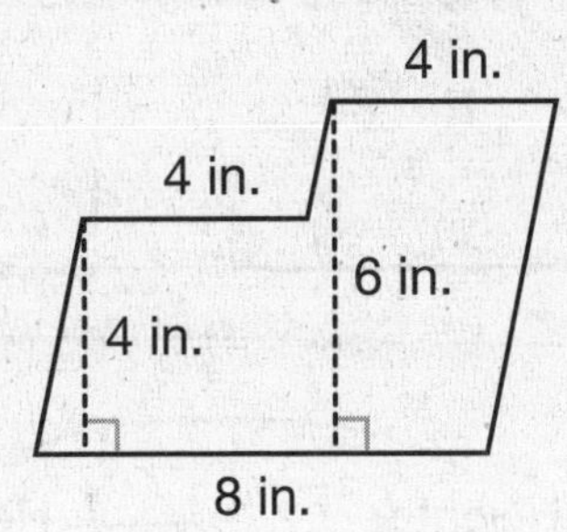

4 in.
4 in.
6 in.
4 in.
8 in.

HINT: Separate the figures in 4 & 5 into two figures first.

4. $A =$ ____ square inches **5.** $A =$ ____ square inches

Calculate these in your mind and fill in the answers.

6. $40 + 40 =$ ____ **7.** $30 + 40 =$ ____ **8.** $20 + 30 =$ ____ **9.** $40 + 50 =$ ____

10. $90 - 20 =$ ____ **11.** $90 - 70 =$ ____ **12.** $80 - 50 =$ ____ **13.** $80 - 30 =$ ____

14. $15 + 15 =$ ____ **15.** $32 + 32 =$ ____ **16.** $23 + 23 =$ ____ **17.** $41 + 41 =$ ____

18. $18 - 9 =$ ____ **19.** $16 - 7 =$ ____ **20.** $14 - 6 =$ ____ **21.** $14 - 5 =$ ____

22. $6 \times 6 =$ ____ **23.** $6 \times 7 =$ ____ **24.** $6 \times 8 =$ ____ **25.** $6 \times 9 =$ ____

26. $30 \div 6 =$ ____ **27.** $24 \div 6 =$ ____ **28.** $18 \div 6 =$ ____ **29.** $12 \div 6 =$ ____

Reflection and Discussion

Are the four height lines in this parallelogram the same?

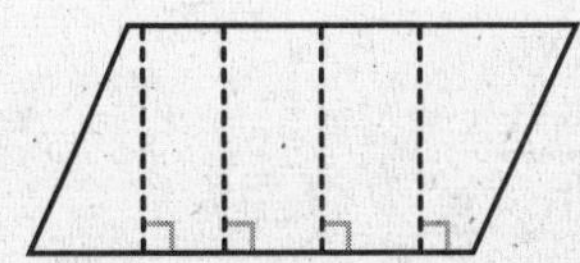

Warm-up Exercises				
	$10 \div 2 + 4 =$ ____	$9 \div 3 - 3 =$ ____	$14 \div 2 + 3 =$ ____	$16 \div 4 - 2 =$ ____
	$4 + 10 \div 2 =$ ____	$3 + 9 \div 3 =$ ____	$3 + 14 \div 2 =$ ____	$2 + 16 \div 4 =$ ____

6-7 Further along the trail . . .

Mathematical Conversation

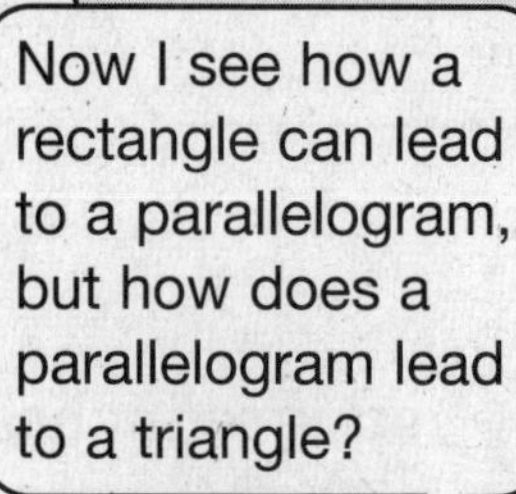
Now I see how a rectangle can lead to a parallelogram, but how does a parallelogram lead to a triangle?

Good question. Let's work on finding the answer. Here are two congruent triangles; they're exactly the same size and shape. Can you make them into a parallelogram?

This is what I got:
Hey, it works! Look at what I got:

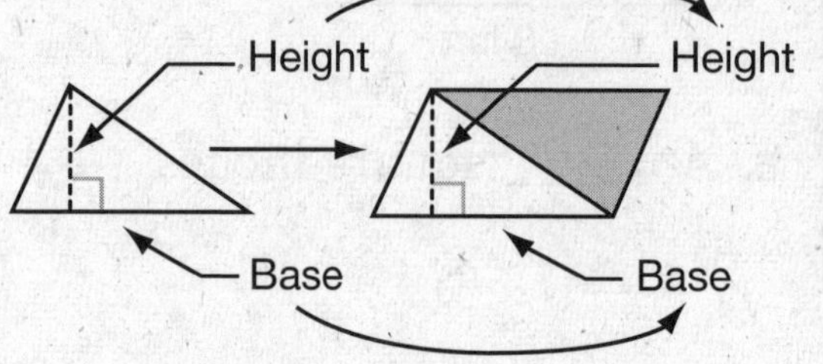
Now carefully compare the triangle and parallelogram. Tell me what you find.
Height
Height
Base
Base
Aha! The base and height of the triangle are equal to the base and height of the parallelogram, while the area of the triangle is half the area of the parallelogram.

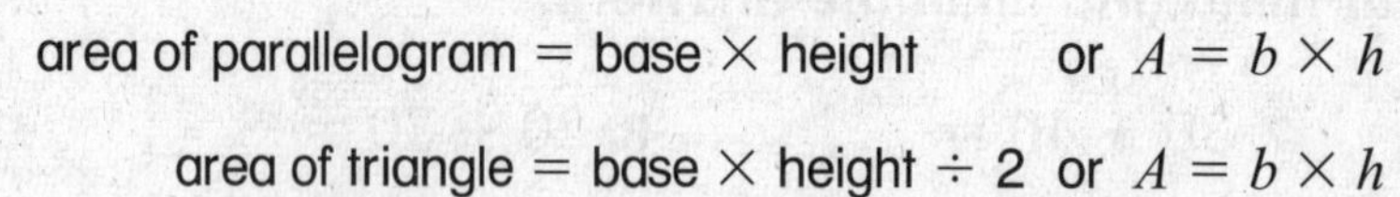

area of parallelogram = base × height or $A = b \times h$

area of triangle = base × height ÷ 2 or $A = b \times h \div 2$

Does what C.J. said make sense to you?

Yes!

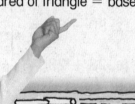

Guided Practice

Find the areas of these triangles and fill in the answers.

A.

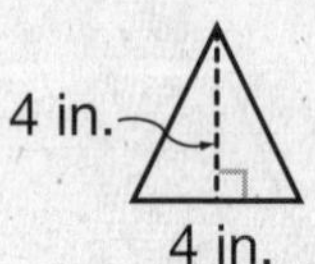
4 in.
4 in.

____ square inches

B.

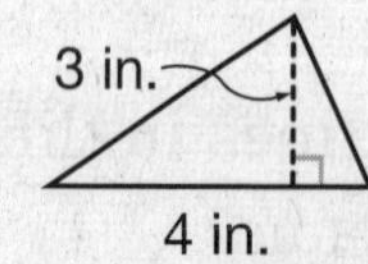
3 in.
4 in.

____ square inches

C.

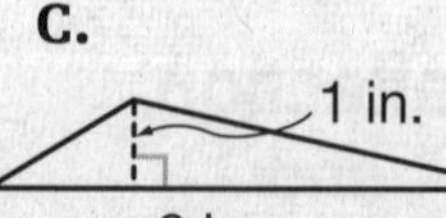
1 in.
6 in.

____ square inches

Lesson 6–7 Exercises

Find the areas of these figures and fill in the answers. The results will be in square inches.

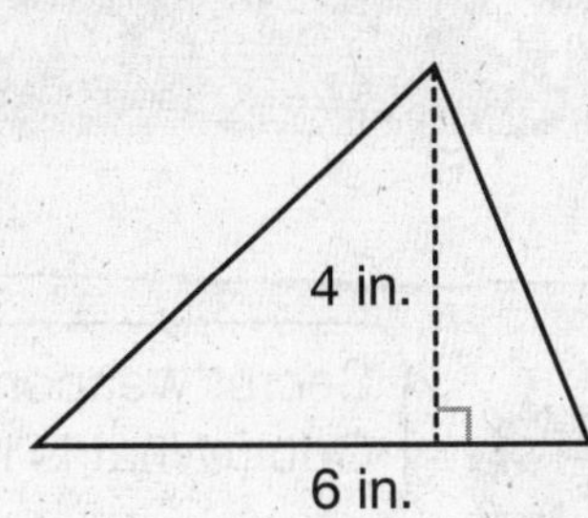
4 in.
6 in.

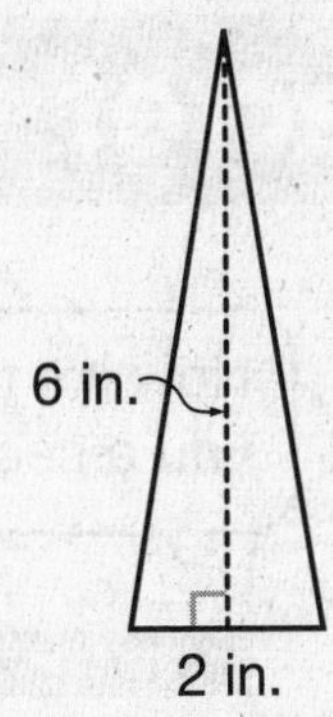
6 in.
2 in.

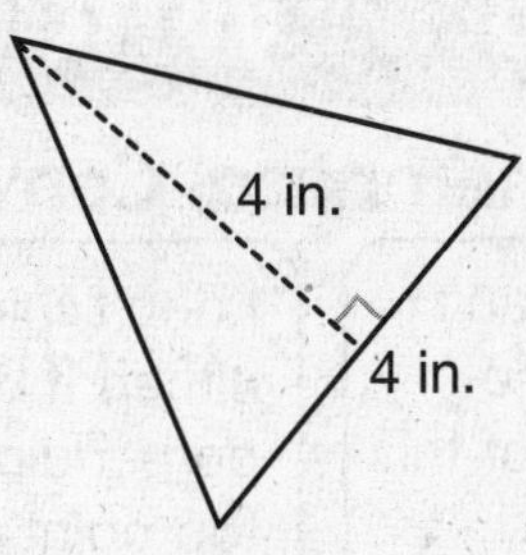
4 in.
4 in.

1. $A =$ ____ square inches **2.** $A =$ ____ square inches **3.** $A =$ ____ square inches

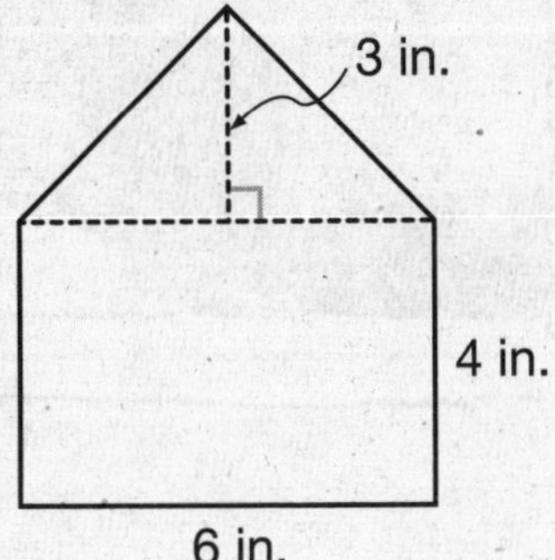
3 in.
4 in.
6 in.

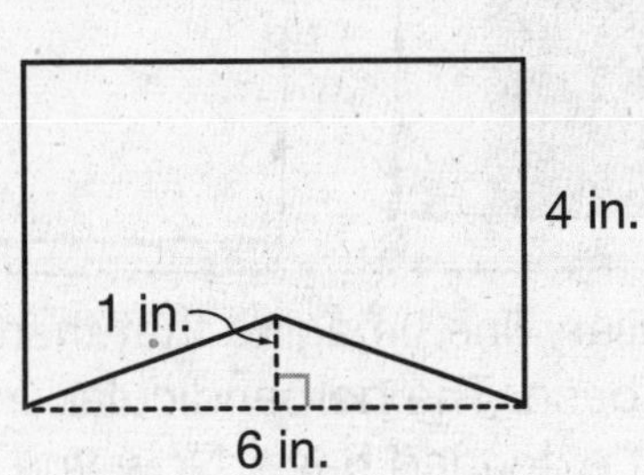
4 in.
1 in.
6 in.

HINT: Sometimes you need to subtract.

4. $A =$ ____ square inches **5.** $A =$ ____ square inches

Calculate these in your mind and fill in the answers.

6. 6 + 7 = ____ **7.** 5 + 8 = ____ **8.** 9 + 4 = ____ **9.** 4 + 7 = ____

10. 13 − 7 = ____ **11.** 14 − 6 = ____ **12.** 16 − 7 = ____ **13.** 13 − 5 = ____

14. 5 + 7 = ____ **15.** 6 + 8 = ____ **16.** 7 + 5 = ____ **17.** 8 + 6 = ____

18. 17 − 9 = ____ **19.** 11 − 6 = ____ **20.** 13 − 8 = ____ **21.** 12 − 4 = ____

22. 5 × 9 = ____ **23.** 5 × 8 = ____ **24.** 5 × 7 = ____ **25.** 5 × 6 = ____

26. 25 ÷ 5 = ____ **27.** 20 ÷ 5 = ____ **28.** 15 ÷ 5 = ____ **29.** 10 ÷ 5 = ____

Reflection and Discussion

People say that to find the area of a right triangle, we don't need to draw a height line. Do you agree?

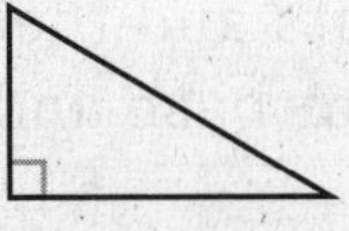

Warm-up Exercises

$15 \div 5 + 3 =$ ____	$12 \div 3 - 2 =$ ____	$16 \div 2 - 2 =$ ____	$18 \div 3 - 2 =$ ____
$7 + 15 \div 5 =$ ____	$6 + 12 \div 3 =$ ____	$2 + 16 \div 2 =$ ____	$4 + 18 \div 3 =$ ____

6-8 What is the secret weapon?

Mathematical Conversation

Lily, I can't draw the height of this triangle.
I don't think that I can either! If we draw a perpendicular line from the top point of the triangle, it won't even touch the base!

Now it's time to show you a secret weapon!
Secret weapon? Cool! What is it?

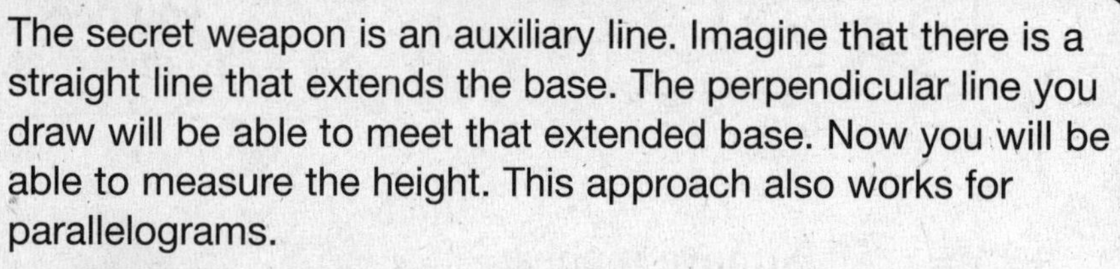
The secret weapon is an auxiliary line. Imagine that there is a straight line that extends the base. The perpendicular line you draw will be able to meet that extended base. Now you will be able to measure the height. This approach also works for parallelograms.

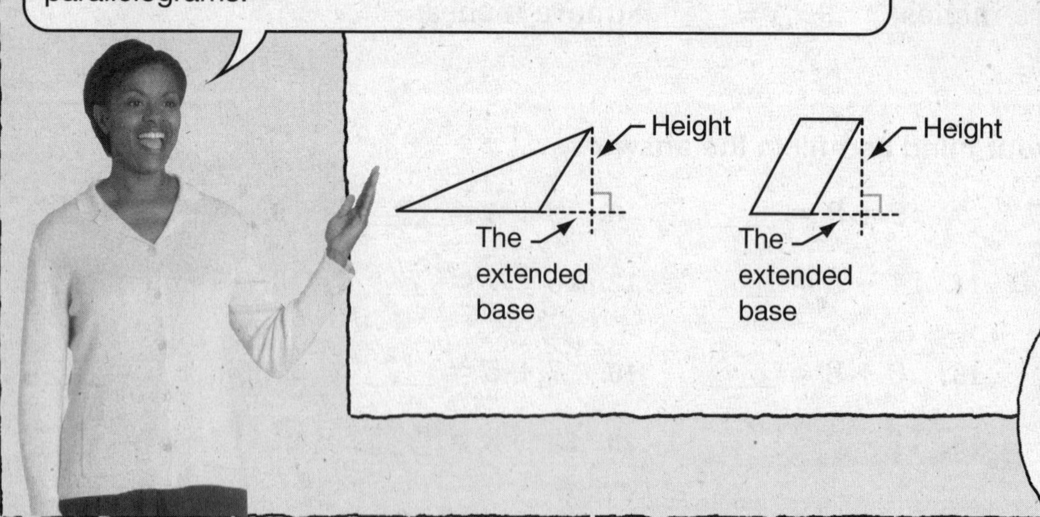
Height
The extended base
Height
The extended base
Do you have a secret weapon?
Now I do!

Guided Practice

Every triangle has three bases and three heights. Look at these congruent triangles. Find the three heights and their corresponding bases (write "*b*" for base and "*h*" for height).

Lesson 6–8 Exercises

1. Draw the three heights of this triangle. Label each one "height."

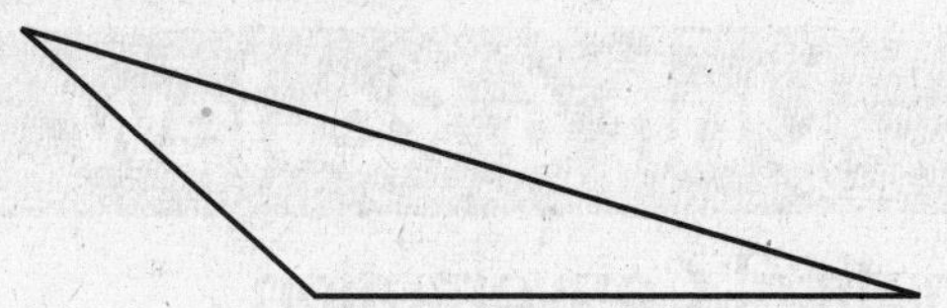

Find the areas of these figures and fill in the answers. The results will be in square inches.

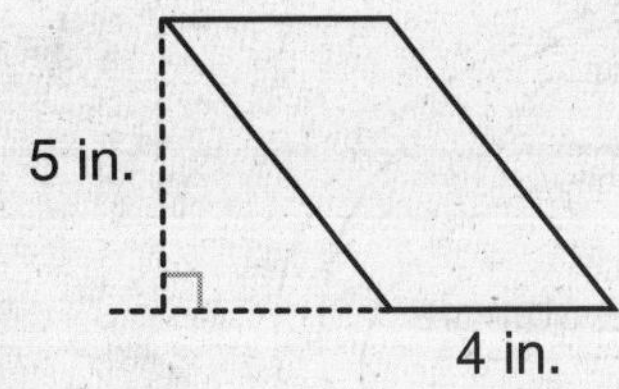
5 in.
4 in.

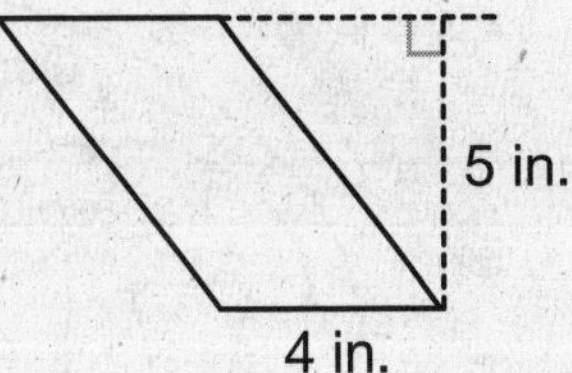
5 in.
4 in.

2. $A =$ ____ square inches **3.** $A =$ ____ square inches

Bonus:

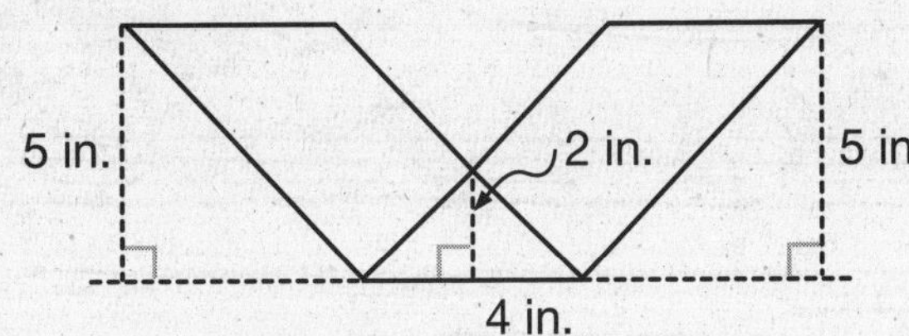
5 in.
2 in.
5 in.
4 in.

4. $A =$ ____ square inches

Calculate these in your mind and fill in the answers.

5. $18 + 7 =$ ____ **6.** $15 + 9 =$ ____ **7.** $13 + 8 =$ ____ **8.** $17 + 5 =$ ____

9. $25 - 8 =$ ____ **10.** $26 - 7 =$ ____ **11.** $22 - 9 =$ ____ **12.** $24 - 8 =$ ____

13. $24 + 8 =$ ____ **14.** $23 + 7 =$ ____ **15.** $26 + 5 =$ ____ **16.** $28 + 7 =$ ____

17. $30 - 9 =$ ____ **18.** $33 - 6 =$ ____ **19.** $35 - 8 =$ ____ **20.** $31 - 7 =$ ____

21. $4 \times 9 =$ ____ **22.** $4 \times 7 =$ ____ **23.** $4 \times 8 =$ ____ **24.** $4 \times 6 =$ ____

25. $240 \div 4 =$ ____ **26.** $160 \div 4 =$ ____ **27.** $120 \div 4 =$ ____ **28.** $80 \div 4 =$ ____

Reflection and Discussion

Before this lesson, had you ever seen an auxiliary line? What was it used for?

Warm-up Exercises

$3 \div 3 + 1 =$ ____	$4 \div 2 - 2 =$ ____	$6 \div 3 + 10 =$ ____	$7 \div 7 + 9 =$ ____
$4 + 3 \div 3 =$ ____	$5 + 4 \div 2 =$ ____	$3 + 6 \div 3 =$ ____	$9 + 7 \div 7 =$ ____

6-9 Unit 6 Review

Mathematical Conversation

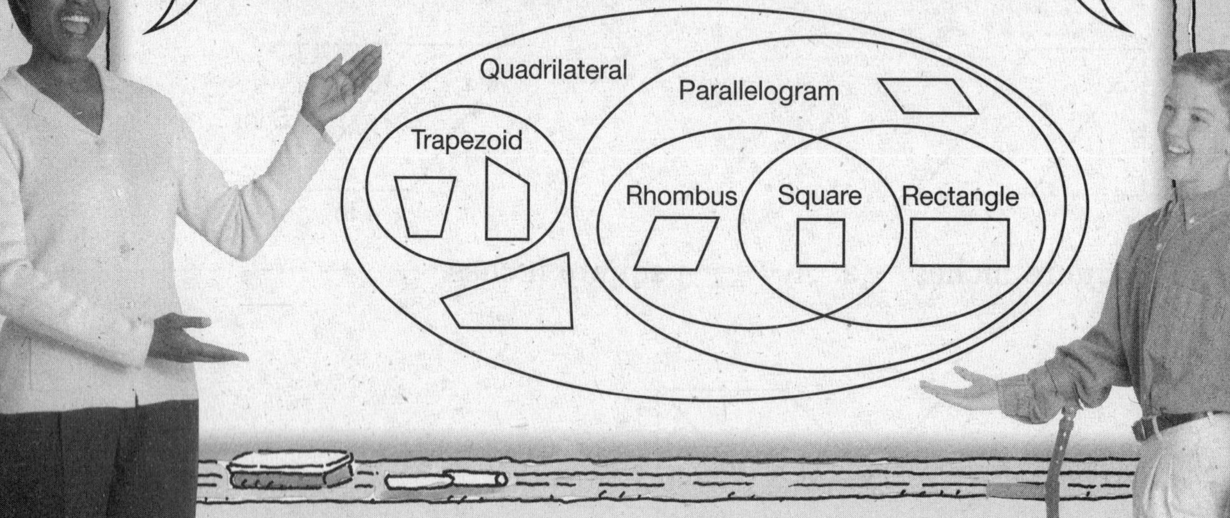
In the first lesson of this unit we had a page of geometry terms. On that page there was a set of quadrilaterals. The following diagram is a way of organizing those quadrilaterals.
Cool! Now we know how to find the perimeter of these quadrilaterals and the area of many of them.
Quadrilateral
Parallelogram
Trapezoid
Rhombus
Square
Rectangle

We also know how to find the perimeter and area of a triangle! Let's make a summary list of all the formulas we learned in this unit.

Geometry formulas

To find the perimeter of a rectangle: $P =$ ____________

To find the perimeter of a square: $P =$ ____________

To find the area of a rectangle: $A =$ ____________

To find the area of a square: $A =$ ____________

To find the area of a parallelogram: $A =$ ____________

To find the area of a triangle: $A =$ ____________

See, there are so many things they learned in this unit!

Learning is fun!

Lesson 6–9 Exercises

Write the names of these figures on the lines provided below.

LINES

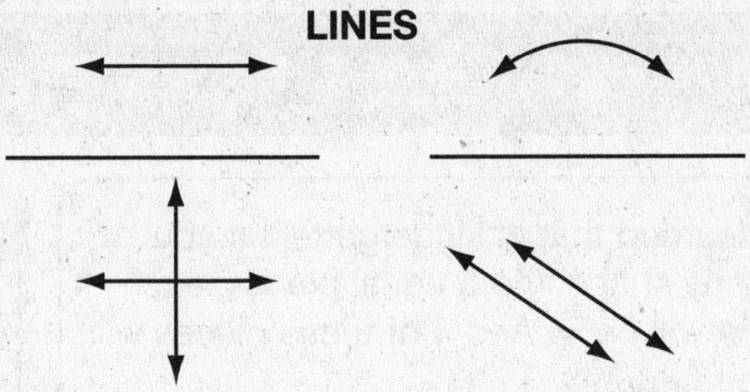

ANGLES

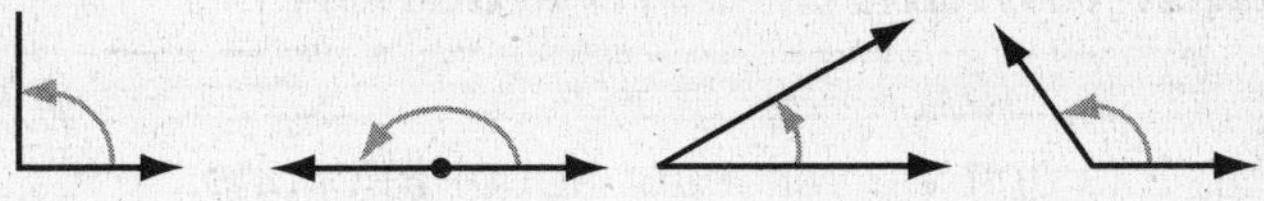

CLASSIFYING TRIANGLES ACCORDING TO SIDES

CLASSIFYING TRIANGLES ACCORDING TO ANGLES

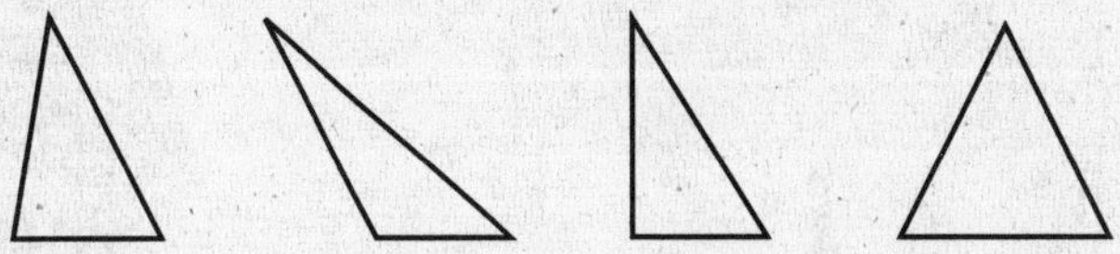

POLYGONS

QUADRILATERALS

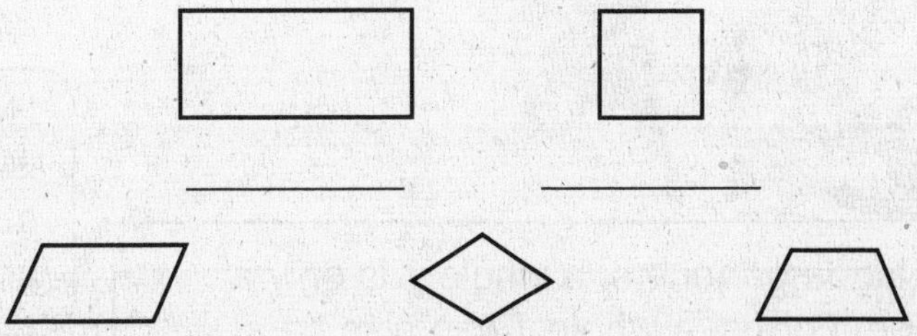

SOLID SHAPES

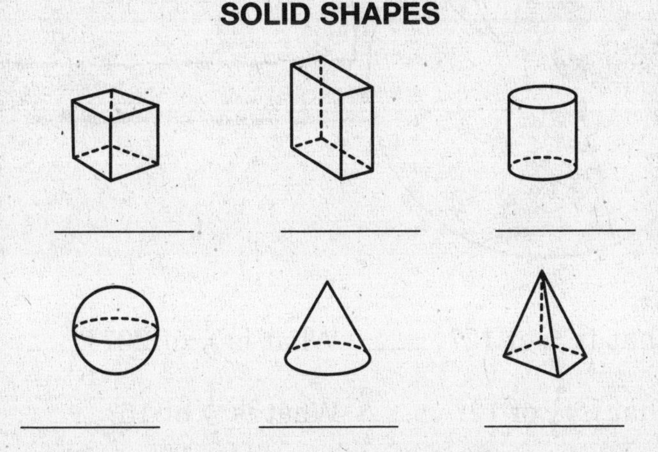

CIRCLE

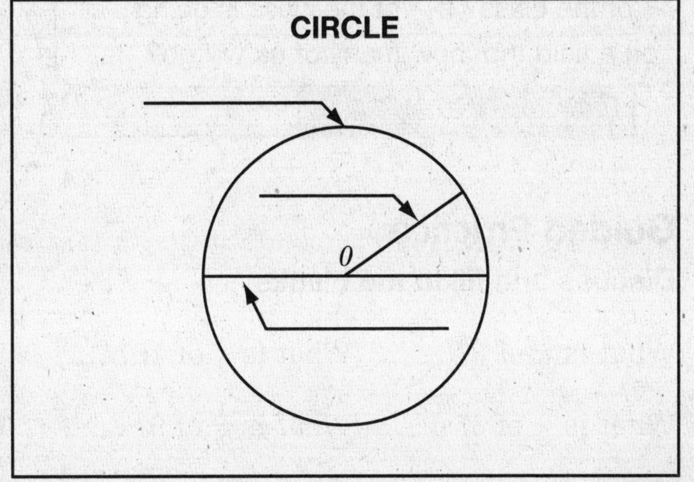
0

Warm-up Exercises

$8 \div 4 \times 3 =$ ____	$10 \div 5 \times 2 =$ ____	$8 \div 4 \times 2 =$ ____	$12 \div 4 \times 3 =$ ____
$9 \div 3 \times 2 =$ ____	$10 \div 2 \times 3 =$ ____	$12 \div 6 \times 3 =$ ____	$12 \div 4 \times 2 =$ ____

7-1 What is $\frac{1}{2}$ of 6?

Mathematical Conversation

In this unit we will learn about fractions. Do you know what "fraction" means? For example, what does $\frac{1}{5}$ mean?
We learned that in kindergarten! If you cut any shape into 5 equal pieces, each piece will be $\frac{1}{5}$. And 4 of those pieces will equal $\frac{4}{5}$, right?
Danny, you are still thinking like a kindergartener!

You mean that we should understand fractions differently?
For kindergarteners, a whole 1 is only a shape. For us, a whole 1 can also be a number! For example, there are 25 students in our class. How many students make up $\frac{1}{5}$ of the class? If $\frac{4}{5}$ of the class is going on a field trip, how many of us will go?

Here, the number 25 is the whole 1. Think about how to find $\frac{1}{5}$ and $\frac{4}{5}$ of that whole.

$\frac{1}{2}$ of 6 is 3.

Fractions of a shape

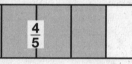

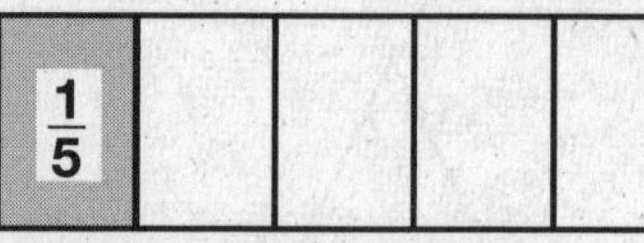

$\frac{1}{5}$
$\frac{4}{5}$

Fractions of a number

What is $\frac{1}{5}$ of 25?

What is $\frac{4}{5}$ of 25?

Guided Practice

Discuss and fill in the blanks.

What is $\frac{1}{2}$ of 8? ____	What is $\frac{1}{2}$ of 10? ____	What is $\frac{1}{2}$ of 12? ____	What is $\frac{1}{2}$ of 20? ____
What is $\frac{1}{3}$ of 3? ____	What is $\frac{1}{3}$ of 9? ____	What is $\frac{1}{3}$ of 12? ____	What is $\frac{1}{3}$ of 15? ____

Lesson 7–1 Exercises

Fill in the parentheses and the blanks. The first two problems are done for you.

1. One third ($\frac{1}{3}$) of 6 is 2.
2. Two thirds ($\frac{2}{3}$) of 6 is 4.
3. Half ( ) of 20 is ___.
4. One third ( ) of 15 is ___.
5. Two thirds ( ) of 15 is ___.
6. One fifth ( ) of 15 is ___.
7. Two fifths ( ) of 15 is ___.
8. Three fifths ( ) of 15 is ___.
9. Four fifths ( ) of 15 is ___.
10. Half ( ) of 12 is ___.
11. One third ( ) of 12 is ___.
12. One fourth ( ) of 12 is ___.
13. One sixth ( ) of 12 is ___.
14. Three fourths ( ) of 12 is ___.
15. One fourth ( ) of 20 is ___.
16. Three fourths ( ) of 20 is ___.
17. One fifth ( ) of 20 is ___.
18. Two fifths ( ) of 20 is ___.
19. Three fifths ( ) of 20 is ___.
20. Four fifths ( ) of 20 is ___.

Reflection and Discussion

5 is $\frac{1}{2}$ of what number? $\frac{1}{4}$ of what number? $\frac{1}{3}$ of what number?

Warm-up Exercises

$15 \div 5 =$ ____ $12 \div 6 =$ ____ $32 \div 4 =$ ____ $10 \div 5 =$ ____

$16 \div 4 =$ ____ $24 \div 8 =$ ____ $40 \div 5 =$ ____ $35 \div 7 =$ ____

7-2 How can 4 people share 3 tortillas?

Mathematical Conversation

I brought 3 big tortillas today. How can we share them equally among the 4 of you?
With division! Dividing 3 tortillas by 4 . . . Wait a minute; how can we do 3 ÷ 4? I know that 6 ÷ 2 = 3, 10 ÷ 5 = 2, but what is 3 ÷ 4 equal to?

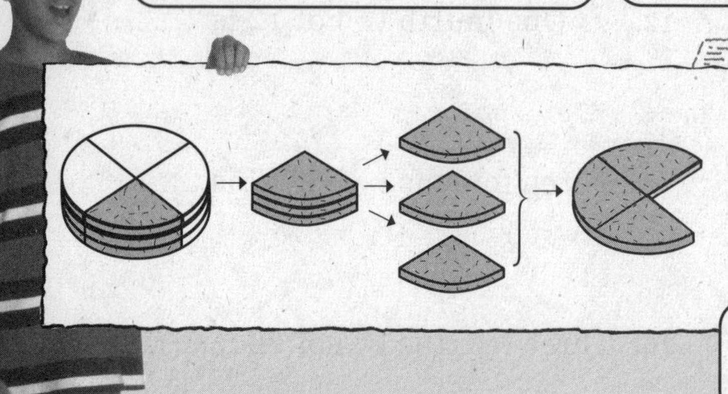

Let's just try it! . . . I can divide 3 tortillas into 4 equal shares. Here is the answer: 3 ÷ 4 = 3/4
That's cool! The next time I don't know how to do a division, I will just write it as a fraction. 2 ÷ 7 = 2/7; 3 ÷ 8 = 3/8
Yes, it's true that you can write a division as a fraction, and vice versa.

Check out my fraction poster!

dividend → 3, divisor → 4

$$3 \div 4 = \frac{3}{4}$$

numerator ← 3, denominator ← 4

Numerator corresponds to Dividend

Denominator corresponds to Divisor

Fraction Line corresponds to Division Sign

Lesson 7–2 Exercises

Write these fractions as divisions and write the divisions as fractions. The first one is done for you.

1. $\frac{1}{4}$ = 1 ÷ 4 2. $\frac{2}{5}$ = ______ 3. $\frac{3}{7}$ = ______ 4. $\frac{2}{3}$ = ______

5. $\frac{3}{4}$ = ______ 6. $\frac{3}{10}$ = ______ 7. $\frac{4}{9}$ = ______ 8. $\frac{5}{8}$ = ______

9. $\frac{5}{6}$ = ______ 10. $\frac{1}{7}$ = ______ 11. $\frac{2}{7}$ = ______ 12. $\frac{3}{7}$ = ______

13. $\frac{7}{8}$ = ______ 14. $\frac{8}{9}$ = ______ 15. $\frac{1}{10}$ = ______ 16. $\frac{9}{10}$ = ______

17. 1 ÷ 2 = ____ 18. 1 ÷ 3 = ____ 19. 1 ÷ 4 = ____ 20. 1 ÷ 5 = ____

21. 2 ÷ 3 = ____ 22. 3 ÷ 4 = ____ 23. 4 ÷ 5 = ____ 24. 5 ÷ 6 = ____

25. 3 ÷ 5 = ____ 26. 1 ÷ 6 = ____ 27. 2 ÷ 7 = ____ 28. 3 ÷ 7 = ____

29. 7 ÷ 10 = ____ 30. 5 ÷ 11 = ____ 31. 6 ÷ 11 = ____ 32. 3 ÷ 20 = ____

33. 5 ÷ 5 = ____ 34. 9 ÷ 9 = ____ 35. 10 ÷ 10 = ____ 36. 4 ÷ 4 = ____

37. $\frac{5}{5}$ = ____ 38. $\frac{9}{9}$ = ____ 39. $\frac{10}{10}$ = ____ 40. $\frac{4}{4}$ = ____

41. 7 ÷ 7 = ____ 42. 6 ÷ 6 = ____ 43. 11 ÷ 11 = ____ 44. 8 ÷ 8 = ____

45. $\frac{7}{7}$ = ____ 46. $\frac{6}{6}$ = ____ 47. $\frac{11}{11}$ = ____ 48. $\frac{8}{8}$ = ____

Word Problems

Draw a model and a mathematical expression to represent these problems. Then calculate and answer the questions.

49. Danny used 4 cups of flour to make 5 cakes of the same size. How many cups of flour did he use for each cake? ____________

Model:

Mathematical expression:

50. In Mary's class there are 25 students. $\frac{2}{5}$ of them are girls. How many girls are there in the class? ____________

Model:

Mathematical expression:

Reflection and Discussion

What is $\frac{1}{2}$ of 8? What is $\frac{2}{4}$ of 8? What is $\frac{4}{8}$ of 8?
What pattern do you notice? How can you explain it?

Warm-up Exercises

$3 \div 4 =$ ____ $4 \div 7 =$ ____ $5 \div 8 =$ ____ $7 \div 9 =$ ____

$9 \div 10 =$ ____ $8 \div 11 =$ ____ $5 \div 12 =$ ____ $7 \div 13 =$ ____

7-3 Are fractions connected to decimals and percents?

Mathematical Conversation

You know what, Ana? I found out something very interesting about fractions. Tell me, how do you say this: 0.1?

I say zero point one, or one tenth. Oh, I know what you are trying to tell me! One tenth is also $\frac{1}{10}$. So $\frac{1}{10} = 0.1$! The fraction can be changed into a decimal!

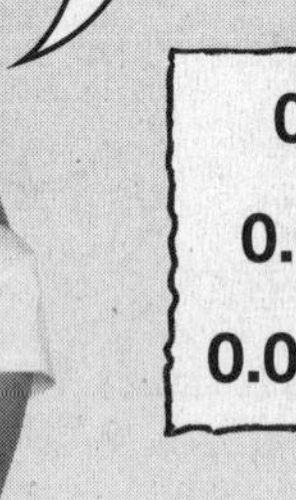

$0.1 = \frac{1}{10}$

$0.01 = \frac{1}{100}$

$0.001 = \frac{1}{1,000}$

Decimals are special kinds of fractions. They are fractions with denominators of 10 or powers of 10.

You reminded me of something, Ms. Park! Percents are also special kinds of fractions. Percents are fractions with denominators of 100!

Yes! 1% means $\frac{1}{100}$,
5% means $\frac{5}{100}$,
20% means $\frac{20}{100}$,
75% means $\frac{75}{100}$, and
99% means $\frac{99}{100}$.

I thought of something else!
$1 \div 4 = 0.25$
$1 \div 4 = \frac{1}{4}$
$\frac{1}{4} = 0.25$
What do you think of my poster?
Good job!
$1 \div 100 = \frac{1}{100}$
$0.01 = \frac{1}{100}$
$1\% = \frac{1}{100}$

Guided Practice

Complete the following table.

Fraction	Decimal	Percent	Fraction	Decimal	Percent
$\frac{1}{2}$				0.33	
$\frac{1}{5}$				0.51	

Lesson 7–3 Exercises

Write these fractions as decimals or whole numbers.

1. $\frac{3}{10}$ = ____ **2.** $\frac{3}{100}$ = ____ **3.** $\frac{3}{1,000}$ = ____ **4.** $\frac{1}{10}$ = ____

5. $\frac{7}{10}$ = ____ **6.** $\frac{17}{100}$ = ____ **7.** $\frac{9}{10}$ = ____ **8.** $\frac{99}{100}$ = ____

9. $\frac{1}{2}$ = ____ **10.** $\frac{1}{5}$ = ____ **11.** $\frac{2}{5}$ = ____ **12.** $\frac{3}{5}$ = ____

13. $\frac{4}{5}$ = ____ **14.** $\frac{8}{8}$ = ____ **15.** $\frac{6}{6}$ = ____ **16.** $\frac{10}{10}$ = ____

Write these decimals as fractions.

17. 0.1 = ____ **18.** 0.7 = ____ **19.** 0.9 = ____ **20.** 0.3 = ____

21. 0.11 = ____ **22.** 0.19 = ____ **23.** 0.13 = ____ **24.** 0.17 = ____

25. 0.121 = ____ **26.** 0.259 = ____ **27.** 0.666 = ____ **28.** 0.999 = ____

Write these numbers as percents.

29. 0.05 = ____ **30.** 0.08 = ____ **31.** 0.01 = ____ **32.** 0.02 = ____

33. 0.15 = ____ **34.** 0.75 = ____ **35.** 0.1 = ____ **36.** 0.7 = ____

37. $\frac{27}{100}$ = ____ **38.** $\frac{17}{100}$ = ____ **39.** $\frac{91}{100}$ = ____ **40.** $\frac{57}{100}$ = ____

41. $\frac{33}{100}$ = ____ **42.** $\frac{41}{100}$ = ____ **43.** $\frac{83}{100}$ = ____ **44.** $\frac{99}{100}$ = ____

Word Problems

Draw a model and write a mathematical expression to represent these problems. Then calculate and answer the questions.

45. 5 people are going to share 4 bottles of water evenly. How many bottles of water will each person get? ____________

Model:

Mathematical expression:

46. Carmen has 20 friends. $\frac{2}{5}$ of them are boys. How many boys are her friends?

____

Model:

Mathematical expression:

Reflection and Discussion

Write 25 cents as a fraction of a dollar. Write that fraction as a decimal.

Warm-up Exercises

$5 \div 4 =$ ____	$10 \div 3 =$ ____	$7 \div 2 =$ ____	$6 \div 4 =$ ____
$9 \div 2 =$ ____	$16 \div 3 =$ ____	$15 \div 2 =$ ____	$20 \div 6 =$ ____

7-4 Have you heard about "fake fractions"?

Mathematical Conversation

I have a question. We know that $8 \div 4 = 2$. However, since a division can be a fraction, it means that $8 \div 4 = \frac{8}{4}$. So, what is $8 \div 4$? Is it 2 or $\frac{8}{4}$?

$\frac{8}{4}$ looks weird to me. Shouldn't a fraction have a numerator that is less than its denominator?

You are right, Ana. For a fraction, the numerator should be less than the denominator. But Danny is right, too. $8 \div 4$ can be written as $\frac{8}{4}$. Look, $\frac{8}{4}$ is actually 2. And 2 is a whole number.

$\frac{1}{4}$	$\frac{1}{4}$
$\frac{1}{4}$	$\frac{1}{4}$

$\frac{1}{4}$	$\frac{1}{4}$
$\frac{1}{4}$	$\frac{1}{4}$

$$\frac{8}{4} = \frac{4}{4} + \frac{4}{4} = 1 + 1 = 2$$

We call fractions like $\frac{8}{4}$ that have greater numerators than denominators "improper fractions." Some people in other parts of the world call them "fake fractions."

"Fake fractions"! That's a funny name but it makes sense! They are not really fractions, but whole numbers!

But what about $\frac{5}{4}$? I don't think it can be a whole number. It has a 1 and a $\frac{1}{4}$.

1 plus $\frac{1}{4}$ is $1\frac{1}{4}$; it consists of a whole number and a proper fraction. We call a number like $1\frac{1}{4}$ a mixed number.

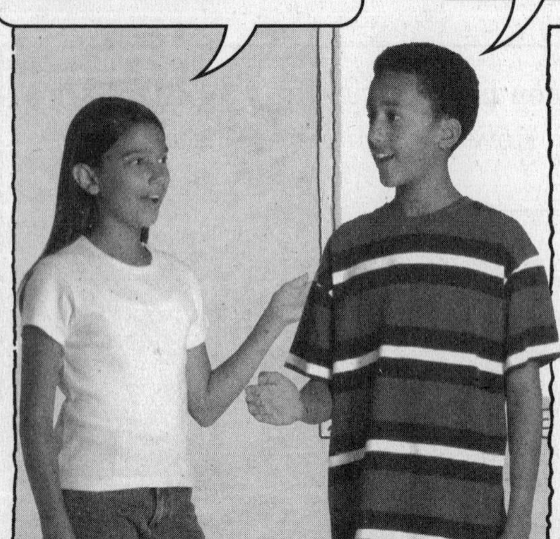

Converting improper fractions

$$\frac{a}{b} = a \div b$$

When you convert an improper fraction, if there is a remainder, the result will be a mixed number. The remainder is the numerator of the fraction in the mixed number.

$$\frac{9}{4} = 9 \div 4 = 2R1 = 2\frac{1}{4}$$

Lesson 7–4 Exercises

Investigate the following fractions. Write a "P" after a proper fraction, an "I" after an improper fraction, and a "W" after a whole number.

1. $\frac{3}{10}$ ____ **2.** $\frac{10}{3}$ ____ **3.** $\frac{7}{6}$ ____ **4.** $\frac{6}{7}$ ____

5. $\frac{10}{10}$ ____ **6.** $\frac{12}{11}$ ____ **7.** $\frac{9}{10}$ ____ **8.** $\frac{25}{21}$ ____

9. $\frac{3}{2}$ ____ **10.** $\frac{5}{5}$ ____ **11.** $\frac{2}{5}$ ____ **12.** $\frac{3}{5}$ ____

Convert these improper fractions into mixed numbers or whole numbers.

13. $\frac{3}{2} =$ ____ **14.** $\frac{4}{3} =$ ____ **15.** $\frac{7}{5} =$ ____ **16.** $\frac{8}{3} =$ ____

17. $\frac{10}{10} =$ ____ **18.** $\frac{22}{11} =$ ____ **19.** $\frac{10}{9} =$ ____ **20.** $\frac{21}{7} =$ ____

21. $\frac{16}{5} =$ ____ **22.** $\frac{44}{7} =$ ____ **23.** $\frac{81}{9} =$ ____ **24.** $\frac{50}{9} =$ ____

Write these divisions as fractions. If the fraction is improper, convert it into a mixed number or a whole number.

25. $3 \div 5 =$ ____ **26.** $11 \div 12 =$ ____ **27.** $5 \div 3 =$ ____ **28.** $25 \div 24 =$ ____

29. $20 \div 4 =$ ____ **30.** $30 \div 5 =$ ____ **31.** $20 \div 21 =$ ____ **32.** $21 \div 20 =$ ____

33. $9 \div 4 =$ ____ **34.** $5 \div 4 =$ ____ **35.** $4 \div 5 =$ ____ **36.** $24 \div 8 =$ ____

37. $36 \div 6 =$ ____ **38.** $37 \div 6 =$ ____ **39.** $32 \div 8 =$ ____ **40.** $15 \div 4 =$ ____

Word Problems

Draw models and write out a mathematical expressions to represent these problems. Then calculate and answer the questions.

41. If 10 people share 3 pizzas equally, how much will each person get?

____

Model:

Expression:

42. Derek poured 4 quarts of oil into 5 bottles equally. How many quarts of oil are in each bottle?

____

Model:

Expression:

Reflection and Discussion

C.J. has 100 books. His older brother has $1\frac{1}{2}$ times as many books as C.J. How many books does his older brother have?

Warm-up Exercises

$5 \div 4 =$ ______ $10 \div 3 =$ ______ $7 \div 2 =$ ______ $7 \div 6 =$ ______

$9 \div 2 =$ ______ $16 \div 3 =$ ______ $15 \div 2 =$ ______ $19 \div 6 =$ ______

7-5 Review, Reflection, and Quiz 7

Mathematical Conversation

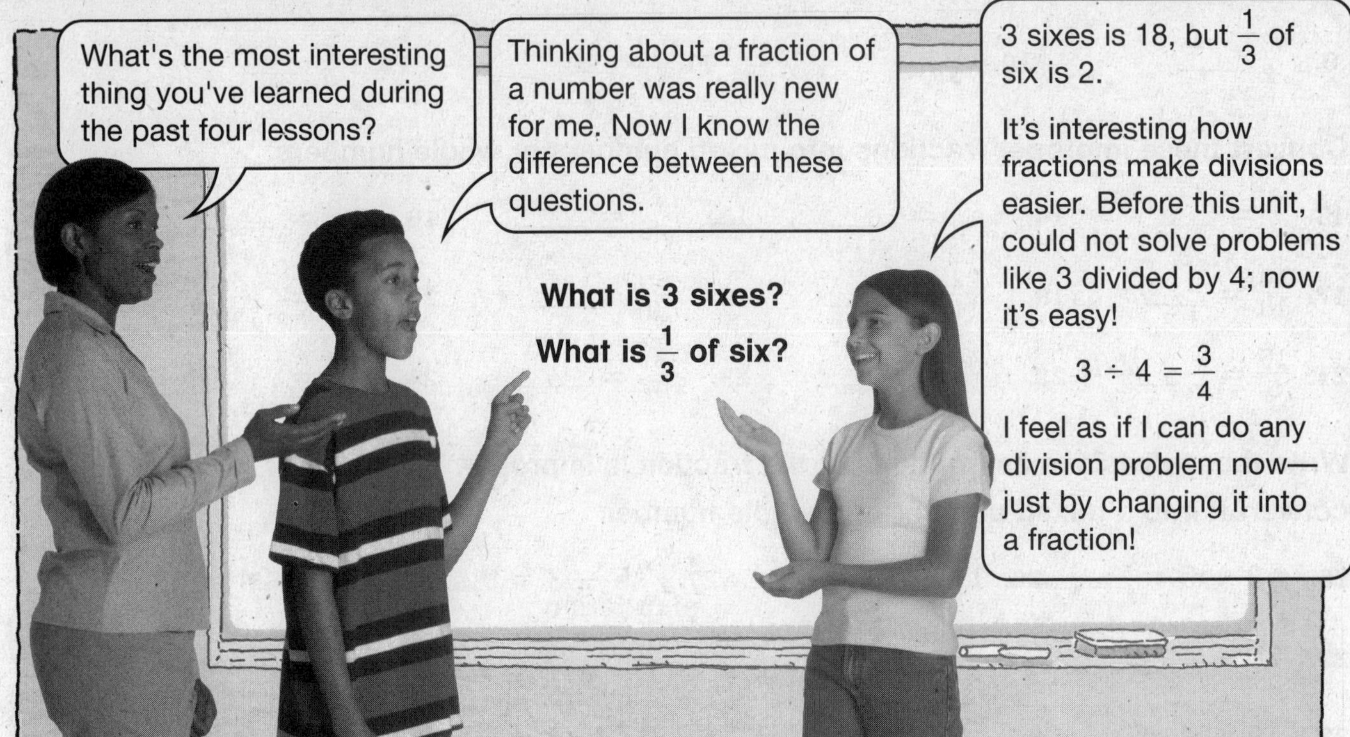
What's the most interesting thing you've learned during the past four lessons?
Thinking about a fraction of a number was really new for me. Now I know the difference between these questions.
What is 3 sixes?
What is $\frac{1}{3}$ of six?
3 sixes is 18, but $\frac{1}{3}$ of six is 2.
It's interesting how fractions make divisions easier. Before this unit, I could not solve problems like 3 divided by 4; now it's easy!
$3 \div 4 = \frac{3}{4}$
I feel as if I can do any division problem now—just by changing it into a fraction!

I also like to convert improper fractions into whole numbers or mixed numbers.

$\frac{4}{4} = 1$

$\frac{5}{4} = 1\frac{1}{4}$

Great! So fractions are fun, hmm?

Of course!

Quiz 7

Score

Fill in the answers.

1. One third ($\frac{1}{3}$) of 12 is ____ 2. Two thirds ($\frac{2}{3}$) of 12 is ____ 3. Half ($\frac{1}{2}$) of 12 is ____

4. One third ($\frac{1}{3}$) of 24 is ____ 5. Two thirds ($\frac{2}{3}$) of 24 is ____ 6. Half ($\frac{1}{2}$) of 15 is ____

Write the fractions as divisions and write the divisions as fractions.

7. $\frac{1}{6}$ = ____ 8. $\frac{4}{11}$ = ____ 9. $\frac{7}{10}$ = ____ 10. $\frac{9}{13}$ = ____

11. 1 ÷ 4 = ____ 12. 1 ÷ 6 = ____ 13. 5 ÷ 9 = ____ 14. 7 ÷ 22 = ____

Investigate these fractions. Write "P" after a proper fraction, "I" after an improper fraction, and "W" after a whole number.

15. $\frac{3}{8}$ ______ 16. $\frac{8}{3}$ ______ 17. $\frac{30}{30}$ ______ 18. $\frac{20}{21}$ ______

Convert the improper fractions into mixed numbers or whole numbers.

19. $\frac{7}{3}$ = ____ 20. $\frac{8}{5}$ = ____ 21. $\frac{9}{9}$ = ____ 22. $\frac{20}{10}$ = ____

Write these divisions as fractions. Convert improper fractions into mixed numbers or whole numbers.

23. 10 ÷ 3 = ____ 24. 5 ÷ 3 = ____ 25. 12 ÷ 5 = ____ 26. 20 ÷ 7 = ____

Word Problem

Draw a model and write a mathematical expression to represent this problem. Then calculate and answer the question.

27. Ten people want to share 1 bottle of cider equally. What fractional part of the bottle will each person get?

____

Model:

Mathematical Expression:

Warm-up Exercises

$15 + 6 =$ ____	$24 + 6 =$ ____	$38 + 8 =$ ____	$69 + 2 =$ ____
$26 - 2 =$ ____	$45 - 6 =$ ____	$14 - 6 =$ ____	$11 - 8 =$ ____

7-6 What is $\frac{1}{3} + \frac{1}{3}$?

Mathematical Conversation

Danny, if you had $\frac{1}{3}$ of a pizza and I had $\frac{1}{3}$ of a pizza, how much pizza would we have in all?

$\frac{2}{3}$ of a pizza! Look.

1 + 1 = 2

$\frac{1}{3} + \frac{1}{3} = \frac{2}{3}$

$\frac{1}{3}$ (Ana) $\frac{1}{3}$ (Danny) = $\frac{2}{3}$

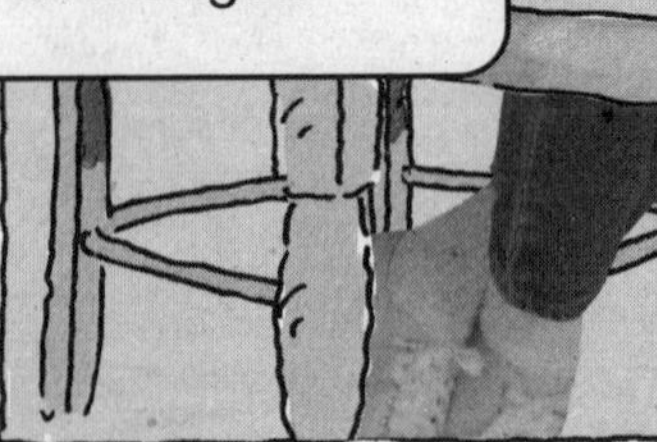

So, we add the numerators and leave the denominator unchanged.

Yes, that's what we do for fractions with like denominators. Also, when we subtract fractions with like denominators, we subtract the numerators. We leave the denominator unchanged, just as we did for addition.

Do $\frac{2}{3}$ and $\frac{2}{5}$ have like denominators?

Guided Practice

Calculate and fill in the answers.

A. $\frac{7}{15} + \frac{7}{15} =$ ____ B. $\frac{3}{7} + \frac{2}{7} =$ ____ C. $\frac{7}{9} - \frac{2}{9} =$ ____ D. $\frac{9}{11} - \frac{7}{11} =$ ____

Lesson 7–6 Exercises

Calculate and fill in the answers.

1. $\frac{2}{5} + \frac{2}{5} =$ ____ **2.** $\frac{1}{4} + \frac{3}{4} =$ ____ **3.** $\frac{3}{7} + \frac{3}{7} =$ ____ **4.** $\frac{2}{9} + \frac{5}{9} =$ ____

5. $\frac{3}{8} + \frac{5}{8} =$ ____ **6.** $\frac{3}{11} + \frac{7}{11} =$ ____ **7.** $\frac{9}{21} + \frac{4}{21} =$ ____ **8.** $\frac{5}{17} + \frac{7}{17} =$ ____

9. $\frac{4}{11} + \frac{4}{11} =$ ____ **10.** $\frac{18}{25} + \frac{3}{25} =$ ____ **11.** $\frac{6}{19} + \frac{7}{19} =$ ____ **12.** $\frac{7}{23} + \frac{8}{23} =$ ____

13. $\frac{4}{5} - \frac{2}{5} =$ ____ **14.** $\frac{13}{14} - \frac{13}{14} =$ ____ **15.** $\frac{4}{7} - \frac{3}{7} =$ ____ **16.** $\frac{8}{9} - \frac{7}{9} =$ ____

17. $\frac{14}{15} - \frac{13}{15} =$ ____ **18.** $\frac{7}{11} - \frac{4}{11} =$ ____ **19.** $\frac{9}{21} - \frac{4}{21} =$ ____ **20.** $\frac{7}{17} - \frac{5}{17} =$ ____

21. $\frac{9}{11} - \frac{4}{11} =$ ____ **22.** $\frac{18}{25} - \frac{4}{25} =$ ____ **23.** $\frac{18}{19} - \frac{9}{19} =$ ____ **24.** $\frac{21}{23} - \frac{3}{23} =$ ____

25. 60 + 12 = ____ **26.** 40 + 24 = ____ **27.** 30 + 37 = ____ **28.** 80 + 16 = ____

29. 100 − 15 = ____ **30.** 150 − 30 = ____ **31.** 120 − 20 = ____ **32.** 80 − 20 = ____

33. 50 × 2 = ____ **34.** 40 × 3 = ____ **35.** 30 × 5 = ____ **36.** 60 × 8 = ____

37. 25 ÷ 5 = ____ **38.** 27 ÷ 3 = ____ **39.** 49 ÷ 7 = ____ **40.** 72 ÷ 9 = ____

41. 2 × 2 × 2 = ____ **42.** 3 × 3 × 3 = ____ **43.** 2 × 4 × 4 = ____ **44.** 3 × 2 × 8 = ____

45. 5 × 2 × 8 = ____ **46.** 4 × 2 × 7 = ____ **47.** 2 × 3 × 7 = ____ **48.** 3 × 3 × 5 = ____

Word Problems

Draw a model and write a mathematical expression to represent these word problems. Then calculate and answer the questions.

49. Ana finished $\frac{2}{5}$ of her homework in school. She did another $\frac{2}{5}$ before dinner. How much of her homework has she completed so far?

____

Model:

Expression:

50. In the summer camp that Derek attended last year, $\frac{2}{5}$ of the campers were boys and $\frac{3}{5}$ were girls. How many more of the campers were girls? ____________________

Model:

Expression:

Reflection and Discussion

Ana ate $\frac{1}{3}$ of the cake that her mother gave to her. How much cake is left?

Warm-up Exercises

$37 \div 6 =$ ____	$50 \div 7 =$ ____	$65 \div 8 =$ ____	$92 \div 9 =$ ____
$41 \div 6 =$ ____	$40 \div 7 =$ ____	$33 \div 8 =$ ____	$20 \div 9 =$ ____

7-7 Then, what is $\frac{2}{3} + \frac{2}{3}$?

Mathematical Conversation

If you had $\frac{2}{3}$ of a pizza, and I also had $\frac{2}{3}$ of a pizza, how much pizza would we have?
$\frac{2}{3} + \frac{2}{3} = \frac{4}{3} \ldots \frac{4}{3}$ of a pizza. Wait a minute; that sounds strange!
$1\frac{1}{3}$ pizza sounds better than $\frac{4}{3}$ pizza. Don't you think so?

In everyday life we usually use mixed numbers rather than improper fractions. If your answer is an improper fraction, convert it to a whole number or a mixed number.

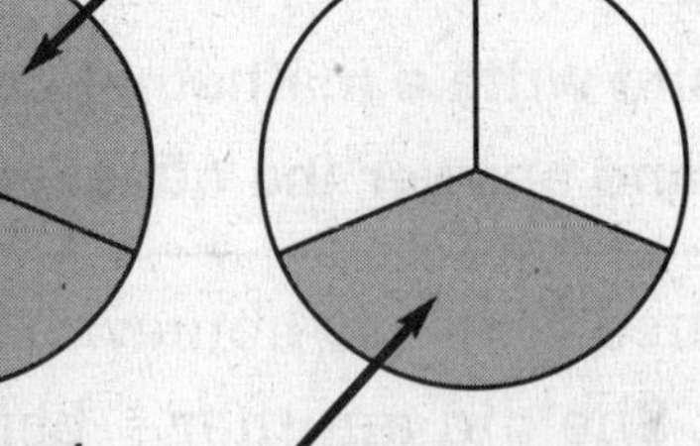

Ana's first $\frac{1}{3}$
Danny's first $\frac{1}{3}$
Ana's second $\frac{1}{3}$
Danny's second $\frac{1}{3}$

$$\frac{2}{3} + \frac{2}{3} = \frac{4}{3} = 1\frac{1}{3}$$

Remember, if your answer is an improper fraction, convert it to a whole number or a mixed number.

OK!

Lesson 7–7 Exercises

Calculate and fill in the answers. If the sum is an improper fraction, convert it to a mixed number or a whole number.

1. $\frac{3}{5}+\frac{1}{5}=$ ____ 2. $\frac{3}{5}+\frac{3}{5}=$ ____ 3. $\frac{5}{7}+\frac{5}{7}=$ ____ 4. $\frac{2}{9}+\frac{5}{9}=$ ____

5. $\frac{7}{9}+\frac{4}{9}=$ ____ 6. $\frac{7}{11}+\frac{9}{11}=$ ____ 7. $\frac{4}{9}+\frac{1}{9}=$ ____ 8. $\frac{5}{7}+\frac{5}{7}=$ ____

9. $\frac{5}{6}+\frac{1}{6}=$ ____ 10. $\frac{11}{18}+\frac{17}{18}=$ ____ 11. $\frac{2}{7}+\frac{3}{7}=$ ____ 12. $\frac{4}{5}+\frac{4}{5}=$ ____

13. $\frac{2}{3}+\frac{2}{3}=$ ____ 14. $\frac{1}{9}+\frac{7}{9}=$ ____ 15. $\frac{7}{12}+\frac{5}{12}=$ ____ 16. $\frac{9}{13}+\frac{7}{13}=$ ____

17. $1+\frac{1}{5}=$ ____ 18. $2+\frac{3}{5}=$ ____ 19. $3+\frac{5}{7}=$ ____ 20. $1+\frac{5}{9}=$ ____

21. $\frac{7}{9}+1=$ ____ 22. $\frac{7}{11}+2=$ ____ 23. $\frac{4}{9}+3=$ ____ 24. $\frac{5}{7}+2=$ ____

25. $\frac{3}{5}-\frac{1}{5}=$ ____ 26. $\frac{3}{5}-\frac{3}{5}=$ ____ 27. $\frac{6}{7}-\frac{5}{7}=$ ____ 28. $\frac{8}{9}-\frac{7}{9}=$ ____

29. $\frac{7}{9}-\frac{2}{9}=$ ____ 30. $\frac{9}{11}-\frac{7}{11}=$ ____ 31. $\frac{5}{9}-\frac{1}{9}=$ ____ 32. $\frac{5}{7}-\frac{5}{7}=$ ____

33. $5\times6=$ ____ 34. $5\times7=$ ____ 35. $5\times8=$ ____ 36. $5\times9=$ ____

37. $7\times6=$ ____ 38. $7\times8=$ ____ 39. $7\times9=$ ____ 40. $8\times8=$ ____

41. $2\times4+2=$ ____ 42. $3\times3+3=$ ____ 43. $2\times4+7=$ ____ 44. $5\times3+5=$ ____

45. $1+2\times7=$ ____ 46. $4+2\times2=$ ____ 47. $2+3\times7=$ ____ 48. $3+3\times5=$ ____

Word Problems

Draw a model and write a mathematical expression to represent these word problems. Then calculate and answer the questions.

49. To make muffins, Ana put $\frac{4}{5}$ of a cup of sugar into the mixing bowl and her sister did the same. How many cups of sugar did they put in the bowl? ________

Model:

Expression:

50. C.J. had $1\frac{3}{5}$ pounds of flour. He used $1\frac{2}{5}$ pounds to make bread. How many pounds of flour are left? ________

Model:

Expression:

Reflection and Discussion

What mixed number is equal to the improper fraction $\frac{28}{9}$?

Warm-up Exercises

$4 + 7 =$ ____ $5 + 9 =$ ____ $7 + 8 =$ ____ $6 + 6 =$ ____

$16 - 7 =$ ____ $15 - 9 =$ ____ $13 - 6 =$ ____ $18 - 8 =$ ____

7-8 What is $1 - \frac{1}{3}$?

Mathematical Conversation

I've got a question. What if Ms. Park brought in 1 whole pizza and Ana ate $\frac{1}{3}$ of it. How much would be left for me?
We would write it $1 - \frac{1}{3}$. But how do we subtract a fraction from 1?
To subtract a fraction from 1, we first convert 1 into an improper fraction with the same denominator as the fraction we are subtracting, so they have the same fractional unit. Then we can do the subtraction. Sometimes we need to convert a mixed number before we can do the subtraction.
Improper fractions helped us this time!
$1 - \frac{1}{3} = \frac{3}{3} - \frac{1}{3} = \frac{2}{3}$
Every one is special and can be helpful!
Yes!

Guided Practice

Calculate and fill in the answers. Show your work.

A. $1 - \frac{2}{9} =$ ____ **B.** $2 - \frac{4}{9} =$ ____ **C.** $1\frac{2}{9} - \frac{7}{9} =$ ____

Lesson 7–8 Exercises

Calculate and fill in the answers.

1. $1 - \frac{3}{5} =$ ____ **2.** $1 - \frac{1}{8} =$ ____ **3.** $1 - \frac{5}{7} =$ ____ **4.** $1 - \frac{5}{9} =$ ____

5. $1 - \frac{5}{6} =$ ____ **6.** $1 - \frac{9}{11} =$ ____ **7.** $1 - \frac{11}{14} =$ ____ **8.** $1 - \frac{5}{7} =$ ____

9. $2 - \frac{1}{6} =$ ____ **10.** $2 - \frac{17}{18} =$ ____ **11.** $2 - \frac{3}{7} =$ ____ **12.** $2 - 1\frac{4}{5} =$ ____

13. $1\frac{1}{5} - \frac{3}{5} =$ ____ **14.** $1\frac{3}{7} - \frac{5}{7} =$ ____ **15.** $1\frac{4}{9} - \frac{5}{9} =$ ____

16. $1\frac{7}{11} - \frac{9}{11} =$ ____ **17.** $1\frac{1}{9} - \frac{8}{9} =$ ____ **18.** $1\frac{7}{13} - \frac{9}{13} =$ ____

19. $1\frac{3}{5} + \frac{1}{5} =$ ____ **20.** $\frac{3}{5} + \frac{3}{5} =$ ____ **21.** $\frac{6}{7} + \frac{5}{7} =$ ____ **22.** $\frac{8}{9} + \frac{8}{9} =$ ____

23. $\frac{7}{9} + \frac{2}{9} =$ ____ **24.** $\frac{9}{11} + \frac{7}{11} =$ ____ **25.** $1\frac{1}{9} + \frac{1}{9} =$ ____ **26.** $\frac{5}{7} + \frac{5}{7} =$ ____

27. $8 \times 7 =$ ____ **28.** $8 \times 6 =$ ____ **29.** $8 \times 9 =$ ____ **30.** $8 \times 4 =$ ____

31. $4 \times 9 =$ ____ **32.** $4 \times 7 =$ ____ **33.** $4 \times 5 =$ ____ **34.** $3 \times 9 =$ ____

35. $3 \times 4 + 2 =$ ____ **36.** $3 \times 3 + 5 =$ ____ **37.** $4 \times 4 + 1 =$ ____ **38.** $3 \times 5 + 2 =$ ____

39. $0 + 3 \times 7 =$ ____ **40.** $4 + 2 \times 3 =$ ____ **41.** $2 + 4 \times 7 =$ ____ **42.** $1 + 3 \times 5 =$ ____

Word Problems

Draw a model and write a mathematical expression to represent these word problems. Then calculate and answer the questions.

43. Ana and her sister are still making muffins. Ana put a whole cup of flour in a bowl, but she only needs $\frac{3}{5}$ cup. How much flour should she take out of the bowl? ____

Model:

Expression:

44. Ana's sister put $1\frac{2}{3}$ cups of oatmeal in the muffin batter. Ana added $\frac{2}{3}$ of a cup more. How much oatmeal in all is in the batter? ____

Model:

Expression:

Reflection and Discussion

What are the fractional units of these fractions?

$\frac{1}{5}$ $\frac{2}{3}$ $\frac{3}{4}$ $\frac{7}{5}$

Warm-up Exercises				
	26 ÷ 5 = ____	15 ÷ 7 = ____	26 ÷ 8 = ____	30 ÷ 9 = ____
	20 ÷ 6 = ____	10 ÷ 3 = ____	13 ÷ 4 = ____	32 ÷ 5 = ____

7-9 Unit 7 Review

Mathematical Conversation

In the last few days we learned how to do addition and subtraction with fractions. But something bothers me: all the fractions had the same denominators . . .

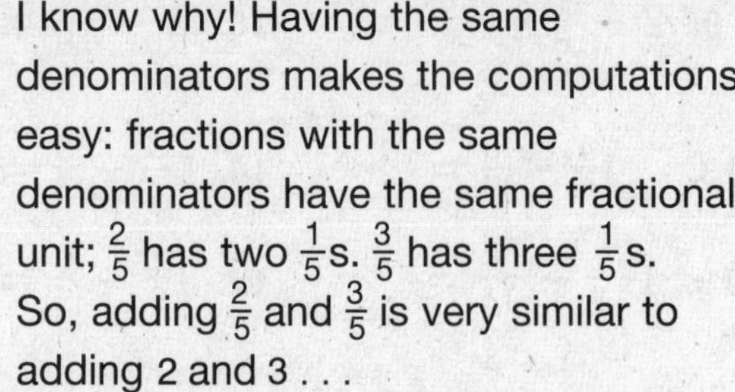
I know why! Having the same denominators makes the computations easy: fractions with the same denominators have the same fractional unit; $\frac{2}{5}$ has two $\frac{1}{5}$s. $\frac{3}{5}$ has three $\frac{1}{5}$s. So, adding $\frac{2}{5}$ and $\frac{3}{5}$ is very similar to adding 2 and 3 . . .

But what do we do when the denominators are not the same? How can we add and subtract fractions that have different denominators?

Good, you two! Having the same denominator, or formally, "common denominator," is the key to addition and subtraction with fractions. Eventually you will learn how to convert fractions with unlike denominators to fractions with like denominators.

$\frac{2}{3} + \frac{3}{4} = ?$
+
= ?
Are you looking forward to learning about common denominators of fractions?
Of course I am!

Lesson 7–9 Exercises

Calculate and fill in the answers

1. $\frac{2}{5} + \frac{2}{5} =$ ____
2. $\frac{1}{4} + \frac{3}{4} =$ ____
3. $\frac{3}{7} + \frac{3}{7} =$ ____
4. $\frac{2}{9} + \frac{5}{9} =$ ____
5. $\frac{3}{5} + \frac{1}{5} =$ ____
6. $\frac{1}{11} + \frac{7}{11} =$ ____
7. $\frac{2}{9} + \frac{2}{9} =$ ____
8. $\frac{1}{7} + \frac{1}{7} =$ ____
9. $\frac{3}{4} + \frac{1}{4} =$ ____
10. $\frac{1}{18} + \frac{17}{18} =$ ____
11. $\frac{6}{7} + \frac{6}{7} =$ ____
12. $\frac{3}{5} + \frac{4}{5} =$ ____
13. $\frac{1}{3} + \frac{2}{3} =$ ____
14. $\frac{7}{9} + \frac{7}{9} =$ ____
15. $\frac{1}{12} + 1 =$ ____
16. $2 + \frac{5}{13} =$ ____
17. $\frac{3}{4} - \frac{3}{4} =$ ____
18. $\frac{4}{5} - \frac{3}{5} =$ ____
19. $\frac{6}{7} - \frac{2}{7} =$ ____
20. $\frac{3}{5} - \frac{1}{5} =$ ____
21. $\frac{7}{9} - \frac{2}{9} =$ ____
22. $\frac{10}{11} - \frac{3}{11} =$ ____
23. $\frac{8}{9} - \frac{1}{9} =$ ____
24. $\frac{15}{17} - \frac{6}{17} =$ ____
25. $1 - \frac{1}{5} =$ ____
26. $1 - \frac{2}{9} =$ ____
27. $1 - \frac{1}{10} =$ ____
28. $1 - \frac{3}{7} =$ ____
29. $1\frac{1}{9} - \frac{2}{9} =$ ____
30. $1\frac{1}{3} - \frac{2}{3} =$ ____
31. $1\frac{2}{5} - \frac{3}{5} =$ ____
32. $1\frac{3}{7} - \frac{4}{7} =$ ____

Word Problems

Draw a model and write a mathematical expression to represent these word problems. Then calculate and answer the questions.

33. Julia took 3 hours to read 1 book. What portion of the book did she read each hour? ____________

Model:

Mathematical expression:

34. Julia took 3 hours to read 2 books. What portion of a book did she read each hour? ____________

Model:

Mathematical expression:

Reflection and Discussion

Is $\frac{1}{3} + \frac{1}{2}$ greater than 1? Explain.

Warm-up Exercises

$9 \times 4 =$ ____ $9 \times 5 =$ ____ $9 \times 6 =$ ____ $9 \times 7 =$ ____

$18 \div 9 =$ ____ $27 \div 9 =$ ____ $72 \div 9 =$ ____ $81 \div 9 =$ ____

8-1 Why is there only half of a car?

Mathematical Conversation

This pictograph shows the kinds and the number of vehicles that belong to the families of students in our class. Each drawing stands for 4 vehicles. Can you tell how many vehicles of each kind there are?

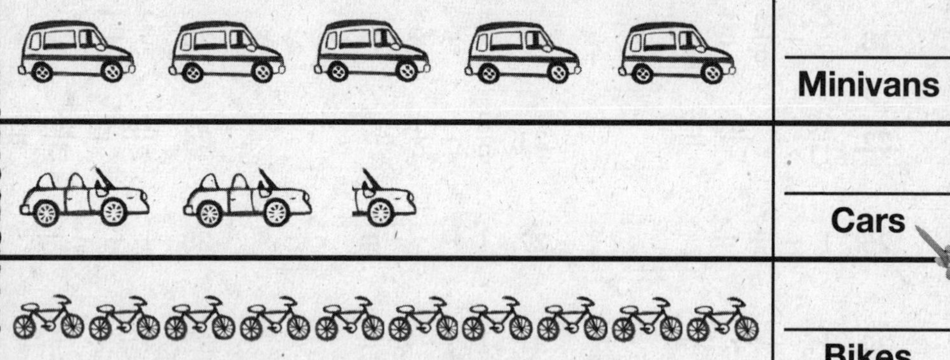

Minivans
Cars
Bikes

Hey, Ana, you forgot to complete the last car! It only has a front half.

Ana told me that she did that on purpose. Do you know why?

I bet the number of cars is not a multiple of 4. Maybe half a car stands for 2—half of 4.

Oh! I bet it does!

Guided Practice

Calculate and fill in the answer.

If each drawing stands for 10 bicycles, how many bicycles does this pictograph stand for? ____________

Lesson 8–1 Exercises

1. Choose three kinds of writing tools such as ballpoint pens, markers, and pencils. Make a pictograph showing how many of each kind you have. Each drawing in your pictograph should stand for at least two writing tools.

- Collect the data.
- Draw the graph.
- Plan the graph.
- Label the graph (title, writing tool type, key).

2. As a group, count the different kinds of writing tools that you and your classmates own. Then make a pictograph of the information on the blank graph below for three of them. Each drawing in your pictograph should stand for at least four writing tools.

- Collect the data.
- Draw the graph.
- Plan the graph.
- Label the graph (title, writing tool type, key).

Reflection and Discussion

What ways besides pictographs could we use to show the numbers and kinds of things?

Warm-up Exercises

$8 \times 6 =$ ____	$8 \times 7 =$ ____	$8 \times 8 =$ ____	$8 \times 9 =$ ____
$48 \div 8 =$ ____	$56 \div 8 =$ ____	$64 \div 8 =$ ____	$72 \div 8 =$ ____

8-2 Do you agree with C.J.?

Mathematical Conversation

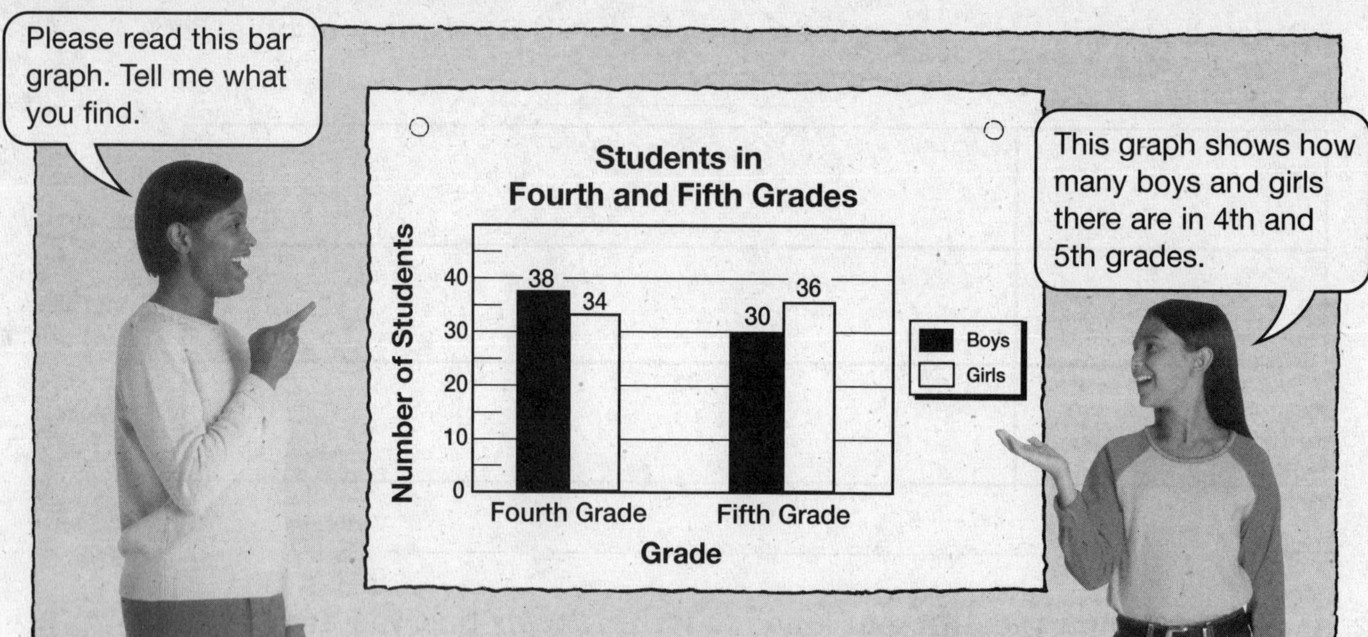
Please read this bar graph. Tell me what you find.
Students in Fourth and Fifth Grades
Number of Students
0
10
20
30
40
38
34
30
36
Fourth Grade
Fifth Grade
Grade
Boys
Girls
This graph shows how many boys and girls there are in 4th and 5th grades.

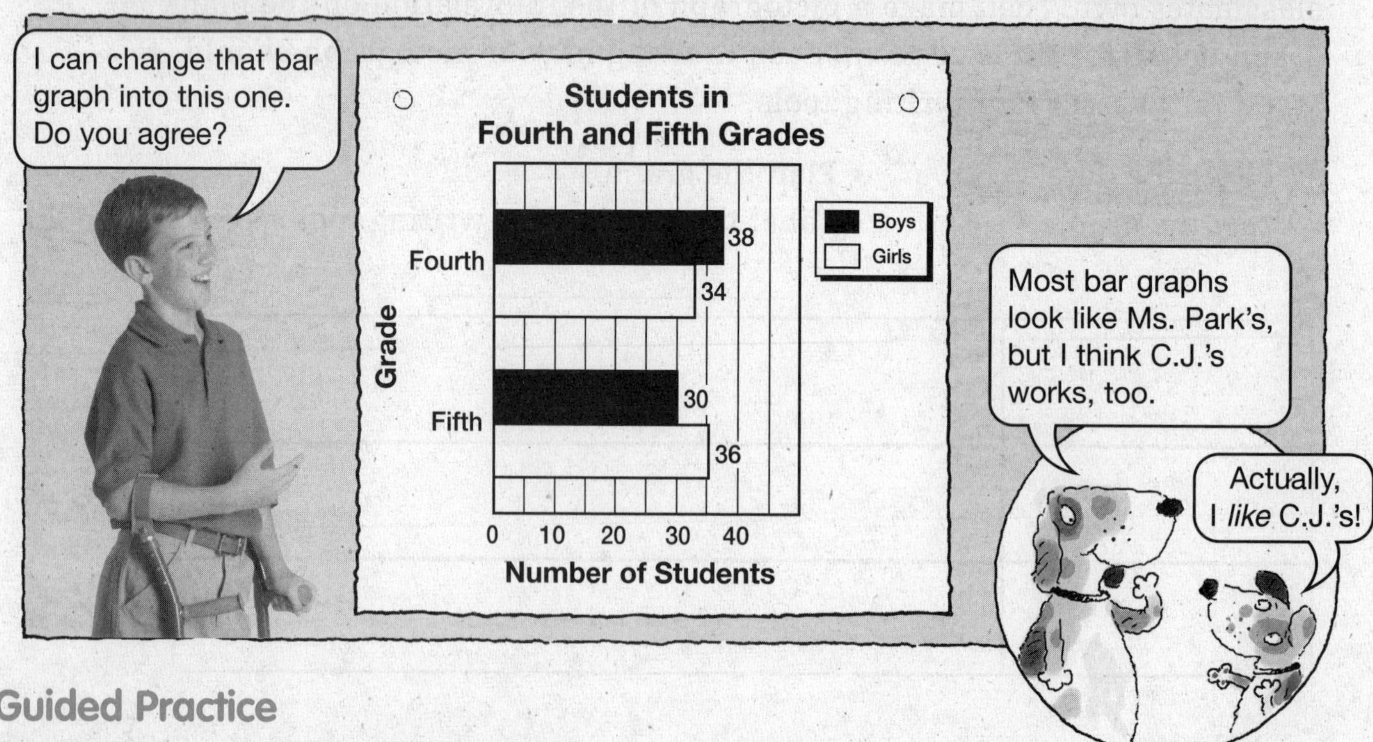
I can change that bar graph into this one. Do you agree?
Students in Fourth and Fifth Grades
Grade
Fourth
Fifth
38
34
30
36
0
10
20
30
40
Number of Students
Boys
Girls
Most bar graphs look like Ms. Park's, but I think C.J.'s works, too.
Actually, I *like* C.J.'s!

Guided Practice

Read the graphs and fill in the answers.

According to these graphs, the total number of girls in fourth and fifth grades is ____ and the total number of boys in fourth and fifth grades is ____.

Lesson 8–2 Exercises

For each problem: collect the data, plan the graph, draw the graph, and label the graph.

1. When he was younger, C.J. went to a very small preschool. There were 12 girls and 15 boys altogether.

A. Make a bar graph to show the number of boys and girls in C.J.'s preschool.

B. Make a pictograph to show the number of boys and girls in C.J.'s preschool.

2. Find out how many girls and boys there are in the third and fourth grades of your school. Then make a bar graph to show your findings.

Reflection and Discussion

There were more boys than girls in C.J.'s preschool. Can you tell how many more from the bar graph? From the pictograph?

Warm-up Exercises

$7 \times 5 =$ ____ $7 \times 6 =$ ____ $7 \times 7 =$ ____ $7 \times 8 =$ ____

$14 \div 7 =$ ____ $21 \div 7 =$ ____ $28 \div 7 =$ ____ $63 \div 7 =$ ____

8-3 What do "up" and "down" mean?

Mathematical Conversation

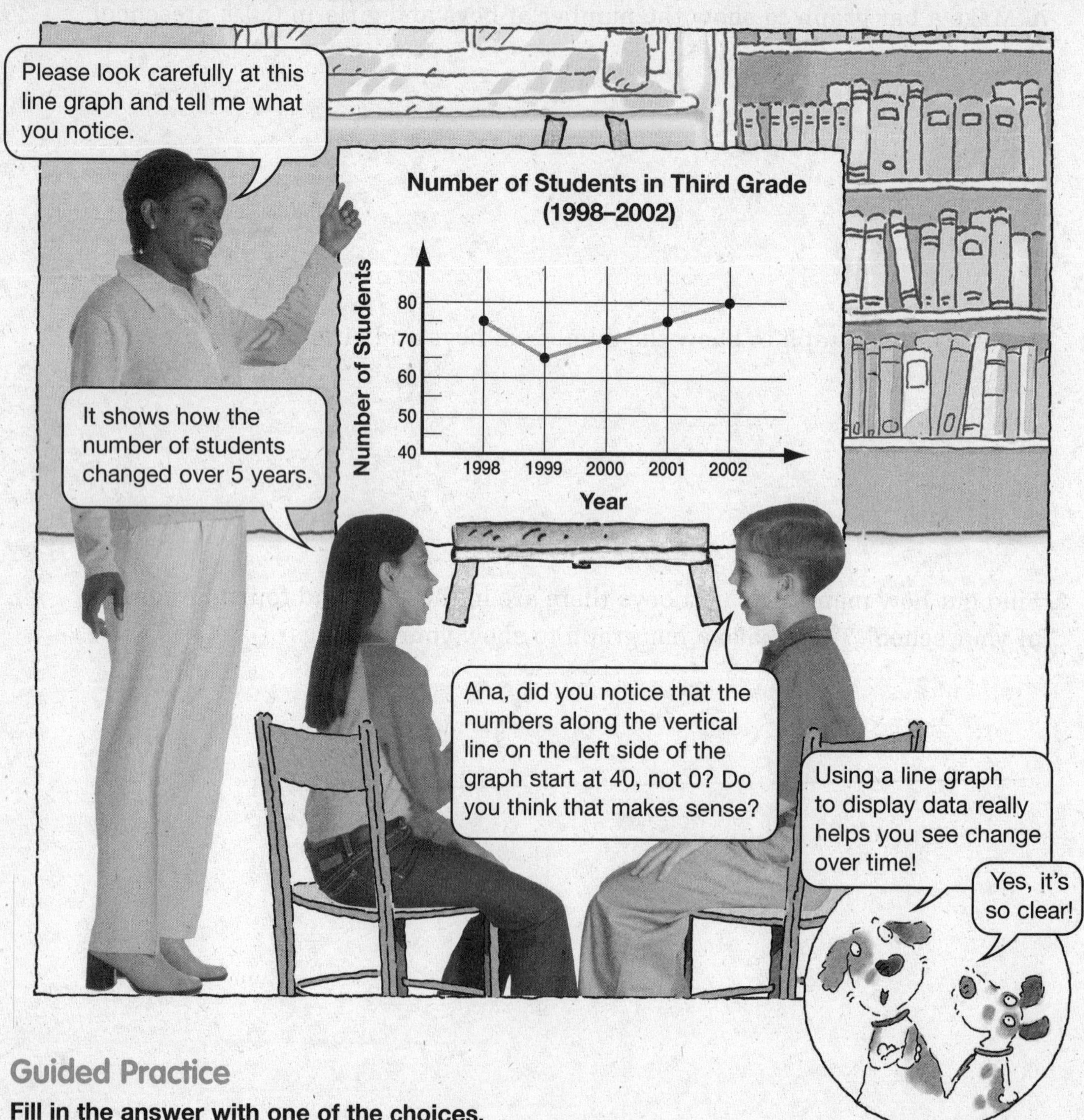
Please look carefully at this line graph and tell me what you notice.
Number of Students in Third Grade (1998–2002)
Number of Students
80
70
60
50
40
1998
1999
2000
2001
2002
Year
It shows how the number of students changed over 5 years.
Ana, did you notice that the numbers along the vertical line on the left side of the graph start at 40, not 0? Do you think that makes sense?
Using a line graph to display data really helps you see change over time!
Yes, it's so clear!

Guided Practice

Fill in the answer with one of the choices.

According to the line graph, the number of third-grade students is going ______ (down, up, or not changing).

Lesson 8–3 Exercises

For each problem: collect the data, plan the graph, draw the graph, and label the graph.

1. On the grid provided, make and label a bar graph to show the information from Ms. Park's line graph.

A. There were 70 third-grade students in 2000. How many more third-grade students were there in 2001? ____________________

B. How many more third-grade students were there in 2002 than in 2000?

____

2. Find out how many students attended your school each year for the past five years. On the grid provided, make a line graph to show your findings.

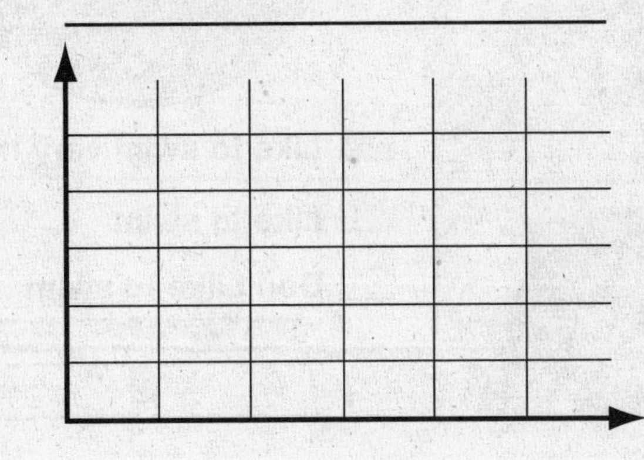

Reflection and Discussion

Why did Ms. Park use a bar graph in the last lesson, but a line graph in this lesson?

Warm-up Exercises

$6 \times 6 =$ ____ $6 \times 7 =$ ____ $6 \times 8 =$ ____ $6 \times 9 =$ ____

$12 \div 6 =$ ____ $18 \div 6 =$ ____ $24 \div 6 =$ ____ $30 \div 6 =$ ____

8-4 Do you like circle graphs?

Mathematical Conversation

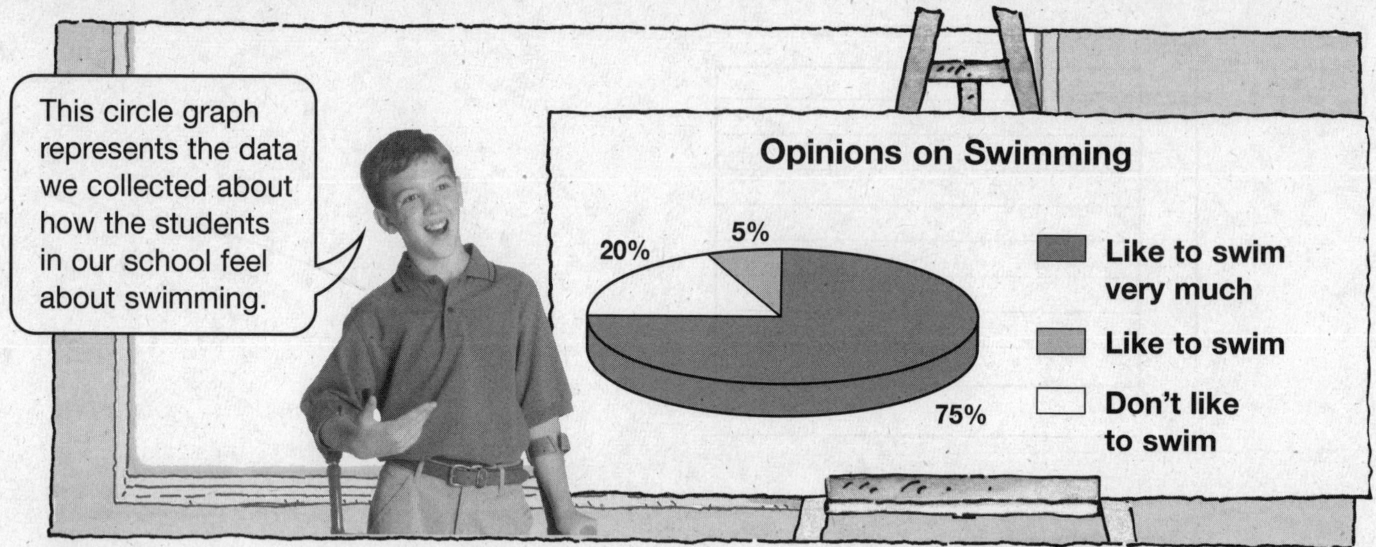
This circle graph represents the data we collected about how the students in our school feel about swimming.
Opinions on Swimming
20%
5%
75%
Like to swim very much
Like to swim
Don't like to swim

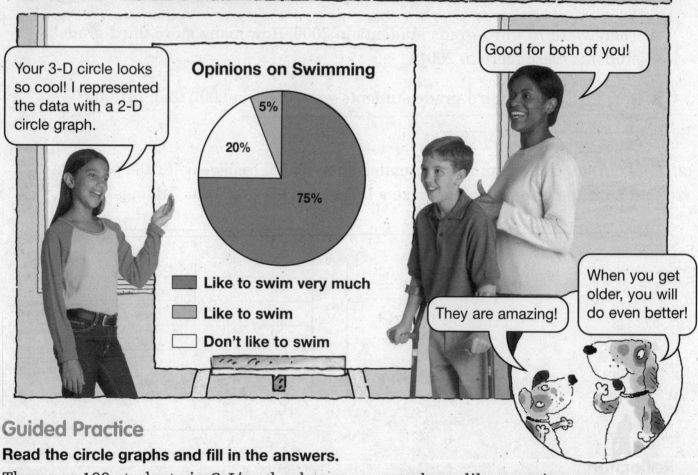

Your 3-D circle looks so cool! I represented the data with a 2-D circle graph.

Opinions on Swimming

5%

20%

75%

Like to swim very much

Like to swim

Don't like to swim

Good for both of you!

They are amazing!

When you get older, you will do even better!

Guided Practice

Read the circle graphs and fill in the answers.

There are 100 students in C.J.'s school, so ____ students like to swim very much, ____ students like to swim, and ____ don't like to swim at all.

Lesson 8–4 Exercises

1. In Ana's school, 60% of the girls like to dance very much, 25% of the girls like to dance, and 15% of the girls don't like to dance.

   Use the circle graph below to show this information. Remember to make a key.

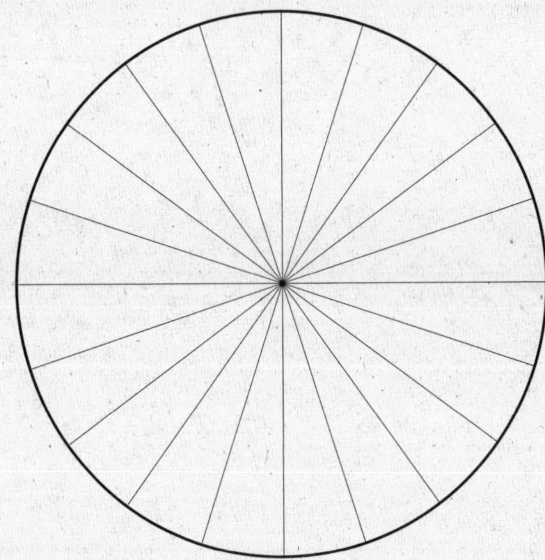

2. Last week, 40% of the students in Ana's school read more than 3 books, 30% read 3 books, 15% read 2 books, 10% read 1 book, and 5% didn't read any books.

   Use the circle graph below to show this information. Remember to make a key.

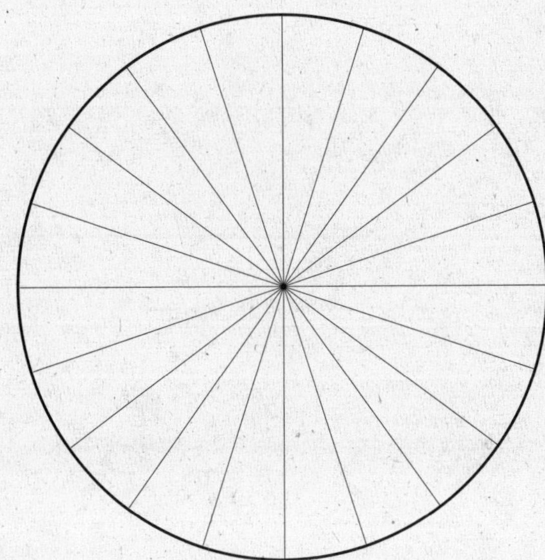

Reflection and Discussion

In each graph above, what does the whole circle represent?